Sociology and Canadian Society

SECOND EDITION

Geoffrey Johnstone and Kathryn Bauer

2004
EMOND MONTGOMERY PUBLICATIONS LIMITED
TORONTO, CANADA

Printed in Canada.

Edited, designed, and typeset by WordsWorth Communications, Toronto.
Cover design by Susan Darrach, Darrach Design.

We acknowledge the financial support of the Government of Canada through the Book Publishing Industry Development Program (BPIDP) for our publishing activities.

Statistics Canada information is used with the permission of the Minister of Industry, as Minister responsible for Statistics Canada. Information on the availability of the wide range of data from Statistics Canada can be obtained from Statistics Canada's Regional Offices, its World Wide Web site at http://www.statcan.ca, and its toll-free access number 1-800-263-1136.

Library and Archives Canada Cataloguing in Publication

Johnstone, Geoffrey, 1947–
    Sociology and Canadian society / Geoffrey Johnstone and Kathryn Bauer.—2nd ed.

Includes bibliographical references and index.
ISBN 1-55239-111-6

    1. Sociology—Textbooks.   2. Canada—Social conditions—1991—Textbooks.   I. Bauer, Kathryn G.C., 1950–   II. Title.

HN103.5.J63 2004   301   C2004-903782-X

Contents

Preface

This book provides students with new perceptions about the connections between the individual and his or her social world and makes sense of social life. It is designed to provide a basic understanding of theories, themes, and concepts in sociology. This approach allows instructors and students to apply their own contemporary issues to these basics. We begin by examining the foundations of the discipline and proceed to the social base of society, how the individual fits into society, the social institutions that give it structure, and the process of continual changes to society.

Many of the statistics in the text come from Canada's 2001 census. The Canada Census is a survey carried out by the Canadian government every five years. This census is not just a bunch of numbers. It is vital for planning communities of the future to ensure that government programs are changing along with the changing needs of society. All the planning that deals with Canadians, from immigration policies to transportation needs, housing, hospitals, schools, and other social agencies, depends on the data from the census. The 2001 census revealed the growing influence of immigration in overall population patterns; as Canada's population growth is slowing, immigration is responsible for the majority of new growth. In addition, Canadians are becoming more urban.

ABOUT THE AUTHORS

Kathryn Bauer and Geoffrey Johnstone are professors at Conestoga College in Kitchener, Ontario. Kathryn teaches courses in sociology and psychology. She has a BA in psychology and sociology, an MSc in health behaviour from the University of Waterloo, and an Ontario Teacher's Certificate. Geoff teaches sociology and multiculturalism. He has a BSc in sociology and statistics from University College Swansea, University of Wales, and an MA in sociology from McMaster University.

CHAPTER 1

Theoretical Background

This chapter probes the nature of sociology. It examines the idea of a social science, the development of sociological theory, the subject matter of sociology, and current perspectives in sociology. Some of the fundamental concepts of sociology are also introduced.

Chapter Objectives

After completing this chapter, you should be able to:

- Examine the sociological perspective through which you conduct your life.

- Examine the degree to which scientific methods can be appropriately used in sociological inquiry.

  Identify possible uses of sociological knowledge in your chosen field of specialization.

- Define the primary concepts of sociology.

THE SCIENCE OF SOCIETY

As construction workers were putting the finishing touches on the "Luminous Veil," a suicide barrier on the Bloor Street Viaduct in March of 2003, someone tried to jump. A construction worker was successful in convincing the person to stop. The Viaduct, built in 1919, is one of Toronto's grandest civic structures, rising 140 feet above the Don Valley. It is second only to the Golden Gate Bridge in San Francisco as a choice spot for suicide in North America. An estimated 480 people have voluntarily leapt to their deaths from this bridge.

How would sociologists explain this attempt at suicide prevention? They would look for recurring patterns of behaviour to explain the causes of suicide. We encounter many important questions and issues about ourselves and our social environment. Sociology offers a better understanding of a wide range of social phenomena in our complex and ever-changing world by explaining recurring patterns in group life. It encourages us to look beyond our personal experiences and to think sociologically about how social interaction and membership in a variety of groups, both large and small, shape us.

We start with a definition of the term sociology itself. **Sociology** is the scientific study of human relationships. The words "scientific" and "relationships" may present

sociology
the scientific study of human relationships

some difficulties in this definition. Because we focus on relationships between people rather than the individual people themselves, sociology can often appear to be dealing with abstractions and generalizations. At the same time, we are dealing with the dynamic, two-way process of communication that always goes on between two individuals, between groups, or between individuals and groups. The study of sociology can therefore be interesting and exciting.

Every time one person (A) meets another person (B), some interaction takes place:

Person (A) acts:

$$(A) \longrightarrow (B)$$
$$\text{Action}$$

Person (B) reacts:

$$(A) \longleftarrow (B)$$
$$\text{Reaction}$$

Each person makes a subjective assessment of the nature of the interaction that has taken place. Thus, **interaction** refers to the two-way process of communication between people and their assessment of the nature of that communication.

Our daily lives involve interactions with others in many different social situations. Skill is needed in analyzing these situations in order to handle these interactions successfully. Sociology has a significant practical application in that it assists us in understanding the complexities of numerous social situations.

Because sociologists study the interaction between individuals rather than the behaviour of one individual, it follows that the basic unit of study for sociologists is the group, not the individual. For most sociologists, the family unit is the basic unit of society.

Sociology studies all *human relationships*. It follows that it is a sociologist's job to study both normal and abnormal behaviour. In fact, sociologists would not use the terms normal and abnormal; they are more likely to talk in terms of normative and deviant behaviour. **Normative behaviour** refers to behaviour that is within socially accepted boundaries, and **deviant behaviour** refers to behaviour that is outside socially accepted boundaries. The general public often confuses the study of sociology with the study of deviant behaviour. The vast majority of our population stays within society's rules the vast majority of the time. Theoretically, then, the vast majority of sociological study should concentrate on normative behaviour, and for the most part it does.

There is, however, an overemphasis in sociological study on deviant behaviour for basically the same reason that there is an overemphasis in the news media on deviant behaviour: most people find deviant behaviour more interesting than normative behaviour. There can, however, be negative consequences of this overemphasis. It often gives the public the impression that there is a lot more deviant and criminal behaviour in society than there actually is. It also helps to promote a fortress mentality in which people shut themselves off because of their suspicions of others.

The simple social facts are that the majority of teenagers survive adolescence without acquiring addictions, criminal records, or sexually transmitted diseases (STDs). Most of our population still believes in and takes part in the institutions of

interaction
the two-way process of communication between people and their assessment of the nature of that communication

normative behaviour
behaviour that is within socially accepted boundaries

deviant behaviour
behaviour that is outside socially accepted boundaries

marriage and the family (and most frequently in that order), and the vast majority of our senior citizens are mentally and physically competent. We should not be deceived by media images of our rapidly decaying society. Look around you and reflect on the large number of decent, law-abiding, socially conscious people you know.

The second debatable term in our definition of sociology is the term *scientific*. **Science** is the pursuit of objective knowledge accumulated from observation. The **scientific method** is the process involved in acquiring objective knowledge.

Sociologists study society by asking questions about social phenomena, observing social life, and developing theories from their systematic observations to explain the social phenomena. **Theories** are broad explanations and predictions concerning phenomena of interest. They provide the basis for ways of organizing and making sense of the phenomena we experience. One theory could offer an explanation of how public opinion is altered by the media and social institutions. For example, as a result of O.J. Simpson's trial, he has been branded as an unconvicted murderer. This label has erased people's perception of him as a successful broadcaster and one of the best running backs in the history of the game of football.

The term society is such a common word in our language, we tend not to think about its definition. It encompasses concepts such as territory, relationships, self-efficiency and culture. **Society** is "the totality of social relationships and interactions among a collectivity of people occupying a territory who, over time, survive by meeting their needs and solving their problems" (Knuttila, 1993, p. 51).

It is open to debate just how far sociology can claim to be a science. In our everyday dealings with other human beings, we constantly assess and judge them. This is simply part of the process of being human. As a result, social scientists face a problem when they try to apply the principles of science to their studies. The essence of the scientific method is that the scientist should maintain his **objectivity** about his subject matter — that is, he should be able to see things as they are, not as he thinks they ought to be. It is not easy — some say it is impossible — to view something (that is, other humans) objectively when you have always previously used subjective perceptions in assessing them. Even a scientist in the more traditional fields has some difficulties with this effect. If she looks for something under a microscope, she desperately wants to see it there, and this subjective desire to make the discovery increases the probability that she will mistakenly see something there when, in fact, it is not present. For a social scientist, this difficulty is compounded by the fact that his subject matter is people. He will have normal emotions about them, and he will also be conscious that they too will have feelings about him.

A further difficulty in applying the scientific method to social phenomena is the fact that it is virtually impossible to determine all of the variables that might affect a person's behaviour. Therefore, it is difficult to isolate and focus on the behaviour that you want to know about. Even if one were able to know everything that contributes to a person's behaviour, it is both impractical and unethical to experimentally control that portion of the person's life to see what makes him or her tick.

THE SOCIAL SCIENCES

The social sciences are a related set of subjects that study various aspects of human behaviour. All of the social sciences (sociology, psychology, anthropology, political science, and economics) study humans from a different perspective. Sociology examines

science
the pursuit of objective knowledge accumulated from observation

scientific method
the process involved in acquiring objective knowledge

theories
broad explanations and predictions concerning phenomena of interest

society
"the totality of social relationships and interactions among a collectivity of people occupying a territory who, over time, survive by meeting their needs and solving their problems" (Knuttila, 1993)

objectivity
seeing things as they are, not as they ought to be

human interaction. Psychology deals with mental processes, focusing on individual behaviour. Anthropology often concentrates on the study of small, pre-literate societies where the society is studied as a whole. Political science is divided into the study of government and the study of political ideologies. Economics looks at the production, distribution, and consumption of goods.

The distinction between psychology and sociology can be demonstrated in the following way. When considering why a student does not apply herself in school or why a young adult is depressed over a layoff at work, a psychologist might try to understand their behaviour by analyzing their beliefs, attitudes, and personalities. However, many people have similar experiences and similar behaviours. A sociologist might try to understand the common social forces that influence people in situations such as these. Perhaps the student belongs to a lower social economic class that does not value the pursuit of knowledge, and perhaps the young adult sees little opportunity for a future job because of the current economic climate.

THE DEVELOPMENT OF SOCIOLOGY

Sociological thinking began to thrive in the late 18th and early 19th centuries with the social upheaval brought about by industrialization and urbanization. France, Germany, and England underwent the most rapid change with the impact of the Industrial and French revolutions. Attention was drawn to the study of society as progressive political ideas took shape, a new industrial economy emerged, a radically new organization of work developed, and cities burgeoned. No longer was social order based on family and tradition in simple, rural communities. People increasingly lived in more complex, heterogeneous societies in urban areas. However, sociologists reacted differently to this change in social order.

Auguste Comte

Auguste Comte (1798–1857), a French philosopher, coined the term sociology. He was interested in how the French Revolution affected social order and social change in society. He believed the answers to questions, such as what held society together and what caused it to change, lay in applying the scientific method to social life. Comte referred to sociology as the scientific study of the natural laws governing social phenomena. Comte further believed that sociology was destined to become the master science that would give us final solutions to all social ills and would help us shape and, consequently, improve society. Nowadays, we see sociology as being just one science that takes its place alongside many others in a concerted effort to tackle social problems. Comte's lasting contribution, then, is the introduction of the term sociology.

Karl Marx

Perhaps the best known (although for the wrong reasons) of the 19th-century founding fathers of sociology was Karl Marx (1818–1883). Marx was a German philosopher and social theorist who spent most of his life in England. He believed that society was a continuous, historical struggle between opposing interests. At every stage of history, he suggested, society could be divided into classes with unequal power: a ruling class and an exploited, powerless majority — in other words, the haves and the have-nots. He believed that the workers are exploited by the small number of elite who control most of the wealth without actually producing it themselves. Marx believed it was an inexorable law of history that the ruling class would start to crumble from within and be overturned by the growing alienation of the exploited classes.

Marx described social relationships in terms of exploitation, conflict, and antagonism. He suggested that if we want to understand social relationships, we should look for the current conflict groups in society and analyze the nature of the conflict.

This theory of conflict is rooted in the writings of Marx, although not everyone who believes in this theory accepts all of Marx's arguments. **Conflict theory** is a theoretical perspective that stresses conflict, power differences, and social change as permanent characteristics of society. In general, society is seen as a delicate balance of power groups trying to hang on to or improve their positions. These groups usually work at cross purposes, in constant conflict. The goals of one group are frequently at odds with the goals of another. Stability occurs for brief periods when one group dominates the rest or some groups have a balance of power. *Coercion* is always present — that is, in every society some people have more power than others do.

Critics assert that the limitation of the conflict theory is that it suggests that one group's gain is, inevitably, another group's loss. It assumes that when someone gets ahead, it is always at the expense of another. Although this does happen at times, this belief discourages one from looking for ways to cooperate and serve everyone.

conflict theory
a theoretical perspective that stresses conflict, power differences, and social change as permanent characteristics of society

Émile Durkheim

Émile Durkheim (1858–1917), a Frenchman, was concerned mainly with establishing sociology as a discipline and a science distinct from psychology. Durkheim studied the way in which social institutions and people in society are mutually interdependent; that is, everyone needs others to be performing their function appropriately. Durkheim viewed society as a living organism that needs all of its parts working in harmony. This theoretical perspective is called **functionalism**, and it stresses the way in which each part of society functions to meet the needs of society as a whole.

Society, Durkheim believed, is made up of integrated parts or social systems, such as families, religion, industry, the armed forces, and other institutions. Each social system of society contributes to, and has an effect on, the whole society. Social systems tend to be relatively stable, and change usually is gradual. Functionalism emphasizes order. When the requirements of the system are met, it is in a state of balance or equilibrium. A society cannot survive unless its members share common beliefs and values, which are required to hold the society together. Functionalism analyzes institutions such as the family, education, and religion according to the way they help meet the needs of society and the role they play in maintaining stability.

Both conflict theory and functionalism agree that a society, if it is to hold together, needs shared values. The differences between these perspectives arise in their theories of how shared values are attained and maintained. The functionalist view sees shared values as a cohesive element that is adopted by members in order to contribute to harmony in society. Conflict theorists focus on the ability of dominant groups to force their views on others.

functionalism
a theoretical perspective that stresses the way in which each part of society functions to meet the needs of society as a whole

Critics of functionalism say that social systems are never in a perfect state of balance; that this kind of harmony does not exist any more. In large, complex societies such as Canada, there are groups whose interests and values are opposed. However, functionalism continues to exert a strong influence on sociology. It has contributed a great deal to the analysis of shared values and assumptions in cultures, and theories of the structures of institutions.

The social theories of Marx and Durkheim exactly paralleled their own experiences in society. Marx's life was one of constant conflict. He left his native Prussia (northern Germany) because of his dislike for its militaristic regime and the discrimination that stopped him from receiving a university position. Marx voluntarily moved to France to make a new start, but his political views and activities quickly drew the attention of the French authorities and he was forced to leave the country in 1848. He settled in London, England, but he was never fully accepted by the British government. There is a record at Somerset House in Britain that Karl Marx became a British citizen in 1871. However, as recently as 1981, the British government denied that it was *the* Karl Marx that became a naturalized subject; rather, the government asserted, it was someone else of the same name. It is not surprising, then, that a man whose personal history had seen so much conflict would take a conflict view of social relationships.

Durkheim, in contrast, was born into a comfortable, middle-class family and lived a fairly stable, secure life. He spent most of his life as a university professor at Bordeaux and the Sorbonne (in Paris), initiated the first department of sociology without major opposition, and was accorded substantial amounts of government and private money to produce sociological documents. It appeared that society worked effectively for Durkheim, and this led him to believe that society is functional. Social ills indicate that the social system is simply slightly askew and just needs some patching up. Marx, on the other hand, would say these ills are a manifestation of exploitation in society.

Durkheim focused on how individuals in modern society could achieve consensus and create the conditions for social solidarity. He saw social problems as a product of social differentiation, arising from the increasingly complex division of labour. As people perform more and more specialized tasks, their social obligations change. In traditional societies, consensus and solidarity are achieved through common experiences, values, attitudes, and norms that override freedom of thought and action. This type of solidarity in which individuals resemble each other in all aspects of their lives he termed **mechanical solidarity**. Individuals feel the same emotions, cherish the same values, and are governed by strict rules and proscriptions.

As modern society became organized, with a strict division of labour and the specialization of functions, there was a transition to **organic solidarity**, in which the parts of society perform different functions and are interdependent. Individualism is valued. Everyone is free to believe, act, and have independent thoughts and desires. Durkheim was interested in how individuals could achieve integration in a society that had such social diversity and weakened social bonds.

Durkheim made two other major contributions to the beginnings of sociology.

First, he was the person who initially pointed out that there were things that could be called **social facts**, things that are outside the individual but that coerce or constrain him or her in some way. These social facts exist because (and only because) of the fact of human social interaction, and they cannot be explained psychologically. Hence, social facts are the main components of sociology. Some social facts are

mechanical solidarity
solidarity in which individuals resemble each other in all aspects of their lives

organic solidarity
solidarity in which the parts of society perform different functions and are interdependent

social facts
things that are outside the individual but that coerce or constrain him or her in some way

customs, traditions, obligations (for example, of husbands, brothers, wives, and daughters), rights, duties, laws, roles, religious beliefs, and language.

Second, Durkheim suggested that sociologists, to obtain social facts, should analyze the rates of certain human behaviours (births, deaths, marriages, divorces, and so on). Thus, it was Durkheim who showed us the steps and procedures that have to be undertaken in any social research. It was in his classic work *Suicide* (first published in 1897) that Durkheim illustrated the steps of social research.

THE STEPS OF SOCIAL RESEARCH

1. First, we must recognize that social facts are real, that such things as duties or customs can cause people to behave in certain ways. In this way, we can generate a hypothesis for our study. A **hypothesis** is a suggestion or an assumption that two social facts are related in a previously unsuspected way. In *Suicide*, Durkheim suspected that the very nature of a society's organization could cause suicide rates to be high or low. Once this hypothesis was established, it followed that it must be tested.

hypothesis
a suggestion or an assumption that two social facts are related in a previously unsuspected way

2. Then, we have to *collect data* about our topic. Durkheim collected his data on suicide from many Western countries, where information on the topic has been well documented for centuries.

3. Durkheim realized that raw data on their own were useless — we have to *pick out generalizations or sequences* in the data. He discovered that the data on suicide had some remarkable consistencies. For example, suicide rates for married people were lower than for singles; rates for urban dwellers were higher than for rural; rates for Roman Catholics were lower than for Protestants; rates for males were higher than for females; and rates were higher at certain times (for example, in early morning hours, in the spring, and at Christmas) than at others.

4. Having extracted these generalizations, Durkheim had to *find suitable explanations for each generalization*. For example, do people commit suicide in the spring because the season of renewed hope arrives and they are still without hope, thus increasing the emotional gap between these individuals and those who are feeling renewed by the new season?

5. Once we have come up with explanations for each of our generalizations, we must, as the final step, look for *theoretical explanations that will subsume all of these isolated cases*. Durkheim suggested that the patterns of suicide were so consistent across so many distant societies that it must be something more than individual moral choices of private citizens that drive them to suicide. There must also be external pressure from some more general agent of social control. Durkheim theorized that this external agent was the degree to which an individual was integrated into his society and the amount of regulation society imposed on the individual. He suggested that when the degree of integration and regulation was balanced, the individual was shielded from suicide. On the other hand, when an individual lacked an active integrated role that was consistent with what was considered socially desirable, or when an individual was overly controlled by society, he or she was more prone to suicide.

FOUR TYPES OF SUICIDE

Durkheim, on the basis of his theory that social integration and regulation were factors in suicide, suggested that there were four types of suicide.

1. *Altruistic suicide*   An individual commits altruistic suicide when he feels that his group (family, friends, community, or society) would benefit from his death. Thus, the hold that society has on the individual is seen to be so excessive that the individual ends his life for the good of the group. Altruistic suicide is more common in societies or smaller social groupings in which the sense of community is strong. Similar work and social activities, shared values and beliefs, and close social bonds encourage individuals to place the group's welfare ahead of their own.

2. *Fatalistic suicide*   An individual who commits fatalistic suicide feels that the society or group is overregulated, or restricts the person too much. Norms are set down with little opportunity for freedom of thought or action. Lacking choices and achievement possibilities, the individual feels trapped with nothing new to anticipate in life. If the future looks bleak, then suicide might present itself as a way out. Traditional examples of fatalistic suicides are prisoners or slaves who kill themselves to escape their situation. The fastest rising rate of suicide in industrially advanced countries is among teenagers. One wonders how many of these young people perceive a bleak future from which they must escape.

3. *Egoistic suicide*   An individual who commits egoistic suicide lacks integration into her society, and usually lacks support systems, such as kinship or friendship networks. The person feels painfully isolated from the rest of society, and as though she does not have a meaningful role to play. In modern industrial societies, which are characterized by an overemphasis on individualism, the person feels diminishing attachment to, and is less influenced by, social norms. If the ties that bind a person to society are slack, then at a time of crisis she lacks a lifeline to help her through the crisis. Married people are more fully integrated into our society's demands than single people are, and the Roman Catholic church permeates more dimensions of its members' lives than most Protestant churches do. It is interesting to note that members of the Anglican church (a Protestant church, that, of all Protestant churches, bears the closest resemblance to the Roman Catholic church) have lower rates of suicide than do members of other Protestant churches in which individualism is more strongly stressed. Suicide rates are higher among males than among females, perhaps because society has long emphasized that males should be more independent and less group-oriented than females. This emphasis on independence may leave males with less of a feeling of integration into society.

   Thus, egoistic suicide can be seen as the polar opposite of altruistic suicide. In egoistic suicide, the individual feels socially isolated; in altruistic suicide, the individual feels overobligated to the social group.

4. *Anomic suicide*   It is often the case that in modern society the crisis from which we suffer is neither too much or too little social integration, nor social regulation that is too strict or not strict enough. Instead, the problem centres on the contradictions within society. This is most apparent in

industrialized societies at times of rapid social change. Often, times of change mean that traditional norms and values are eroding yet no coherent set of new norms and values have arisen to take their place. Anomic suicide is often associated with the loss of a particular way of life. The individual can feel rootless, uncertain, and disoriented with no familiar guidelines.

In a complex, modern, multidimensional society where everything is right to one group and everything is wrong to another, it becomes increasingly difficult to make individual choices. One situation with two possible responses (for example, virginity, staying on at school, or the use of non-prescription drugs) can be decided by appeal to two sets of contradictory rules; each set of rules may have its attractions, but each will also have its disadvantages. **Anomie** is a state in which the individual is chronically unable to make choices. Durkheim maintained that anomie puts the individual in a position of having no set of social regulations by which to make decisions, and that being confused and spending a long time in this indecisive state could lead to suicidal behaviour in order to avoid the need to make a decision.

anomie
a state in which the individual is chronically unable to make choices

Thus, anomic suicide can be seen as the polar opposite of fatalistic suicide. In anomic suicide, the individual feels rootless; in fatalistic suicide, the individual feels smothered.

Durkheim looked at suicide, which had been seen as uniquely psychological, and treated it instead as uniquely sociological. In 1982, the federal government of Canada commissioned a study of suicide in Canada to report on and make recommendations about current trends. At a distance of 3000 miles and 85 years from Durkheim's study, the data reported by the commission showed exactly the same trends in suicide statistics.

In Canada, the suicide rate remained fairly stable between 1979 and 1998. The suicide rate for males was four times that of females (see figure 1.1).

The suicide rate among the aboriginal population for all age groups is about three times higher than the rate for the Canadian population as a whole. Among aboriginal youth, the suicide rate is five or six times higher than the suicide rate of the general Canadian youth population (Standing Senate Committee on Social Affairs, Science and Technology, 2002). The anomic state produced by the conflict between their traditional culture and the pull of the European culture produces a sense of rootlessness in young aboriginals. Being a stranger in a strange land is to be expected, being a stranger in your own land is unfathomable.

Herbert Spencer

A contemporary of Marx was the Englishman Herbert Spencer (1820–1903). Although Spencer and Marx both wrote in and studied Dickens' England, the picture they drew was entirely different and the social theories they propounded were contradictory. Marx had seen the squalor, rigours, and brutality of the poorhouse, the workshop, and the slums, and thought these features of society were the result of the exploitation of the masses by the ruling business class. He concluded that it was inevitable that the deprived would rise up and take over.

In contrast, Spencer sought his explanation of social deprivation in Charles Darwin's theories of evolution. Spencer maintained that Darwin's ideas on the

FIGURE 1.1   **Age-Specific Suicide Rates, by Sex, Canada, 1998**

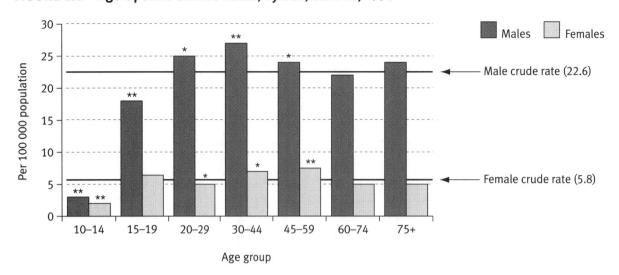

Notes
* Significantly different from sex-specific crude rate (p < 0.05).
** Significantly different from sex-specific crude rate (p < 0.01).

Source: Adapted from Statistics Canada (2001).

evolution of species, through a process in which the fittest survived and adapted to new conditions while the weak died off, could be readily adapted to explain human development. Thus, Spencer suggested that the strong and talented would (and should) always win out over the weak and stupid. He claimed that those with superior intelligence and willingness to work would become powerful and wealthy, while the less worthy would sink to the slums and the poorhouse. Spencer added that any interference in this process, such as providing welfare and sustenance for the weak, would only result in the general weakening of society, because these policies would encourage the weak to remain that way.

Sociology and many other disciplines have been telling us for half a century or more that Spencer's idea has no foundation at all. People are more often deprived by circumstances than they are by weakness, laziness, or stupidity, and the people who achieve do not always do so by ability, hard work, and intellect. It is interesting to note that Spencer was brought to America in 1882 on a speaking tour. The tour was paid for by the great "robber barons" of the day, many of whom had gained their wealth and power by stealth, dishonesty, illegality, and ruthlessness. Spencer's ideas seemed to justify their actions no matter how abhorrent they had been. This conservative outlook, with the belief that competition results in progress because it eliminates weaker individuals, has been called **social Darwinism**. Critics say that this view of society does not promote equality and, although it claims to support progress, actually blocks reform and change.

social Darwinism
the belief that competition results in progress because it eliminates weaker individuals

Max Weber

Max Weber (1864–1920), a German contemporary of Durkheim, also put forward a slightly different theory of how society works. Weber suggested that it is inappropriate to view human relationships in terms of social forces directing our behaviour. For Weber, general theories of society, whether conflict theory, functionalism, or social

Darwinism, are not a useful way to interpret people's actions. Instead, Weber postulated that we should only interpret an individual's behaviour by examining how he himself evaluates the behaviour. In Weber's social theory, the individual is the basic unit of study. He emphasized a need to understand a setting from the point of view of the people in it. For this reason, Weber's social theory, as well as theories that were inspired by it, is called **microsociology** — the study of individuals and small groups. The other major social theories, conflict theory, functionalism, and social Darwinism, are termed **macrosociology** because they concentrate on the study of large groups and social processes that affect the whole society.

Weber was concerned with the meanings people attach to events in social life. For example, when sociologists study a nation, they should concern themselves with what the nation means to its individual members, because it is from the members that a nation gets its reality. Canada means different things to someone in Newfoundland and to someone else in Alberta. In contrast, Durkheim would say that a nation is a social fact with a reality in and of itself and cannot be explained by individual members.

Weber's theories have since been expanded upon by sociologists who are called symbolic interactionists. Symbolic interactionists are not inclined to treat society as a set of real structures distinct from people. Rather, they view individuals as feeling, thinking people who attach meaning to situations and behave according to their interpretations. People are not seen as being coerced by social structures but as being creators of society. They are capable not only of learning the attitudes and values of their society, but also of discovering, inventing, and initiating new attitudes and values. They react to their environment and they act upon it.

Symbolic interactionism is a theoretical perspective that seeks to describe how individuals interpret their environments and how these personal distinctions and meanings affect their interactions with others. Most interactions between human beings are *symbolic* (that is, the meanings of words and gestures are deeper than is first evident). Humans are able to represent themselves, others, ideas, and objects in symbols. They communicate effectively because they agree on and share the meanings of symbols. These meanings are learned through social interaction. Millions of these interactions build up a social system, and as individual interactions change, society also changes.

Social interactionism focuses on the processes by which people interpret and respond to the actions of others. In the process of interaction, we learn to anticipate each other's responses and viewpoints and adjust to them. This ability is called role taking. We take on many roles in the course of our lives and develop a sense of self through the process of role taking. In this way, our identity is dependent on interaction with others in our society.

In short, social interactionists focus on social behaviour in everyday life and on how people behave in social units such as families and schools, and they try to understand how people create and define the situations they experience.

Critics of symbolic interactionism argue that it is so preoccupied with the trees that it loses sight of the forest. Focusing on the smallest details of daily life does not take sufficient account of the larger context, the society in which they occur.

We are all born into a pre-existing society with its culture and into particular communities and social classes that shape us. The three perspectives of functionalism, conflict theory, and symbolic interactionism give us a well-rounded understanding of social life (see table 1.1).

microsociology
the study of individuals and small groups

macrosociology
the study of large groups and social processes that affect the whole society

symbolic interactionism
a theoretical perspective that seeks to describe how individuals interpret their environments and how these personal distinctions and meanings affect their interactions with others

TABLE 1.1   The Three Major Theoretical Perspectives

Theoretical perspective	Orientation	Explanation of society	Explanation of social change
Functionalism	• macrosociology (we are shaped by the large groups to which we belong)	• society shapes the individual • society has interrelated structures • each structure has a function that helps meet the needs of society • consensus and cooperation within each structure lead to harmony and relative stability	• society changes by peaceful evolution
Conflict theory	• macrosociology (we are shaped by the large groups to which we belong)	• society shapes the individual • conflict is deep-rooted in society due to power differences and coercion between groups • as groups gain and lose power, social change occurs	• society changes through revolution
Symbolic interactionism	• microsociology (societies are shaped by the individuals within them)	• society is shaped by the individual • face-to-face, small-group social interactions in daily activities influence society • interaction is based on symbolic communication	• individuals change through adaptation to new situations

CONTEMPORARY THEORIES

Contemporary conflict theorists examine how social structure profits a portion of society while depriving another portion. They investigate the links among factors such as age, gender, race, and ethnicity with the unequal distribution of factors such as income, power, social prestige, and level of education. Contemporary functionalists have made advances in how institutions with shared core values that encourage stability make adjustments to the changing needs of society. They recognized that as value systems shift and change, the entire social structure is impacted. Contemporary symbolic interactionists examine how society is created by people as they go about their daily lives. Their focus is on how individuals interact with each other on the basis of shared symbols.

Beyond the three mainstream approaches, new challenges in social life have been examined in the feminist perspective and in Anthony Giddens's work on structuration.

Feminist sociologists address the inability of the major perspectives to deal adequately with the important issues of sex and gender. The women's perspective continues to re-examine our social world, searching for the causes and solutions of gender inequality in terms of social status, power, and wealth. Many have become politically active to raise public awareness of how gender crosscuts all aspects of social life.

British sociologist Anthony Giddens developed the structuration theory based on what he calls the "duality of structure," the fact that we are simultaneously the product and producer of our social structures (Giddens, 1984, chap. 1). We develop social structures with their institutions, statuses, roles, value systems, and so on, as we act socially to solve social problems and meet our needs. These social activities he refers to as social practices which become routine and structured as they are successful in meeting our needs. Once these structures are developed, they in turn determine our subsequent behaviour.

Multiple Perspectives

Each reader of these positions carries her or his own theory about the way society is structured. You may well find that your own social theory approximates one of the above, but it is also possible that your social theory actually contains some element of a number of these positions, or that different situations appear to fit different social theories.

All of the major sociological theories have been useful in helping us come to an understanding of society. All are based on different assumptions, which lead to different questions and different answers. Each theory is concerned with particular aspects of social existence, but by focusing only on certain aspects, each theory leaves other aspects in the dark. People need to know how institutions and the relationships among them are moulded by processes of cooperation (functionalism) and conflict (conflict theory). However, it is also important to discover how individuals interpret situations and how these interpretations influence behaviour (symbolic interactionism).

NORTH AMERICAN SOCIOLOGY

In the early 20th century, schools of sociology started to appear in American universities, and they owed much to the ideas of Herbert Spencer. During the 1920s and 1930s, Chicago emerged as the centre of sociology in the United States. The Chicago school of sociology, which was very influential in the history of American sociology, focused on pragmatic problems, such as industrial relations and urban problems. The Chicago school also insisted on quantitative research. Everything had to be concrete and measurable, and there was little room for speculation.

It was not until the 1950s and 1960s that good-sized sociology departments began to appear in Canada. The 1960s saw the production of the two most internationally recognized pieces of Canadian sociology, the Blishen scale and John Porter's vertical mosaic.

Bernard Blishen

Bernard Blishen noted that Canadians most often assessed each other's social standing by the social prestige of their occupations. "And what do you do?" was and is an important part of initial encounters between two Canadians. Blishen set about measuring the relative importance of all Canada-wide occupations as viewed

Blishen scale
a measure of the relative social prestige of occupations

through the eyes of a cross-section of the population. These measures became known as the **Blishen scale**.

Blishen eventually ranked over 400 occupations, taking into account both income and education. Occupations that require a high degree of specialized training along with a great deal of responsibility (for example, a judge or a physician) were accorded the highest social prestige.

Blishen divided occupations into seven classes. The requirements for the highest social class, class 1, were high levels of education and high earning power. Judges, doctors, lawyers, engineers, and architects were some of the occupations in class 1. Class 2 included high-level white-collar workers such as professors, company managers, and pilots. Occupants of the middle classes (3, 4, 5) had increasingly less education and earning power and were skilled white-collar workers and blue-collar workers. Jobs in these classes ranged from purchasing agents and factory supervisors to skilled tradespeople. The bottom classes consisted of semi-skilled workers such as masons and carpenters and, finally, unskilled workers such as janitors and other labourers.

According to Blishen's scale, occupations that required a high level of education but paid poorly could rank higher than occupations that did not require a lot of education but paid well.

Blishen's scale and its derivatives have become the standard way of attributing social standing in most Western countries.

John Porter

John Porter, like Blishen, was interested in the fact that Canada had a distinct social ladder, a vertical scale of social rank. Porter, however, also noted that Canada's social scale was not just a simple, vertical social class system, but was also affected by the other great social fact of Canadian existence, one's ethnicity or cultural heritage. Certain ethnic groups seemed to have clearly marked positions on the social ladder and seemed to have great difficulty rising above that status; so the social ladder was a **vertical mosaic**, interspersed with a diversity of ethnic groups restricted to their appointed positions on the scale.

vertical mosaic
a social ranking that is affected by ethnicity or cultural heritage

According to Porter, the formation of social classes in Canada was influenced by the immigration of various ethnic groups. In his book *The Vertical Mosaic* (1965), he gives evidence of this influence. The two colonizing groups, the English and the French, have retained their elite group status. Certain ethnic groups, of less preferred immigrants, were given an "entry status" by the charter groups. This status indicated lower-level occupational roles. Most of Canada's minority groups have, at some time, had this entry status.

Porter gave many examples of Canada's immigration policies. Many immigrants in Canada's early history filled the labour force for large-scale construction projects. They became a source of cheap labour. For example, Ukrainians and Chinese assisted in nation building in western Canada by constructing and maintaining the railroad. The famine-stricken Irish were hired to build the canals of the St. Lawrence.

Some ethnic groups eventually moved out of their entry status. Others, with cultural barriers such as different language and customs, often settled in ethnic enclaves and found it difficult to improve their entrance status. Yet other groups such as the Germans and Dutch were initially ranked more highly. These groups had desirable traits closely resembling the charter groups. They were Christians who valued cleanliness and military bravery. Many Asian immigrants had to be professionals such as engineers and scientists in order to enter Canada. Many Italians entered Canada as labourers.

THE USES OF SOCIOLOGY

As we have already seen, science is the pursuit of objective knowledge accumulated through observation. The natural and social sciences assume that there is an underlying order to the universe — that the activities of atoms and humans are not random. The main search of science, then, is for laws and generalizations, for knowledge that uncovers and embodies this order. The search for laws and generalizations is called **pure science**, and the major goal of pure science is the pursuit and discovery of new knowledge simply for the sake of finding new knowledge. In this sense, sociology is a pure science, because it seeks laws and generalizations about human interaction and human society.

pure science
the search for laws and generalizations; the pursuit and discovery of new knowledge simply for the sake of finding new knowledge

In contrast, the **applied sciences** take the knowledge gained in pure science and put it to everyday, practical use. It may not be the job of the sociologist to find practical and beneficial uses for sociological knowledge, but other disciplines such as law enforcement, medicine, nursing, social work, urban planning, consumer behaviour, and community planning can put the findings of sociology to work on behalf of the society.

applied science
the application of the knowledge gained in pure science to everyday, practical use

The fact that sociology is a pure and not an applied science places the sociologist in a dilemma. All knowledge that can be used can also be abused. Heroin can be used therapeutically to alleviate pain, or it can be abused to create a debilitating addiction. Psychotherapy can be used to restore emotional stability, or abused to permanently unbalance it. Education can be used to open up minds or to confine learning to narrow areas of specialization. Most sociologists believe that their pursuit of knowledge should be **value-free**; in other words, they believe that their personal biases should be kept out of their work, and that the potential misuse of their data is not their responsibility. An increasing number of sociologists have taken an **action involvement** approach to this dilemma; they believe that scientists should try to retain some control over their findings to make sure the findings are not misused. In practice, the action involvement position is almost impossible to maintain, because most scientific knowledge is published and, therefore, available for use by others.

value-free
the absence of personal biases in sociological work

action involvement
the deliberate attempt by scientists to exercise some control over the way in which their findings are used

BASIC CONCEPTS

Some terms in sociology are used more frequently than others; they are part of the language of sociology. Although these terms will be fully explained in the chapters in which they are most appropriate, they are so common that it is useful now to introduce them.

A **norm** is an established pattern of behaviour or an appropriate response to a social situation. An **institution** is like a big norm; it is an established way of dealing with a social need. A hospital is an institution not because it is a large building, but because it is a cluster of norms, values, beliefs, statuses, and roles concerning the delivery of health care in society.

norm
an established pattern of behaviour or an appropriate response to a social situation

institution
an established way of dealing with a social need

value
a socially shared idea about what is good, right, and desirable

value judgment
an opinion based on personal biases about what is good, right, and desirable

beliefs
ideas that tell people what should exist or happen in a particular situation

status
the social position of an individual in a group

role
a set of expected behaviours attached to a certain status

Values are socially shared ideas about what is good, right, and desirable; a **value judgment** is an opinion based on personal biases about what is good, right, and desirable. In the same realm as values are **beliefs**, which are people's ideas of what should happen in a particular situation. **Status** describes the position of an individual in a group, and status determines a person's **role**, or a set of expected behaviours attached to a certain status.

CHAPTER SUMMARY

Sociology is the study of human interaction. It is the job of the sociologist to look at all human relationships, normative and deviant. Auguste Comte coined the term sociology. There are three major schools of thought in sociology. Conflict theory emphasizes the divisions between the major groups within society and examines the exploitation that results from these divisions. Functionalism looks at the way society's major systems are interrelated and interdependent, and emphasizes social harmony. Symbolic interactionism takes a microsociological view and looks specifically at how individuals interpret their social situation. Two major Canadian sociologists have made notable contributions to sociology: Bernard Blishen, with the Blishen scale, and John Porter, with the notion of the vertical mosaic. Social research develops through a five-step process: the generation of a hypothesis; data collection; data analysis; the search for interpretation; and the development of theoretical explanations. Some concepts and terms are essential to sociology.

KEY TERMS

action involvement	organic solidarity
anomie	pure science
applied sciences	role
beliefs	science
Blishen scale	scientific method
conflict theory	social Darwinism
deviant behaviour	social facts
functionalism	society
hypothesis	sociology
institution	status
interaction	symbolic interactionism
macrosociology	theories
mechanical solidarity	value
microsociology	value judgment
norm	value-free
normative behaviour	vertical mosaic
objectivity	

REFERENCES

Blishen, B.R. (1967). A socio-economic index for occupations in Canada. *Canadian Review of Sociology and Anthropology, 4,* 41-57.

Comte, A. (1896). *The positive philosophy* (H. Martineau, Trans.). London: George Bell & Sons.

Durkheim, É. (1933). *The division of labor in society.* Glencoe, IL: The Free Press.

Durkheim, É. (1951). *Suicide: A study in sociology* (J.A. Spaulding & G. Simpson, Trans., G. Simpson, Ed.). New York: The Free Press.

Durkheim, É. (1964). *The rules of sociological method.* New York: The Free Press.

Giddens, A. (1984). The constitution of society: Outline of the theory of structuration. Cambridge, UK: Popity Press.

Knuttila, M. (1993). *Sociology revisited.* Toronto: McClelland & Stewart.

Marx, K. (1933). *Capital* (E. Paul & C. Paul, Trans.). London: J.M. Dent & Sons.

Porter, J. (1965). *The vertical mosaic: An analysis of social class and power in Canada.* Toronto: University of Toronto Press.

Spencer, H. (1851). *Social statics.* London: Chapman.

Standing Senate Committee on Social Affairs, Science and Technology. (2002, January). *The health of Canadians — The federal role: Interim report,* Vol. 2, *Current trends and future challenges.* http://www.parl.gc.ca/37/1/parlbus/commbus/senate/com-E/SOCI-E/rep-e/repjan01vol2-e.htm.

Statistics Canada. (2001). *Health reports.* Vol. 13, no. 2. Catalogue no. 82-003-XPE CAISTC VH142.

Weber, M. (1946). *From Max Weber: Essays in sociology* (H.H. Gerth & C.W. Mills, Eds. & Trans.). New York: Oxford University Press.

CHAPTER 2

Population Studies

This chapter examines population size, distribution, composition, and change. Fertility, mortality, and migration in Canada are explored in detail and compared with other societies. The chapter shows how fertility, mortality, and migration are affected by, and, in turn, affect the social fabric.

Chapter Objectives

After completing this chapter, you should be able to:

- Describe the general trends of worldwide population growth, including the demographic transition model.

- Identify the factors that contribute to different fertility rates.

- Identify factors that contribute to changes in mortality rates.

- Trace changes in the distribution of disease in the 20th century and the effects on society.

- Describe the worldwide trends in migration and their effect on Canadian society.

> *Demography, the study of human populations, is the most powerful — and most underutilized — tool we have to understand the past and foretell the future.*

This quotation is taken from Boom, Bust & Echo: Profiting from the Demographic Shift in the New Millennium, written by David Foot, a Canadian demographer and professor of economics at the University of Toronto. David Foot has an impressive record in projecting trends. Many of his predictions are related to Canada going through the "loudest" baby boom in the industrialized world. Every aspect of our society has been profoundly affected by the boomers and now by the children of these boomers, the echo boomers. He explains how the entry of these two boomer generations into the workplace and market continues to redefine society's needs. In his book, he talked about an aging spectator sport audience with empty seats, bankruptcies of sports teams and ticket rebellions. He predicted that these people would pursue other leisure activities, such as bird watching. He actually saw that once the baby boomers' babies were grown, SUVs would replace the minivan and that home renovations, gardening, laser *eye surgery, and golf were about to soar. He points to the falling birth rate and less demand for day care and reduced annual sales for toy companies in the future. This projection has prompted Mattel to look ahead. The company saw a big profit margin in redefining Barbie as a collectable doll from the youth of 45–55 year old women at $650 each. He was right on cities, on education, and the coming crunch in health care (MacGregor, 2003; Constantineau, 2002; Foot, 1996).*

BACKGROUND

demography
the study of populations

The study of populations is called **demography**. The term demography comes from two Greek words — *demos*, or people, and *graphos*, or writing — hence, writings about people. Demography is not the exclusive domain of sociology; it also incorporates aspects of economics, political science, geography, history, and psychology. The basic processes that are dealt with in population studies are birth, death, and migration, as well as the factors that influence these processes. Demography, then, is an attempt to trace and explain the increases, decreases, and shifts in human numbers.

There have been some very drastic changes in population size over the centuries. In 1801, the estimated population of the world reached one billion people for the first time. In 1926, 125 years later, the world's population was estimated at two billion. The third billion arrived by 1961, less than four decades later. By 1975, there were four billion people living on the planet, and by 1987 five billion. By 2003, the world's population reached 6.3 billion and is projected to grow to 8.9 billion by 2050 (United Nations, 2003). More people have lived on this earth in the 20th century than in all the rest of time combined.

The current numbers of this "population explosion" are somewhat misleading. Most European, North American, and other westernized countries have birth rates that are below the replacement levels for their own societies. A situation in which birth and immigration simply replace death and emigration has become known as **zero population growth (ZPG)**. The accepted calculation of ZPG is that each reproductive couple has to produce, on average, 2.1 children. This calculation allows for the fact that a proportion of the population does not reach reproductive age, and that a further group that does either cannot reproduce or chooses not to. The average fertility rate in some western European nations is low. The rate in Italy has plummeted to 1.1 children per woman, the lowest rate recorded in human history (United Nations, 2003). Industrialized nations as a whole are at 1.58 (United Nations, 2003). Canada as a nation is now at about 1.52, compared with a rate of 3.5 during the baby-boom years. The US rate is 2.08 (Statistics Canada, 2002). In contrast, the world rate is now 2.83 per reproductive couple, yet, of 192 countries, 24 have levels of 6 children or higher and 7 countries have fertility rates greater than 7 children per woman (United Nations, 2003). Rwanda is the highest at about 8.5 (United Nations, 2003). In explaining the continued explosion in worldwide population growth, we must keep in mind that population increases at a geometric rate.

zero population growth (ZPG)
a situation in which birth and immigration simply replace death and emigration

Countries such as China and Cuba have taken on massive educational programs and increased the availability of free contraception, resulting in drastic cuts in their birth rates. In many cases, however, distributing contraceptives and teaching about family limitation are insufficient to have a real effect. What is needed is also a massive change in value systems. If it is culturally ingrained that having a large family is a good thing, then teaching contraception and handing out condoms is not enough. People will also have to be convinced of the benefits of controlling their birth rates. Hence, in large parts of Asia, most of Africa, and nearly all of Latin America population levels are still soaring. When we add to these trends the fact that more people are living longer, then we still tend to have growing populations. Despite these growth rates, demographers are predicting declines in western populations commencing around the year 2035.

THEORETICAL PERSPECTIVES

Thomas Malthus

Thomas Malthus was the central historical figure in the attempt to formulate a theory of the interrelationship between population and social and economic change. In 1798, Malthus published his most important work, *An Essay on the Principles of Population*, in which he put forth three theories:

1. Population increases at a faster rate than food supply.

2. Nature will produce "positive checks" on population growth if the imbalance between population size and food supply gets too lopsided. These positive checks are poverty, misery, vice, disease, famine, war, and, ultimately, a rapid increase in the death rate.

3. The only way to avoid positive checks is to encourage "preventive checks" or "moral restraint" — that is, no premarital sex, delayed marriage, or celibacy within marriage. He did not believe in contraception, because he considered it immoral to intercede in God's decisions.

Malthus's predictions gained him the title "the gloomy parson." His preventive checks were intended chiefly for the lower classes, which he maintained were overbreeding and, because of their low social status and their increasing numbers, were weakening the social fabric. All the same, he despaired of the success of preventive checks, because he thought that the lower classes were too strongly driven by their "base" instincts ever to practise moral restraint. Malthus foresaw a time when population would far outstrip food supply and nature would intercede. Malthus could not, however, have predicted the massive agricultural changes that have made it possible to greatly increase food supply, or the opening up of the great "bread baskets" of the world — the American and Canadian prairies, the Ukrainian steppes, the Argentinian pampas, and the other great food-producing regions (in Brazil, New Zealand, South Africa, and Australia) that were in a primitive state of development when he wrote. Perhaps a more liberal appreciation of the role of contraception would have given some hope to his writings.

Demographic Transition Theory

Different societies in the world are at different stages of the **demographic transition theory** of population growth. The demographic transition theory, which is more a descriptive picture than a theory, provides a model of how societies

demographic transition theory
a model of how societies progress from a state of balanced populations as a result of high birth rates and high death rates, through periods of rapid population growth, to a state of balanced population with low birth and death rates

progress from a state of balanced populations as a result of high birth rates and high death rates, through periods of rapid population growth, to a state of balanced population with low birth and death rates (see table 2.1). The demographic transition model divides population growth into four eras or stages.

STAGE 1: THE PRE-INDUSTRIAL ERA (PRE-1760)

In Western societies, the pre-industrial era is taken to have ended with the onset of the Industrial Revolution, around 1760. This is the point at which manual industry started to give way to power-machine-driven industry. Specifically, 1760 saw the harnessing of steam to drive an engine by James Watt, the Scottish inventor. Some societies are still very much in this era.

The pre-industrial era was typified by high birth rates; contraception was available but it was not very effective and, more important, it was not highly valued. Large families were considered desirable. In a hand-operated agricultural society, field workers had to be bred. A large number of pregnancies were needed to ensure a reasonable birth rate. It is estimated, for example, that in Europe in the 1700s, only 4 children out of 10 would survive to adulthood. The death rate, especially among infants and children, was very high. Sanitation was poor; water often was drawn from sources that had been contaminated by human and other animal feces. Nutritional knowledge was virtually non-existent; in many countries children would progress from breast-feeding to drinking beer or wine that was unrefined and of a very high alcohol content. Disease was rampant and medical knowledge was rudimentary. Thus, a natural balance kept birth rates and death rates equal and population grew only slowly.

STAGE 2: THE INDUSTRIALIZING ERA (1760–1899)

As society started to industrialize, urban areas started to grow and a factory culture developed. From the 1830s onward, a rapid transition from a predominantly rural population to a mainly urban one occurred. Scientific and technological advances started to affect the life expectancies of citizens. Nutritional knowledge improved. Factories greatly enhanced the real income of people. The growth and development of cities brought advancements in techniques of waste disposal. The introduction of sewer systems may well have had the single greatest impact on increasing life expectancy of any invention. Medical knowledge also greatly advanced. The role of bacteria and viruses in causing disease was uncovered. All of these factors meant that life expectancy started to increase greatly for a growing proportion of the population. The death rate started to decrease rapidly. The birth rate, meanwhile, was decreasing, but at a much slower pace. The population found it easier to accept things that could increase their life expectancy than to accept things that would challenge their cultural tradition of having as many children "as God sends," so they continued to avoid the usage of contraception. Population growth started to mushroom, but this was not yet problematic. With empires to be conquered, settled, and staffed, and with virtually deserted regions like Australasia, Africa, and North and South America to take the overflow, the escalation was barely noticed. Nobody, of course, bothered to ask the Indian or Inuit, the Aboriginal or Maori, the Azande or Zulu, the Inca or Aztec if they considered their regions to be deserted.

TABLE 2.1   The Demographic Transition Model

Stage	Birth rate	Death rate	Growth
Pre-industrial	High	High	Slow
Industrializing	Slow decrease	Rapid decrease	Very rapid
Industrialized	Rapid decrease	Rapid decrease	Medium
Post-industrial	Low	Low	Slow

STAGE 3: THE INDUSTRIAL ERA (1900–1960)

Between 1900 and 1960, in North America and Europe, industrialization reached its peak. Large, labour-intensive factories based on assembly-line technology appeared all over the landscape. In fact, the first use of the assembly line marks the beginning date of this era. Industrial cities, with elaborate sewer systems and water-cleansing plants, grew rapidly and people flocked to them. The industrial explosion and the contingencies of two experiences of global warfare accelerated the need for new scientific and medical knowledge. Soldiers returning from war demanded that their sacrifices be rewarded with a better system of educational, social, and health care safeguards. The greatly increased technologization of agriculture, and the increasing application of science to farming, yielded bigger and better harvests.

The trade union movement and law reform protected workers from many of the more deadly consequences of the workplace, especially guarding children against commercial exploitation. Fleming's discovery of penicillin in the 1930s and the subsequent production of other antibiotics in the '40s and '50s enhanced our ability to fight disease. This was followed by the massive inoculation campaigns, beginning in the 1950s, that would eventually rid the world of smallpox and exercise great control over polio, whooping cough, measles, tuberculosis, diphtheria, and other diseases. Consequently, the death rate started to drop to record lows and the biblical limit of life expectancy — "three score and ten," or 70 years — became a reality for the great majority of the population.

People started to realize the benefits of smaller families. This trend was reinforced by the pioneering work of such people as Margaret Sanger in the United States and Elizabeth Bagshaw in Canada. Sanger, troubled by the despair she had witnessed as a public health nurse, opened a birth control clinic in the Hell's Kitchen area of New York City in 1916. She did so in direct contravention of the sanctimonious Comstock Laws, enacted in the 1870s, as an attempt to govern people's moral behaviour. Dr. Elizabeth Bagshaw later set up a birth control clinic in Hamilton, Ontario, despite massive opposition from both the Anglican and the Roman Catholic churches. The birth rate did begin to drop, but it did not drop nearly as quickly as the death rate, in spite of a depression, two world wars, and many more minor conflicts.

Population still increased at a fairly rapid rate. To a certain extent, Western culture still favoured large families and the contraceptives available still were not completely effective and not completely accepted by society. Acquiring contraceptives seemed to carry more social taboos than the sex act itself. Governments, too, were afraid to be seen to be encouraging sex by supporting contraceptive research. A century and a half after Malthus's essay, no world government was significantly concerned about the rate of population increase or what to do about it. Sanger and others approached many governments to try to finance the beginning work on the birth control pill, but none dared to get involved for fear of being ejected from office on a morals issue.

A very unusual demographic event took place immediately following World War II. A reproductive generation is usually a five-year age group, but two groups had for the most part postponed relationships, marriages, and childbirth because of the uncertainties of the Great Depression and World War II. Shortly after the cessation of hostilities in 1945, both these generations started to make up for lost time in generating families, while the generation due to have children in the normal course of events had their kids on time. Three reproductive generations started to reproduce simultaneously, and the two older generations quickly followed their first child with a second. The massive cohort of babies born between 1945 and 1963, but especially between 1947 and 1966, with a peak blip in 1960, is usually referred to as the baby boom. Thus, a **baby boom** is an unusually large cohort of infants born in a relatively short period of time.

baby boom
an unusually large cohort of infants born in a relatively short period of time

This baby boom was the biggest ever. The impact of this unusual birth rate is with us still. One reason that jobs often were scarce in the '80s and '90s is that this large group had not moved on in the job market as much as previous groups. As this group is retiring, the economy again is having difficulty adjusting. There is now a shortage of potential replacement workers for retiring boomers in some occupational fields such as nursing. If your local radio station has become an "oldies" station, it probably did so because the boomers represent the biggest target audience around, and it is their music that is playing. In fact, 1050 CHUM changed to an all sports channel, then changed back when it was unsuccessful. Over the 1980s, the baby boomers moved through their prime child-bearing years and produced an "echo" generation of boomer children that mitigated slower growth (see figure 2.1).

STAGE 4: THE POST-INDUSTRIAL ERA (1961–PRESENT)

In 1961, the world of demography changed forever. For the previous two years, a significant clinical trial had been going on in Puerto Rico. A sample of young women had been daily swallowing a pill claimed to prevent them undergoing unwanted pregnancies. The clinical trial was a scientific triumph, the pill worked, and there were no significant side effects. In 1961, the pill was marketed in the United States and in 1962 made its appearance in Canada. Women were suspicious at first and the birth control pill caught on only slowly, but by the end of 1963, it was having a major impact. The decade from 1964 to 1973 has become known as the baby bust years: the birth rate dropped off sharply in 1964 and decreased steadily in Western countries until about 1973.

A small increase in the birth rate was noticed in the mid-1970s; the baby boomers started their own mini baby boom. The boomers who had become the hippie generation put off having their first children until five years after the normal average age for a first child, while the succeeding generation had their first child at the "normal" time, thus again producing two generations at once. This generation has become known as the "echo" — that is, an echo of the original boom. Consequently, we are now in a cycle of booms and busts that makes economic, social, occupational, educational, and health care planning exceedingly difficult.

The effect of the birth control pill was slow to take hold, but once it did, the limitation of family size to two children quickly became the norm. Other factors

FIGURE 2.1   Total Fertility Rate, Canada and the United States, 1940–2000

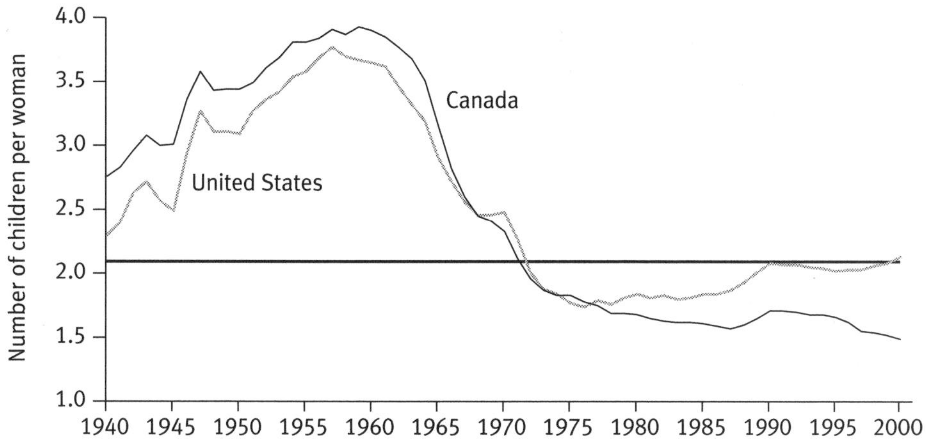

Note: The solid black horizontal line denotes the natural replacement population level of 2.1 children per woman.

Source: Bélanger and Ouellet (2002).

contributed to a decreasing birth rate, such as the need for a family to be compact enough to move easily to seek occupational advancement. The increase in desire for material possessions made it increasingly necessary for a family to have two incomes, and if the mother was going to work, family limitation became important.

On the other side of the ledger, the death rate was again falling at a remarkable rate. Infant mortality has now been reduced to very minor levels. Advances in medicine have greatly increased the life expectancy of people suffering from such diseases as cystic fibrosis and childhood leukemia. Diseases that had previously given a child victim a life expectancy of about 14 can now be controlled into middle age and perhaps beyond. We are now returning to a balance of death rates and birth rates. This time, instead of undergoing eight pregnancies to ensure that four children will become adults, women can go through just two pregnancies and be reasonably sure that both children will survive and replace their parents on this earth.

THE DEMOGRAPHIC TRANSITION OUTLOOK

Many non-Western nations are still only in the beginning phases of the demographic transition model, and even in the Western world different countries are at different phases in the process. So far, the model has proceeded in only one direction, but there is no logical reason why circumstances could not transpire to reverse the process. The incidence of AIDS and the recurring famines in Africa may, for example, be a serious setback for a continent that was making massive strides in undergoing this transition faster than it had happened before.

Western newspapers frequently report that scientists are getting extremely close to making discoveries that may dramatically increase life expectancy. If these breakthroughs are made, how will they affect population growth? The 2035 estimate for population reduction may become obsolete if more and more people start living until they are 92.

BASIC DEMOGRAPHIC CONCEPTS

Demography is the study of three processes:

1. birth and the factors that affect the frequency of birth (fertility)

2. death and its contributing factors (mortality)

3. population redistribution and the reasons people move (migration)

FERTILITY

fertility
the actual reproductive performance of a population

The meaning of fertility for a demographer is considerably different from that for a biologist. In biology, fertility is interpreted in terms of the ability of a male or female member of a species to reproduce. In demography, **fertility** is the actual reproductive performance of a population. Demography makes use of statistics to identify trends in the number of births occurring in the population. The simplest of these statistics is called the **birth rate**, which is calculated as the number of live births per 1000 population per annum. Technically, this is called the *crude birth rate*; it is "crude" because it is the simplest such statistic that can be calculated. The birth rate gives us the ability to compare the reproductive performance of populations of different sizes. By averaging out the crude birth rate to see how many births there are per 1000 people, we can see whether the birth rate of the Greater Toronto Area, with a population in excess of 4 682 897, differs from that of Guelph, with a population of 106 170 (Statistics Canada, 2001).

birth rate
the number of live births per 1000 population per annum

However, not everyone in the population gives birth. If non-reproductive segments of society are overrepresented in a geographical area, then the birth rate for that area will be low. To accommodate this difficulty, more refined versions of the birth rate statistic are necessary. Close to 50 percent of the population are physiologically incapable of giving birth — males. It may be better, then, to measure only the **sex-specific birth rate**, or the number of live births per 1000 women in a population per annum. By using the sex-specific birth rate, we are able to determine whether an imbalance in birth rates between two communities is simply due to a higher proportion of females in the one community. Furthermore, not all age groups take a large part in the reproductive process; typically, the very young and the old are not reproductive. Thus, we may need to calculate an **age-specific birth rate**, or the number of live births per 1000 people of a given age group in a population per annum. As a further refinement, we could produce an age/sex-specific birth rate, which would measure the number of live births per 1000 women within a certain age group. The types of birth rates we could measure are virtually endless — race-specific birth rates, religion-specific birth rates, occupation-specific birth rates, and so on.

sex-specific birth rate
the number of live births per 1000 women in a population per annum

age-specific birth rate
the number of live births per 1000 people of a given age group in the population per annum

fecundity
the maximum biological capacity for reproduction that a population can achieve

The maximum biological capacity for reproduction that a population can achieve is called **fecundity**. The population in question can be one woman, a geographical area, or a country. In modern society, a woman is capable of conceiving between the approximate ages of 13 and 51. This represents close to 500 ovulatory cycles at which a woman is capable of conception. Not surprisingly, there is no known society in which women make a habit of trying to achieve their maximum biological capacity for conception. The reproductive process is influenced by biological factors. After first fertility, it takes a few years for a young woman to ovulate during every cycle. At the other end of the spectrum, menopause is a much more prolonged process than most people think. For seven or eight years before the end of menopause, the number of anovulatory cycles that a woman goes through gradually increases. And any attempt to reproduce at Guinness Book of World Records rates would probably increase the chances of earlier menopause.

It is, however, a result primarily of sociocultural factors that full fertility in the population is inhibited. Factors that affect exposure to intercourse, social norms surrounding virginity and celibacy, taboos about non-marital sexual activity, and age of entry into marital or sexual unions will have an influence on child-bearing. Other factors, such as economic conditions, employment rates, values about family size, and access to and employment of contraceptive devices, will contribute to people's decisions about how many children to have and when. Finally, factors affecting exposure to gestation and birth such as prenatal disorders and the availability of abortion will help determine the actual birth rate.

A growing concern in demography is a marked increase in biological infertility and a decrease in biological fertility. Underdeveloped ovaries, disease-damaged and blocked fallopian tubes, hostile cervical mucus, and inadequate or mistimed sexual relationships can be causes of infertility in females. In males, impaired sperm production, sexually transmitted diseases, high incidence of defective sperm, low motility of sperm, and incomplete, inadequate, or ill-timed sexual activity can cause infertility. In about 40 percent of cases it is the female who is "responsible" for the couple's inability to conceive; in another 40 percent it is the male; in the remaining 20 percent of cases it is a result of the combination of that particular male and that particular female — that is, each would probably be fertile with another partner but are infertile with each other. Changes in the way we live are blamed for perceived increases in infertility. Increases in pollution, emotional stress, and crowded living conditions with their consequent spreading of infections could be affecting the generation of normal and sufficient sperm. So too, some people think, could tight jeans and jockey shorts. Because sperm develop best at a temperature a couple of degrees below body temperature, clothing that holds the testes close to the body cavity will impair sperm development. It is estimated that infertility occurs in 20 percent of the population.

Family Limitation

Since Margaret Sanger (1883–1966) wrote her treatise *Family Limitation* in 1908, the world has become gradually more interested in seeking ways to control fertility. Sanger had been a public health nurse in the Hell's Kitchen area of New York City at the turn of the century. She had witnessed the great misery that women suffered as a result of too many pregnancies, having too many mouths to feed, and the horrific toll of back-street and self-administered abortions. Sanger spoke out in favour of birth control and against the US Comstock Laws of 1873, which forbade the advocating, advertising, distribution, and sale of contraceptives. Sanger and her partner Ethel Byrne were not able to make progress until the death in 1915 of Arthur Comstock, for whom the Comstock Laws were named. After Comstock's death, interest in curtailing the activities of people like Sanger and Byrne declined. In 1916, they were able to open the first birth control clinic in North America.

Contraception and birth control had been around for thousands of years before Sanger. The ancient Egyptians wrote about using small "tampons" soaked in honey, acacia gum, and lemon juice and inserted into the vagina. The gum and honey would slow down the sperm, and the lemon juice would act as a very effective sper-micide. Other Mediterranean cultures also used various mixtures of gum, honey, frankincense, olive oil, and lemon and lime juice. Ancient Hebrews wrote about *coitus interruptus*. The Turks, in AD 200, used vaginal sponges moistened with lemon juice. The condom is thought to have been invented by Fallopius in 1504; it was made out of sheep's intestine and was first propagandized as a way to counter-act venereal disease. In the mid-1700s, Casanova wrote about the usage of cervical caps. By the early 1900s, advocates of birth control such as Francis Place in En-gland and Charles Knowlton in the United States were trying to educate the public about its benefits.

When people talk about family limitation, they use three terms interchangeably — family planning, contraception, and birth control. These terms, however, have slightly different meanings. **Family planning** means the conscious decisions a couple has to make about reproduction. These decisions include whether or not to have sex, whether or not to use contraception, whether or not to have children, how many children to have, how far apart to have children, and how to bring up children. All contraceptives involve birth control, but not all birth control involves contraception. **Contraception** is any device that prevents conception from taking place. If there is no conception, there cannot be a birth. **Birth control** is any tech-nique that prevents the birth of a child. With birth control, conception could have taken place but the birth is thwarted; an example is the use of abortive techniques.

The effectiveness of a contraceptive device is measured in two ways. *Theoretical effectiveness* is a measure of how successful a contraceptive is if it is used properly. Problems associated with theoretical effectiveness are called method failure. The basic statistic that is calculated is our estimate of the proportion of sexually active women who would become pregnant in a given year if they used the device properly. The theoretical effectiveness of most contraceptive devices is very high. The larger problem tends to be associated with user failure. *User effectiveness* is a measure of how many pregnancies in a year are a result of ineffective or inappropriate use of the device. User failure is much higher than method failure. Much user failure can be attributed to the individual's attitude toward using the device as it should be used.

There is a dynamic relationship between a person's social situation and his or her appropriate and consistent use of a contraceptive device. If one partner morally blackmails the other into using a device that he or she does not want to use, then usage will probably be intermittent and sloppy. Similarly, a device must be consistent with a person's lifestyle; if, for example, a person works shifts, it creates an extra strain in trying to take a birth control pill at the same time every day. Lifestyle and attitudinal difficulties are especially predominant among young people. Many mid-teens possess an attitude called the **personal fable** — that is, a belief that the individual is immune to life's crises. This results in risk-taking behaviour such as lack of use, inconsistent use, or improper use of contraceptives. Religiosity can also play a role in teenage pregnancy. The more religious individuals are, the less likely they are to be involved in premarital sex, but if they are involved, they are less likely to use contraceptives.

Reproductive Technology

A growing problem area for social scientists, philosophers, and religious leaders, as well as the legal system, is the massive cultural lag that exists between our rapid ad-vances in reproductive technology and the unanswered ethical and legal questions

family planning
the conscious decisions a couple has to make about reproduction

contraception
any device that prevents conception from taking place

birth control
any technique that prevents the birth of a child

personal fable
a belief that the individual is immune to life's crises

concerning that technology. Surrogate mothering, artificial insemination, in-vitro fertilization, embryo freezing, ovulation-inducing drugs, and sperm banks are already with us. Artificial wombs and **cloning** may not be far away. In fact, an international human cloning company called Clonaid, founded by the Raelian Movement, has claimed to have cloned five babies born around the world by early 2003, although this claim has not been substantiated. Does a frozen embryo have rights? When an artificially inseminated egg is allowed to decay in a petri dish, has an abortion in effect been performed? Is surrogate mothering, even with artificial insemination, a form of adultery? What if the donor sperm that a woman receives turns out to be that of a close relative? These are a few of the moral and legal questions that we have not really even begun to answer. One cannot even begin to tackle the moral issues raised by cloning.

cloning
the technique of producing a genetically identical duplicate of an organism

MORTALITY

Mortality is the number of deaths in a population. Just as fertility is measured by the crude birth rate, so mortality is measured by the crude death rate. The **crude death rate** is the number of deaths per 1000 population per annum. Again, the calculation of deaths per 1000 population allows us to compare otherwise incomparable populations. These populations can be separated by geography or even by time. Once again, calculating sex-specific death rates can refine the crude statistic. This is significant because the life expectancy of the average Canadian male is 76.7, while female life expectancy is 82. Age-specific and age/sex-specific death rates can also be calculated. An important example of an age-specific death rate is the **infant mortality rate**, the number of deaths per 1000 children less than one year of age per annum. Raw statistics can often hide differences within a population. For example, in the United States, infant mortality is relatively low compared with other parts of the world. In some US inner-city areas, however, infant mortality is higher than in many of the poorest Third World countries.

mortality
the number of deaths in a population

crude death rate
the number of deaths per 1000 population per annum

A frequently misunderstood mortality statistic is that of **life expectancy**; the statistic actually refers to the average age of death in the population in a given year. Many people think that very complex calculations go into estimating life expectancy, such as the rate of medical innovation, application of nutritional knowledge, and the lowering of industrial risk. It is, in fact, much simpler than that. It is the sum of the age at death of everybody who died in the year, divided by the number of people who died.

infant mortality rate
the number of deaths per 1000 children less than one year of age per annum

life expectancy
the average age of death in the population in a given year

A popular myth is that life expectancy is rapidly increasing. An Old Testament reference states that the natural life span of mankind is three score and ten — that is, 70 years. The average life expectancy of adults is about 80 years in developed countries. The significant difference between now and biblical times is the fact that a considerably greater and increasing proportion of the population reaches their three score and 10, yet the life expectancy worldwide is only 65 years. In the least developed countries, many of which are highly affected by HIV/AIDS, life expectancy is below 50 years. In eastern Africa, it has dropped to 46.7 years (United Nations, 2003).

Another frequently used demographic concept is **life span**, which is the upper limit of survival of a human body. Many biologists think that the limit is somewhere around 115 years. Recently, though, a woman from Corbeil, Ontario, died at the age of 117. At the time of her death, April 1998, she was thought to be the oldest person on earth, succeeding a French woman who died in August 1997 at the remarkable

life span
the upper limit of survival of a human body

age of 122. These are extremely rare and exceptional circumstances. No claims of ages greater than these have ever been substantiated by independent sources. Remote areas that are out of contact with the mainstream of human history tend not to have benchmark periods or events, such as world wars, against which age can be measured.

Combining mortality and fertility statistics can give us a closer look at population changes in our society. An important way in which population changes can be examined is through the **rate of natural increase (RNI)**, which measures population changes excluding migration. Defined another way, RNI is the birth rate minus the death rate. Because birth rates have been declining steadily over the centuries and are now below the ZPG point, it is estimated that the RNI will be negative by the year 2035. In other words, a natural decline will begin. At present, only the increased longevity of more and more of our population is causing population to continue increasing.

The difference in death rates between males and females produces an imbalance in the **sex ratio**, which is the number of males per 100 females in a population. This ratio is depicted as, for example, 95:100. For a variety of reasons, males die earlier and at a faster rate than females. For example, most miscarriages are of male fetuses; 70 percent of sudden infant deaths occur to male infants; more teenage males than teenage females die through misadventure; and mid-life deaths are more likely to occur to males than to females. For these and other reasons, the normative sex ratio in the population is 95:100.

Morbidity

It is insufficient, of course, to look just at the number of deaths in a society; one must also look at the factors that contribute to the death rate. **Morbidity** is the rate of illness in a population. Morbidity patterns have changed greatly in the last century. In 1900, the majority of people died from opportunistic viral and bacterial disorders that spread as a result of poor sanitation, poor living conditions, and crowded homes and neighbourhoods. Antibiotics to deal with these disorders were 40 years in the future. The only major exception to this pattern was that the chief cause of death for young women was childbirth. Disease control has greatly reduced the risk of whooping cough, diphtheria, tuberculosis, pneumonia, and so on. Smallpox has been eradicated and good prenatal care has greatly cut down the number of maternal deaths. It is interesting to note that smallpox is the only disease that has been eradicated worldwide yet countries are stockpiling vaccines due to terrorist threats. The United States and Russia have the virus in laboratories and there is fear that the virus could leak to terrorists.

Although the relative dangers of these invasive diseases have been reduced and life expectancy has increased, diseases that are more likely to occur to an older population have increased. This is especially the case with diseases that arise from the body itself. Cancer and heart disease are the two main killers in our society, and both destroy the body from within.

Health and Illness

Although the realms of physiology, psychology, and sociology often overlap, social scientists have found it convenient to introduce a distinction between three terms that are often used interchangeably:

---

rate of natural increase (RNI)
the birth rate minus the death rate

sex ratio
the number of males per 100 females in the population

morbidity
the rate of illness in a population

- a **disease** is an objective pathology of the body (that is, it is within the realms of anatomy and physiology);

- an **illness** is the subjective sense that one is not well (that is, it is an internal feeling and thus a psychological process); and

- a **sickness** is the recognition by society that one is unwell (that is, it is a sociocultural phenomenon).

All three sociological perspectives contend that health, illness, and the health care system are social issues.

Symbolic interactionists point out that there are subjective standards of health and illness in every culture. An important pursuit would be to analyze the effects an individual's idea of health and illness have on her or his health. These theorists might assert that how one defines illness will affect how one actually feels. An example would be how our state of mind influences physical sensations. If someone is convinced she or he has a disease, the consequences are real, no matter if she or he actually has the disease or not.

Health and illness are socially defined conditions that are sometimes culturally relative. Obesity, for example, is considered a disorder in North America, whereas it is a sign of beauty in some African tribes. A logical question to ask is: What is health? Most people think of health as simply the absence of disease. In contrast, the World Health Organization (WHO) of the United Nations defines health as "a state of relative physical, mental, and social well-being." The society's culture, technology, and social structure affect the status of a population's health. Health is often defined in terms of the norms and values of the culture. There is, for example, still much controversy in our society over whether we should accept drug addiction, some psychiatric disorders, or hypersexuality as illnesses.

disease
an objective pathology of the body

illness
the subjective sense that one is not well

sickness
the recognition by society that one is unwell

CULTURAL FACTORS

Our culture may make us more susceptible to some illnesses. In our fast-paced, achievement-motivated society, disorders related to stress are on the increase. Many of us are aware of the negative consequences of being involved in the "rat race," and we discuss and scoff at our society's obsessiveness, but very few of us attempt to alleviate the problem by slowing down our pace of life. Fads and fashions can also impair our health. It is reasonable to ask such questions as: Do computer monitors cause birth defects? Do computer games exacerbate attention-deficit problems? Are tight underwear and jeans increasing fertility problems in young males? Is excessive use of pesticides related to recent increases in asthma? Do hip-hugging jeans cause nerve damage? These are just a few of many questions that we could ask about our current way of life.

TECHNOLOGICAL FACTORS

Our technological advances can also help to shape our health. Much of our previous heavy labour has been taken over by machines. At work, machines lift and arrange things for us or transport us from one place to another. At home, machines help us to remove snow, cut lawns, clip hedges, polish floors, and so on. Machines (as well as better laws) have reduced work-related and home accidents considerably. However, the cardiovascular fitness of our population has also declined, and so we encourage people to lift weights and go for walks and generally take part in some physical activity. Machines have also affected the delivery of health care. A great part of the escalation of health care costs can be attributed to the increasing sophistication (and therefore expense) of machinery available to caregivers. We may soon be faced with difficult decisions as a result of this expense, such as whether to let people suffer because the cost of helping them is too great.

SOCIAL FACTORS

Conflict theorists contend that health is related to our social structure, especially to social inequality. This inequality is a major reason that some people are healthier than others. They point out that health and illness are differentially distributed in the society along a number of dimensions: age, sex, social class, ethnicity, race, occupation, etc. This is apparent in capitalistic countries with for-profit health care. As well, the profit orientation of the pharmaceutical industry encourages an overreliance on drugs. Our expectations of quick fixes for many illnesses help to make this industry a very profitable business. On the other hand, many people can't afford the luxury of using expensive drugs when they are needed. The study of the differential distribution of disease among various social groups is called **social epidemiology**. Not all social classes, age groups, ethnic groups, sexes, occupational statuses, races, etc., are prone to the same diseases to the same degree. It is important to demographers and to medical personnel to know which groups are most susceptible to which diseases, because susceptibility to disease will have a significant effect on mortality statistics among these groups.

social epidemiology
the study of the differential distribution of disease among various social groups

Within this framework, it is also important to know whether a disease is spreading or diminishing. Two calculations assist us in determining the course of a disease. The *incidence* of a disease is the number of new cases of the disease in a given year, and the *prevalence* of a disease is the total number of cases of the disease that now exist in a population. Prevalence may also be defined as old cases plus new cases minus the cured and the deceased. By combining incidence and prevalence, we get a picture of the spread of the disease. The fact that 32 256 men and 17 599 women experienced a myocardial infarction in the Canadian fiscal year 1992–93 is an example of incidence (Health Canada, 1997). One in four women and one in eight men over 50 has osteoporosis (Osteoporosis Society of Canada, 2003). This is an example of prevalence.

Patterns of health, illness, and access to health care are also strongly related to social class. Although the universality of medicare in Canada means that we do not see the gross discrepancies in health care delivery that occur in the United States, some groups in Canada do receive better care than others. The vast majority of known diseases attack all social groups, but they do not attack them equally. Lung and chest disorders are much more common among the lower classes; these disorders are probably related to the type of jobs they do, the fact that their homes tend to be in poorer urban areas downwind of factories, and the high incidence of cigarette smoking. The middle class have higher rates of stress-related diseases such as hypertension, ulcers, and heart irregularities. The upper classes have higher levels of disorders related to excess, such as gout and alcoholism. There are pronounced disparities between the health of the general Canadian population and the Canadian aboriginal population. The aboriginal population experiences poorer health, higher rates of some chronic illnesses, higher infant mortality rates, and lower life expectancies. Diabetes is more than three times as prevalent, while hypertension, arthritis, and heart problems are also more common (Standing Senate Committee on Social Affairs, Science and Technology, 2001).

Sick-Role Occupancy

Health and illness can be seen to be social products in the way that individuals, on becoming ill, enter what is called the sick role — patterns of behaviour that are defined as appropriate for those who are ill.

The sick role, as outlined by Parsons and Fox (1961), has four main characteristics:

1. *The person's illness is not deliberate*   Unlike a person who engages in deviant behaviour, the sick person is not considered responsible for his or her illness. Some illnesses — for example, AIDS — cause a dispute in the society as to whether they fit this characteristic.

2. *The sick person is exempted from normal responsibilities*   Healthy people in daily life perform a number of roles that involve various tasks and obligations: writing tests, handing in papers, preparing meals, showing up for practice. The more serious a person's illness is seen to be, the more likely it is that the person will be excused from these obligations. Any attempt to define oneself as ill to escape these obligations is usually treated with suspicion. Approval of entry into the sick role usually depends on recognition of the illness by legitimate experts.

3. *The sick person expresses a desire to get well*   Those who are suspected of feigning illness or injuries, or of unnecessarily prolonging their sick-role incumbency, are usually looked down upon.

4. *The sick person must seek out competent help*   This help must meet with socially accepted notions of competence. Usually, this help must be provided by someone who has been legitimized by accreditation from a scientific medicine-based program.

The concept of a sick role fits into the functionalist perspective in defining the relationship between illness and cultural expectations for the sick. Functionalists claim that the health care system helps keep people healthy in order to perform the social roles necessary for a well-functioning society. When individuals inevitably become ill, rules are necessary to ensure that the disruption of responsibilities in the workplace, in the family, etc., is kept to a minimum.

Health Care

Health care is defined as deliberate activity directed toward improving health. In the past, most health care was provided by the family of the sick person or, in more severe cases of illness, by church-sponsored institutions that were staffed predominantly by nuns. In non-industrial societies, health care is still delivered by people who possess traditional knowledge about the healing properties of plants, herbs, roots, etc., combined with spiritual incantations. Ethnocentric Westerners dismiss these practices as charlatanism, but the fact remains that health often improves after such interventions. More and more in our society, even slight medical problems

health care
deliberate activity directed toward improving health

scientific medicine
the application of scientific methods to the study of disease and injury

are dealt with by highly trained, licensed practitioners, thus escalating the costs of health care delivery. Canadian health care is dominated by **scientific medicine**, which is the application of scientific methods to the study of disease and injury. This view of medicine became dominant as a result of its great success in discovering the role of bacteria and viruses in distributing disease, and the consequent development of vaccines and antibiotics to control the disorders.

Scientific medicine, performed by people with a minimum qualification of a medical doctor (MD), is now a lucrative near-monopoly in Canada. The average MD earns a salary that is in the top 1 percent of the population. Anyone who is caught practising medicine without a licence is subject to criminal proceedings, regardless of the outcomes of their treatments. Many previously respectable treatments (for example, chiropractic, acupuncture, and herbalism) became marginalized and treated with disdain by many health care professionals. To counteract this marginalization, these occupations have established a more scientific model of their processes and have set up training programs and accreditation associations to legitimize their practices.

HOLISTIC MEDICINE

holistic medicine
an approach to health care that directs attention to the whole person as well as to the importance of the social and physical environment

In recent years, there has been a growing interest in alternative kinds of health care. These various interests have been gathered under the title of **holistic medicine** — an approach to health care that directs attention to the whole person as well as to the importance of the social and physical environment. It is interesting to note that aboriginal Canadians have always practised this type of medicine as a part of their culture, with emphasis on the whole person in community with nature and each other. Longstanding criticisms of scientific medicine are that it focuses on the disease or injury; is concerned with symptoms, not people; and is preoccupied with disease, not health. Holistic medicine is not, as some people think, a belief in mumbo jumbo and a turning away from science. There is a growing awareness that scientific medicine is only one dimension of health that must be incorporated into a larger model that includes nutrition, exercise, social support networks, and counselling.

Holistic medicine is based on four major principles:

1. *Patients are people*   Holistic medicine advocates a full understanding of the person, including an understanding of the individual's social and physical environment as possible concurrent factors in the cause and course of a disease.

2. *Responsibility, not dependency*   Holistic medicine places primary responsibility for health decisions on the individuals, and does not treat health as a mystery that only physicians can understand. Physicians and nurses must, of course, be in control of an acute crisis situation, but must also foster a relationship where the individual can proactively promote patterns of behaviour that improve health rather than reactively depend on professionals to control the disease.

3. *Personal treatment environments*   Holistic medicine encourages the individual, wherever possible, to seek health restoration in comfortable surroundings, preferably the home rather than an impersonal and depersonalizing institution.

4. *Optimum health for all*   Holistic medicine promotes "wellness" and encourages lifestyles that are healthy, and thus aims at preventing illness rather than dealing with it after the fact.

The growing holistic health movement has influenced many Canadians. This interest has been stimulated by people's desire to control their health care. The sources they draw on to obtain good health information are expanding. The Internet, health and wellness newsletters, medical bulletins, toll-free nurse phone lines, phone-in counselling services, and other sources are available to fill the need for self-determined, self-managed health care.

The Medicalization of Society

The magnificent achievements of the scientific medicine model include the elimination of smallpox, the widespread control of diphtheria, tuberculosis, and polio, organ transplants, and in-vitro fertilization. These achievements have made this model one to be copied. As a result, non-medical or quasi-medical conditions are now treated as illnesses that need scientific investigation and that can be fixed with scientifically generated "cures." But when addictions, learning disorders, sexual dysfunction, and other disorders are treated as illnesses that need scientific investigation and scientifically generated "cures," are we doing a service or a disservice for the people who suffer from these disorders? Are we blinding ourselves to other, non-medical solutions to the problem?

In 1972, alcoholism was designated a disease, and subsequent research has produced medications and treatments to control the disease. However, many alcoholics have been able to use this disease theory as an excuse for drinking: "I couldn't help myself, my disease got worse." The most effective program for dealing with alcoholism remains Alcoholics Anonymous, whose notions are based on the idea that the disorder is self-inflicted but exacerbated by social situations, and that only spiritual guidance, self-will, and social support can remedy the condition. Education is often seen as a prescription for learning disorders: people go to school as preventive "medicine" against unemployment. This approach implies that the joy of discovery, the acquisition of new knowledge for its own sake, is not a worthy social goal. Learning disorders are "diagnosed" and "treated," while the possibility that the problems stem from the system of education or the IQ of the learner is downplayed or ignored.

Issues in Health Care

AGING

The rapidly falling birth rate, combined with the fact that a growing proportion of the population is surviving beyond 70 years of age, means that the proportion of old people is steadily increasing in society. The pace of this increase will only accelerate as the baby-boom generation advances in years. This process of the population steadily aging is called the "greying of Canada." In response to this process, more and more attention is being given to the science of **gerontology**, the study of the aging process. Greater attention is now being given to maintaining or enhancing the level of physical activity among older people, and to increasing awareness of the

gerontology
the study of the aging process

importance of nutrition and good diet. Geriatric nursing is an area of health care for which demand is likely to increase, and more and more of medical resources may have to be geared to illnesses and injuries associated with old age. Many of our old people are gathering in what have been called "grey ghettos," residential areas (retirement communities, seniors apartments, nursing homes, etc.) that consist almost solely of old people. These social groupings provide some advantages, such as easier access to health care and a built-in peer group to associate with, but they may also be depriving the young of role models and the old of the chance to interact with the young. This aging process has made us more aware of **ageism**, discrimination based on age, including such things as mandatory retirement ages, inadequate provision of age-specific recreational facilities, and condescending behaviours to the old. Not all of the Canadian population is showing this aging trend. Overall, the aboriginal population is growing at twice the rate of the rest of Canada and is younger on average as well. In 1996, the average age of the aboriginal population was 25.5 years, 10 years younger than the average age of the general population. Seniors currently make up a relatively small proportion of the aboriginal population. In 1996 in Canada, just over 4 percent who reported they were North American Indian, Inuit, or Metis were aged 65 and over, compared with 11 percent of the general population (Standing Senate Committee on Social Affairs, Science and Technology, 2001).

ageism
discrimination based on age

DEINSTITUTIONALIZATION

In the late 1960s, government policies toward keeping large numbers of people in permanent, enclosed facilities or institutions started to change. There was a growing realization that a problem was being created that was not readily solved. Institutionalized people were supposed to be involved in the community; however, their involvement was extremely limited when they lived in isolation of that community. Governments thus began the process of **deinstitutionalization**, attempting to return as many institutionalized people to the community as possible, replacing total institutionalized care with outreach programs, community-based services, out-patient clinics, and other programs. Unfortunately, many governments saw deinstitutionalization as an opportunity to cut budgets. Patients were often turned out of institutions when outreach programs were inadequate or non-existent. In the case of ex-psychiatric patients, this lack of planning has left many to fend for themselves in rooming houses in poor urban areas where, moreover, they are often being preyed upon by unscrupulous members of the community.

deinstitutionalization
the attempt to return as many institutionalized people to the community as possible, replacing total institutionalized care with outreach programs, community-based services, out-patient clinics, and other programs

HOSPICES

Forty years ago, Elizabeth Kubler-Ross noted that dying patients did not seem to get adequate care in general hospitals. Nurses, burdened with the demands of many patients, made conscious and unconscious decisions to care more for those who could be helped than for those who were "beyond" help. Meanwhile, relatives feared the dying process and withdrew. Kubler-Ross realized that these final days and months of life may be just the time when individuals are most in need of care and, indeed, specialized care. She proposed (1969) to set up **hospices**, institutions with a homelike atmosphere specifically for the dying and their friends and family. These hospices were to be staffed by professionals specifically trained to deal with the dying. Only the advent of AIDS has made Kubler-Ross's dream a reality.

hospices
institutions with a homelike atmosphere specifically for the dying and their friends and family

Other current issues that impinge on health care include the various aspects of environmental pollution and ozone depletion, the impact of cigarette smoking, increases in sexually transmitted diseases, ethical issues surrounding death (for example, euthanasia, assisted suicide, and definitions of death), and ethical issues surrounding artificial conception (for example, surrogate motherhood and genetic engineering).

MIGRATION

In 1986, 80 percent of the world's population lived in Africa, Asia, and Latin America; the other 20 percent lived in Europe, North America, and Australasia. It is estimated that by 2020, these figures will be 90 percent and 10 percent, respectively. There is tremendous pressure in the overpopulated continents to export many of their excess people, just as Europe did over the past 200 years. Increasingly, then, migratory trends emphasize movement from the Third World to the industrialized countries.

Any movement of a population between two geographical areas is termed **migration**. This movement implies two opposite processes: movement out of a geographical area, or **emigration**, and movement into a geographical area, or **immigration**. There are many reasons people feel a need to leave their country of origin, and just as many reasons they select certain destinations. *Push factors* are the reasons people leave their place of origin. These factors include economic deprivation, political repression, religious intolerance, harsh climate, and health problems. *Pull factors* are the reasons people select a specific place to move to. These factors include economic opportunity, political freedom, religious tolerance, hospitable climate, and good health care. Push factors can exist without pull factors. A refugee, for example, simply knows that he must get out of current danger and does not necessarily give thought to his ultimate destination. Similarly, pull factors can exist without push factors. A person may decide that she simply wants to explore living in a different place, without being dissatisfied with her place of origin.

Originally, most migration flowed from colonized countries in the Third World to the "mother" countries (mostly European) that had done the colonizing. A second wave of migration flowed from European countries to North America and Australasia. There was (and is) also a migratory pattern within these New World host countries — namely, a dense settling of the eastern coastal regions, followed by a gradual drifting to the west. Today, immigration patterns show a more direct route from the Third World to North America. In Canada, most immigrants head for the Windsor–Quebec City corridor and the Victoria–Vancouver area; in the United States, they are concentrated in the Boston–Miami and the Seattle–San Diego corridors. Compounding these international and internal trends is the tendency for the young people of North America to leave rural and small city areas for big city areas. As a result, large North American cities are burgeoning, and burdened, with immigrants from both home and abroad.

The major underlying variables that seem to accompany migration are sex, age, and skill. It is the young that move, often leaving an aging population in the countries, provinces, and areas that they have vacated. The majority of migrants are male. Even in the era of the emancipated woman, the females who migrate tend to do so because their fathers or husbands are migrating. The number of women who are the prime instigators of migration or sole itinerants is, however, rapidly increasing.

migration
any movement of a population between two geographical areas

emigration
movement out of a geographical area

immigration
movement into a geographical area

brain drain
the migration of skilled people from places that need their talents in search of material rewards in places that already have a skilled population

The countries and areas to which people migrate are often in need of scientifically, technically, and academically skilled people, and can often lure such persons to move with the promise of better pay and better living standards. Often these same people cannot get fair reward for their skills in their place of origin and therefore are tempted to sell their skills elsewhere. Thus, we witness a phenomenon that has become known as the **brain drain** — the migration of skilled people from places that need their talents in search of material rewards in places that already have a skilled population. Countries like India or Nigeria can little afford to lose skilled, talented, and motivated people, but they proportionately lose the most. The brain drain does not just apply to Third World countries. Canada loses 75 000 inhabitants to the United States every year, and most of them possess a postsecondary qualification or a skilled trade.

CANADA AND IMMIGRATION

Canada's immigration process and its policies have undergone constant revision in the 20th and 21st centuries. Until the turn of the 20th century, immigration was fairly open. Throughout the 1800s, many Europeans landed on the East Coast and gradually worked their way west, and Asians landed on the West Coast and set up fishing villages and trading centres. It was not until 1885 that the country started to set up immigration policies. The construction of the Canadian Pacific Railway led the government to encourage Asian immigration as a source of cheap labour. Many Asians wanted to stay and bring their families over as well. The *Chinese Immigration Act* of 1885 sought to curtail this immigration. The Act levied a special tax on any Chinese person who wanted to settle in the country. Meanwhile, Europeans were being encouraged to come to Canada with incentives of assisted passages, free rail transportation to underpopulated areas, and free land in the prairie provinces.

From 1901 to 1911, Canada's population increased by one-third. The rate of immigration slowed through the world wars and the interceding depression, and then started to soar again following the end of World War II. The *Immigration Act* of 1952 restricted immigration to a maximum of one percent of the population in any given year. In the 1950s and 1960s, immigration was high. Most immigrants at this time came from Europe, especially from Britain, Italy, Portugal, Ukraine, Yugoslavia, and Holland. World events such as the American defeat in Vietnam, Uganda's expulsion of native-born Asians, the collapsing economies of the West Indies, sporadic outbreaks of war in the Middle East, and right-wing repression in Latin America changed the face of immigration to Canada. In 1976, the British lost their privileged position of easier access to immigration and citizenship.

The *Immigration Act* of 1978 legislated that quotas for immigration were to be set annually, and that attempts must be made to reunite families, provide safe haven for refugees, foster economic development by selecting skilled workers and business people, restore ethnic balance, and give preference to people who wished to migrate to relatively underpopulated areas. The results of this Act have been disastrous. Canada's cities are straining to accommodate more than 1.7 million new immigrants since 1991 while the rest of the country is desperate for skilled labour. Ninety-four percent of these immigrants settled in the largest metropolitan areas. Nearly 44 percent of Toronto's residents are foreign-born. It is one of the most diverse cities in the world, with more than 200 different ethnic groups. Concentration of immigrants in big cities has created two very different Canadas. Regina's residents are largely descended from the first wave of settlers (aboriginals and Europeans). In Richmond, BC, nearly 60 percent of the population are visible minorities, primarily Chinese and South Asians (Statistics Canada, 2001). Canada is a country that needs immigration to stimulate its economy and to maintain its population levels. Immigrants bring new ideas, new products, new markets, and new vitality to a society. Canada has greatly reduced the number of immigrants from traditional sources and thus has greatly reduced the number of people coming in with skills and behaviour patterns adapted to its techno-industrial system. In the last few years, immigrants from Southeast Asia, Central America, and the Caribbean have been the major source of new immigrants. The social upheaval of being displaced into a completely alien culture has resulted in a great deal of social disorganization for the young people of these groups. This built-in alienation has been compounded by a lack of jobs. The depressed economy has been felt the hardest among the socially visible. These youngsters have been extensively exposed, through the media, to the material benefits that are thought to constitute the good life in this culture. Meanwhile, the society seems systemically intent on making sure that avenues to this good life are closed or very narrow. Some have decided that if they can't reach the dream through legal means, they will try illicit means.

The visible minority population is growing far faster than the total population. Under current trends, by 2016, the visible minorities will account for one-fifth of Canada's citizens. Immigrants from Asia, including the Middle East, account for more than half of the immigrants who arrived in the past decade. Among them, the leading birth country was China.

Figure 2.2 and tables 2.2 and 2.3 illustrate how the Canadian population is changing as a result of the immigration trends mentioned above. Figure 2.2 shows the proportion of immigrants born in Europe and Asia by period of immigration, and table 2.2 shows the top 10 countries of birth of immigrants, also by period of immigration. Table 2.3 shows the distribution of 1990s immigrants relative to the total Canadian population. As is evident from the table, Canada's top three census metropolitan areas — Toronto, Vancouver, and Montreal — are home to the majority of Canada's recent immigrants.

CHAPTER SUMMARY

The study of population is called demography. The size and composition of a population have profound effects on the social structure. In the past 200 years, the world has undergone a rapid growth in population. The demographic transition theory explains how a stable population with high birth and death rates and short life expectancy can evolve into a stable population with low birth and death rates and longer life expectancy. The three major variables of population study are fertility, mortality, and migration. All of these variables are profoundly affected by such social variables as values surrounding contraception, the availability of adequate health care, and the availability of viable employment. The changing population affects many social processes. The aging population will have an especially large effect on health care, the economy, and the job market.

FIGURE 2.2　Proportion of Immigrants Born in Europe and Asia by Period of Immigration, Canada, 2001

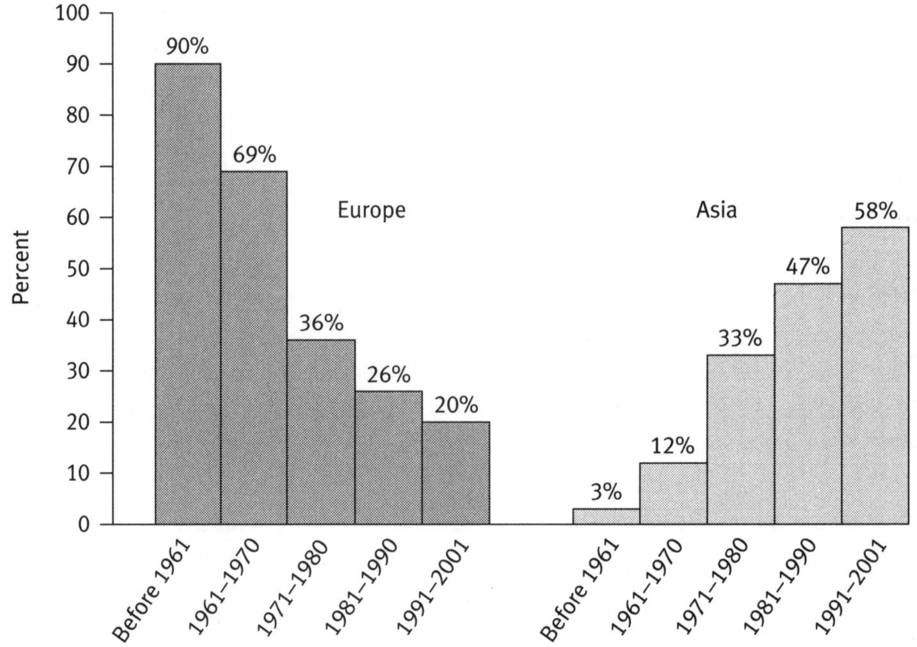

Source: Statistics Canada, http://www12.statcan.ca/english/census01/products/analytic/companion/etoimm/canada.cfm, April 2004.

TABLE 2.2　Top 10 Countries of Birth, Canada, 2001

	Immigrated before 1961			Immigrated 1991-2001[a]	
	Number	%		Number	%
Total immigrants	**894,465**	**100.0**	**Total immigrants**	**1,830,680**	**100.0**
United Kingdom	217,175	24.3	China, People's Republic of ...	197,360	10.8
Italy	147,320	16.5	India	156,120	8.5
Germany	96,770	10.8	Philippines	122,010	6.7
Netherlands	79,170	8.9	Hong Kong, Special		
Poland	44,340	5.0	Administrative Region	118,385	6.5
United States	34,810	3.9	Sri Lanka	62,590	3.4
Hungary	27,425	3.1	Pakistan	57,990	3.2
Ukraine	21,240	2.4	Taiwan	53,755	2.9
Greece	20,755	2.3	United States	51,440	2.8
China, People's			Iran	47,080	2.6
Republic of	15,850	1.8	Poland	43,370	2.4

[a] Includes data up to May 15, 2001.

Source: Statistics Canada, http://www12.statcan.ca/english/census01/products/analytic/companion/etoimm/canada.cfm, April 2004.

**TABLE 2.3   Distribution of 1990s' Immigrants Relative to Distribution of
Total Population, Canada and Census Metropolitan Areas, 2001**

Place of residence	1990s' immigrants	Total population	Ratio of 1990s' immigrants to total population[a]
Canada	**100.0%**	**100.0%**	
Total CMAs	**94.1%**	**64.4%**	**1.5**
Total non-CMAs	**5.9%**	**35.6%**	**0.2**
Toronto	43.3%	15.7%	2.8
Vancouver	17.7%	6.6%	2.7
Windsor	1.3%	1.0%	1.3
Calgary	3.8%	3.2%	1.2
Abbotsford	0.6%	0.5%	1.1
Ottawa-Hull[b]	3.9%	3.5%	1.1
Kitchener	1.4%	1.4%	1.0
Montreal	11.8%	11.4%	1.0
Hamilton	1.9%	2.2%	0.9
Edmonton	2.5%	3.1%	0.8
London	1.1%	1.4%	0.7
Winnipeg	1.4%	2.2%	0.6
Victoria	0.5%	1.0%	0.5
St. Catharines-Niagara	0.5%	1.3%	0.4
Kingston	0.2%	0.5%	0.4
Oshawa	0.4%	1.0%	0.4
Sherbrooke	0.2%	0.5%	0.4
Saskatoon	0.3%	0.8%	0.4
Halifax	0.4%	1.2%	0.3
Regina	0.2%	0.6%	0.3
Quebec	0.5%	2.3%	0.2
Thunder Bay	0.1%	0.4%	0.2
St. John's	0.1%	0.6%	0.1
Greater Sudbury	0.1%	0.5%	0.1
Saint John	0.0%	0.4%	0.1
Trois-Rivières	0.0%	0.5%	0.1
Chicoutimi-Jonquière[c]	0.0%	0.5%	0.1

[a] This ratio shows whether the proportion of 1990s' immigrants living in a given location is higher than the proportion of the total population living in the same location. For example, if 5% of 1990s' immigrants live in a place and the same proportion (5%) of the total population lives there, then the ratio will be 1.0.

[b] Now known as Ottawa-Gatineau.

[c] Now known as Saguenay.

Source: Statistics Canada, http://www12.statcan.ca/english/census01/products/analytic/companion/etoimm/canada.cfm, April 2004.

KEY TERMS

ageism

age-specific birth rate

baby boom

birth control

birth rate

brain drain

cloning

contraception

crude death rate

deinstitutionalization

demographic transition theory

demography

disease

emigration

family planning

fecundity

fertility

gerontology

health care

holistic medicine

hospices

illness

immigration

infant mortality rate

life expectancy

life span

migration

morbidity

mortality

personal fable

rate of natural increase (RNI)

scientific medicine

sex ratio

sex-specific birth rate

sickness

social epidemiology

zero population growth (ZPG)

REFERENCES

Bélanger, A., & Ouellet, G. (2002). A comparative study of recent trends in Canadian and American fertility. In A. Bélanger (Ed.), *Report on the demographic situation in Canada* (pp. 107-136). Statistics Canada catalogue no. 91-209-XPE.

Cable News Network, Inc. (1998). Woman said to be world's oldest person dies at 117. http://cnn.com/WORLD/americas/9804/17/oldest.woman.ap/index.html.

Canada's declining birth rate. (2002, September 27). *The Globe and Mail*, p. A8.

City of Guelph. (2004). Demographic profile. http://www.city.guelph.on.ca/document.cfm?category=252.

Coustantineau, B. (2002, May 3). Boomers aren't dead yet. *Vancouver Sun*, p. C5.

Foot, D.K. (1996). *Boom, bust & echo: Profiting from the demographic shift in the new millennium.* Toronto: Macfarlane Walter & Ross.

Greater Toronto Marketing Alliance. (1996). http://www.greater.toronto.on.ca/pop2031.htm.

Health Canada. (1997). *Heart disease and stroke in Canada 1997*. Population and Public Health Branch.

Kubler-Ross, E. (1969). *On death and dying*. New York: Macmillan.

MacGregor, R. (2003, January 23). How the numbers game revealed the rot in pro sports — and the rise of gardening. *The Globe and Mail*, p. A2.

Malthus, T. (1798). *An essay on the principles of population*.

Model United Nations Far West. (1999). Implications of current population trends. In *Issues before the 49th Session: Building global peace and security in the 21st century*. http://www.munfw.org/archive/49th/agenda.htm.

Osteoporosis Society of Canada. (2003). Things you should know about osteoporosis. http://www.osteoporosis.ca/english/Media%20Room/Background/Things%20You%20Should%20Know%20/default.asp?s=1.

Parsons, T., & Fox, R. (1961). Illness, therapy and the modern urban American family. In S. Lipset & N. Smelser (Eds.), *Sociology: The progress of a decade* (p. 561). Englewood Cliffs, NJ: Prentice-Hall.

Portrait of Canadian immigration. (2003, January 25). *The Globe and Mail*, p. A10.

Sanger, M. (1908). *Family limitation*.

Statistics Canada. (2001). *2001 census*. http://www12.statcan.ca/english/census01/home/index.cfm.

Statistics Canada. (2002, July 3). *The daily*. http://www.statcan.ca/Daily/English/020703/d020703a.htm.

Standing Senate Committee on Social Affairs, Science and Technology. (2001, September). *The health of Canadians — The federal role: Interim report*, Vol. 4, *Issues and options*. http://www.parl.gc.ca/37/1/parlbus/commbus/senate/com-E/SOCI-E/rep-e/repintsep01-e.htm.

United Nations. (2003, February 26). *World population prospects: The 2002 revision*. ESA/P/WP.180.

Weber, M. (1946). *From Max Weber: Essays in sociology* (H.H. Gerth & C.W. Mills, Eds. & Trans.). New York: Oxford University Press.

CHAPTER 3

Social Organization

This chapter explores the ways in which humans organize themselves socially to reach common goals. It examines the nature of organizations and their effect on our lives, and discusses the role of formal organization in Canadian society. This chapter also examines large-scale social behaviour that is unstructured and far from routine.

Chapter Objectives

After completing this chapter, you should be able to:

- Identify the social groups — primary, secondary, and reference — that shape personality and social functioning.

- Draw a multiple-role diagram and the accompanying role sets.

- Demonstrate the interaction between ascribed and achieved factors in social statuses.

- Identify elements of role failure, role conflict, status inconsistency, and subsequent role strain in social life.

- Evaluate techniques for managing role problems.

- Draw the organizational chart of any secondary group.

- Appraise the structure and functioning of any organization, and formulate solutions to the structural weaknesses in the organization.

- Describe how seemingly random patterns of behaviour (for example, crowds, public opinion, and rumour) have an underlying, predictable pattern to them.

Throughout the world in February 2003, there were massive protests against a possible war in Iraq led by US forces. On February 18 alone, it was estimated that 10 million people protested worldwide. This collective behaviour was bigger than the Vietnam War protests of the 1960s and '70s, and on that day the Iraq war was only a threat. Protesters for peace in Vietnam were mainly students; in 2003, the protesters were all ages, from different nations, races, religions, ethnic groups, and social classes. They were much less likely to be labelled as radicals. These two peace protest groups were decades apart and their collective actions arose in very different worlds. Globalization has made possible the international coordination of marches and rallies. Potential protesters can now find out about marches online. However, the goals of the different generations have not changed. Protesters are determined to make a difference. They attempt to capture public opinion, which can lead to a change in public policy.

How would sociologists explain this collective behaviour? It is an attempt to change current social conditions. This goal is only one of many goals for which we organize ourselves into groups.

THE SOCIAL ANIMAL

People are social in that they do not live in isolation from other people; they gather together in groups. There are many reasons for this social tendency:

- At the most basic level, human social behaviour is essential for human survival. Human procreation requires social behaviour, some cooperative action between two individuals. (Some reproduction technologies are an exception.) The human species is one of a few animals, or perhaps the only animal, with a continuous sex drive. Consequently, a minimal human group of two seems biologically necessary.

- Infants are dependent on their parents or other adults for survival. This dependency on others for maintenance and socialization continues until the child is self-sufficient. This dependency also precipitates social action, particularly in a family group.

- Without technology, humans are mere animals and are weak in relation to their environment. Initially, the tendency to collect in large groups was a means of protection and survival.

- Humans rely far less on instinctive behaviour than other animals do. The vast majority of what we are is learned, and a human group is needed to facilitate that learning.

- Some of our higher-order needs, as described by Abraham Maslow, such as ego gratification, and especially social acceptance, can only be fulfilled through group experience.

When people interact with each other, certain mutual dependencies develop. People become dependent on each other for an exchange of services. In a complex society, we are unable to do everything for ourselves. We divide most of the work so that we tend to do those things at which we excel or for which we have special facilities. Consequently, we come to rely on others for additional skills, goods, and services — that is, a basic division of labour results. The **division of labour** refers to the tendency for general tasks and roles to become increasingly specialized.

division of labour
the tendency for general tasks and roles to become increasingly specialized

The division of labour leads to increasing dependency among people, which, in turn, reinforces social behaviour. As development advances in a society, the cycle of interrelationships between skills, goods, and services becomes even stronger, with greater specialization in work. This results in a more complex division of labour, a greater dependency on others, and greater need for social behaviour.

These developments lead to an expanding need for coordination and control of the various elements of society. As this cycle continues, the necessity for organization increases.

THE SOCIAL GROUP

In sociological terms, a **group** is defined as a collectivity of individuals sharing a common interest or bond. A random collection of people at a crosswalk, for example, would not be considered a group; neither would a statistical category like college students or spectators at a sports activity. If these people developed some common identity (for example, a student action group or a sports fan club), they would become a group in sociological terms.

group
a collectivity of individuals sharing a common interest or bond

Sociologists distinguish between two main types of groups: primary and secondary. These groups have fundamentally different bases for action and, therefore, different effects on the behaviour of individuals.

Primary Groups

A **primary group** is a collection of individuals who gather together simply for the sake of being together. This group is people-oriented. It displays characteristics, such as

primary group
a collection of individuals who gather together simply for the sake of being together

- close cooperation between group members,

- a sense of identification with the group,

- a sense of loyalty to the group, and

- regular one-to-one contact.

The relationships among group members serve as an end in themselves; they are not a means of achieving some other purpose. Classic examples of primary groups are friendship groups, peer groups, and close-knit families.

Charles Horton Cooley (1864–1929), a sociologist with a symbolic interactionist approach, called tightly integrated and personal groups primary because they are among the first groups we experience. Family and friends have primary importance in our socialization process, shaping our behaviours, attitudes, and social identity (Macionis, Jansson, & Benoit, 2004, p. 102).

Secondary Groups

A **secondary group** is a collection of individuals who are brought together to achieve a common purpose. This group is goal-oriented. It displays such characteristics as

secondary group
a collection of individuals who are brought together to achieve a common purpose

- potential disbandment on the achievement of the goal,

- greater formal organization than a primary group, and

- potential lack of need for face-to-face contact.

The relationships among group members are impersonal, with emphasis on the role performance of individual members. Examples of secondary groups are a school class with its goal of graduation, a work group, and a sports team (see table 3.1).

TABLE 3.1   Comparison of Group Characteristics

	Primary groups	Secondary groups
Physical features	• generally, small number of members • regular one-to-one contact	• generally, large number of members • potential lack of need for face-to-face contact
Nature of roles	• roles emphasize personal-orientation • role expectations are specific to the individual • emphasis more on status rather than on quality of role performance • members are unique and irreplaceable	• roles emphasize goal-orientation • role expectations are universal instead of being specific to the individual • emphasis on quality of role performance rather than on status; failure to perform adequately may lead to dismissal from status position • members are replaceable
Nature of relationships	• a sense of identification with and loyalty to the group • emphasis on cooperation • relationships in the group are valued for their own sake • relationships are mostly personal, with spontaneity • more uninhibited emotional expression	• identification with and loyalty to the group is valued, yet potential disbandment on the achievement of the group's goal • emphasis of competition and cooperation • often relationships are seen as a means of progress and promotion • relationships are more formal and less personal • more detachment and emotional neutrality expected

Although a group may be formed initially as a secondary group, it is possible, and in fact very common, for a secondary group to evolve into a primary group, or, to be more accurate, a number of smaller primary groups. If you examine your college class, you will notice that this process has already occurred. A large secondary group of strangers at the beginning of the semester has probably by now developed into a number of small primary groups. The secondary group will disperse upon graduation. Many of the primary relationships that you develop in your college years will persist for a much longer period of time, perhaps for the rest of your life.

It is also fairly common in our society for a secondary group to try to coerce its members into acting as if they belong to a primary group. This attempt, however, is grounded on a contradiction: primary groups evolve, they are not manufactured to serve a goal. For example, schools exhort students to show school spirit and attend team pep rallies, even though some students may well hate sports. Bosses may claim that their employees are all one big happy family at the workplace, but they have authority and power and their employees don't.

STATUS AND ROLE

Within all social groups, different people occupy different positions and are required to perform different tasks. These different positions are known as statuses, and the tasks that are to be performed in a given status are known as roles.

A status is the social position of an individual in a group. It describes the relationship that one person has to others in his or her social group. For example, the status of *student* describes that person's position in relation to faculty, support staff, librarians, non-students, etc. Many people assume that they know a great deal about someone because of the statuses she or he occupies (for example, a landlord might think that being a student means being poor and noisy, and so will never rent an apartment to a student).

A role is the behaviour that is expected of an individual because he or she holds a particular status. One's status determines one's role. We expect a student to engage in such activities as attending classes, studying for exams, and doing homework. An individual occupies a number of statuses and, therefore, a number of roles.

The way we arrive at our statuses and roles varies. An **achieved status** is a social position that an individual has gained through his or her efforts and abilities. An **ascribed status** is a social position that society gives to an individual regardless of his or her merit or desire. We are born with some ascribed statuses (for example, Prince Charles was born a prince) and other statuses are given to us as we reach certain age stages. There are prescribed ages for entering school, being able to leave school, drinking, driving, voting, marrying without parental consent, retiring, etc.

Many societies have ceremonies or rituals designed to symbolize or solemnize the passage for an individual from one ascribed status based on age to another. At one time in our society, the age of 21 was very significant because many trappings of adulthood were granted then. Nowadays, we have lost a perspective on what constitutes adulthood. For most things, 18 seems to be the ascribed age, but not for drinking (19) or for driving (16). Any ritual or ceremony associated with a change of age status is called a **rite of passage**.

Most societies also ascribe status on the basis of gender. This process is called sex role typing or, simply, **sex typing**. Certain activities are reserved for males and certain ones for females, and crossing the line is often frowned upon. **Gender roles** are culturally defined positions and activities that are considered sex-appropriate within a society. An activity may be designated as male in one society but designated as female in another. Most sex typing, then, is culturally generated and is not a product of inherent biological distinctions between males and females. Most people conform to the norms of their culture, so it can be very difficult to get across the idea, for example, that boys can be ballet dancers and girls can be construction workers.

It is often the case that a particular ascribed status of an individual can help or hinder one's chances of achieving other statuses. For example, it is demonstrably easier for someone born into a wealthy family to achieve high public office than it is for someone from a poorer background. It is similarly difficult for a male to aspire to the position of chair of an equal opportunity group.

For the most part, occupational roles are achieved statuses. Usually, one pursues a certain occupation because of compatibility between one's perception of one's own talents and personality and the demands of the job. However, the very performance of an occupational role can have a socializing effect. It can sharpen and enhance that part of one's personality and behaviour that is called upon on the

achieved status
a social position that an individual has gained through his or her efforts and abilities

ascribed status
a social position that society gives to an individual regardless of his or her merit or desire

rite of passage
a ritual or ceremony associated with a change of age status

sex typing
the ascription of a status on the basis of gender

gender roles
culturally defined positions and activities that are considered sex-appropriate within a society

job. For example, a teacher may become less self-conscious of public speaking, or a salesperson may become more extroverted.

MULTIPLE ROLES

In modern societies like Canada, individuals tend to belong to many primary and secondary groups. In each of these groups, the individual holds a status, and for each of these statuses, there is a corresponding role to play. Therefore, each individual maintains multiple statuses and performs multiple roles. **Multiple roles** are behavioural patterns associated with the different statuses that an individual holds in his or her many primary and secondary group affiliations. Figure 3.1 shows a typical student's multiple roles.

The group that surrounds an individual in any given role is known as the **role set**. Each role set expects different things from us and has different needs for us to fulfill. Consequently, as we move from one role set to another, we emphasize different aspects of our personality and behave in a slightly different way to accommodate the needs and expectations of the different role sets. We can appear to be different people in our different roles. This is neither a two-faced hypocrisy nor a conscious attempt to disguise our real self. It is simply a response, usually unconscious, to a changed situation.

Figure 3.2 shows the surrounding role set of the role of student.

At times, as we enter one of our role sets, we feel that the group likes us, enjoys our presence, and values our participation. This message of acceptance is relayed in a variety of ways: overt behaviours, more subtle non-verbal communications, and expressions of support. The process by which an individual receives a sense of acceptance by and belonging to a group is called **in-grouping**. Just as it is pleasant to be included in a group, it is painful to be excluded from a group. The process by which an individual receives a sense of rejection by and exclusion from a group is called **out-grouping**. Some examples of out-grouping are avoidance behaviour, lively conversations that fall to silence on our approach, and others' facial expressions and certain body movements that signify our rejection.

For example, this behaviour would be quite evident if you were among the hockey fans at the Air Canada Centre in Toronto for a Toronto Maple Leaf vs. Ottawa Senators game. The in-group are those wearing the Leaf hockey sweaters; their sweaters give these fans a sense of belonging and identity. Those wearing Senators sweaters are clearly the out-group. A vivid example of out-grouping occurred in Nazi Germany when Jews were forced to wear the Star of David so that they could be easily identified.

REFERENCE GROUPS

One group to which people do feel they belong, even if they are not actually members, is termed a reference group. A **reference group** is a group with which people compare themselves when evaluating themselves and their behaviour. We constantly assess our lifestyles, achievements, skills, or appearance and compare them with similar qualities in other people. Reference groups can be as simple as our family or friends. They can be groups to which we aspire to belong, such as a professional group. They can be groups to which we used to belong, such as a community or neighbourhood where we used to live, or even a team for which we used to play.

multiple roles
behavioural patterns associated with the different statuses that an individual holds in his or her many primary and secondary group affiliations

role set
the group that surrounds an individual in any given role

in-grouping
the process by which an individual receives a sense of acceptance by and belonging to a group

out-grouping
the process by which an individual receives a sense of rejection by and exclusion from a group

reference group
a group with which people compare themselves when evaluating themselves and their behaviour

FIGURE 3.1   A Typical Student's Multiple Roles

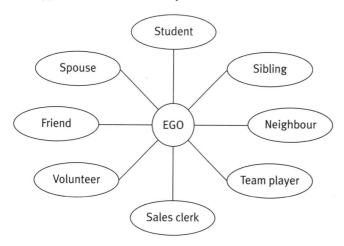

FIGURE 3.2   A Typical Student's Role Sets

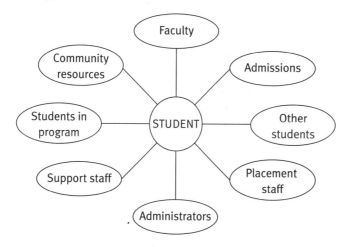

Reference groups can be more unrealistic. For example, consider the inordinate amount of esteem that sports and entertainment figures are given. Reference groups are powerful forces in the socialization process because they can shape individual behaviour and values.

COHESION AND CONFLICT

A group is said to be cohesive when its members strongly identify with the group and when they closely cooperate. Even conflict within a group can often be diminished or removed when the group finds itself in conflict with another group. Group members will drop their differences and unite in the face of external threat.

Many of the better sports coaches of our times have successfully employed the tactic of presenting the opposition, the press, the public, and even the team's own upper management as threatening, conspiring enemies as a means of drawing together the team members. Conflict between groups is often minimized by the fact that most groups in modern society have what are known as *crosscutting ties*. That is, despite differences among groups, there tend to exist relationships on some common ground (for example, agreement on an issue, or mutual interest in a current or potential state of affairs). Primitive societies often settled feuds by marrying off their sons and daughters to the "enemy," thus creating crosscutting ties that would decrease the risk of future hostilities.

When a society is a complex network of many groups, some individuals find themselves on the fringes of many groups but not fully immersed in any one group. Individuals in this position are called **marginal persons**. They can be useful in dealing with conflict between groups by acting as go-betweens because they are somewhat accepted by both groups. Marginal persons, however, can also find themselves being treated as scapegoats by one or both of the conflicting groups.

ROLE PROBLEMS

The social process of allocating statuses and roles can lead to a number of potentially problematic situations. Among the most common role problems are

1. *Role failure*   When an individual has a clearly defined role that he or she is expected to perform but is unable to meet these obligations, he or she is experiencing **role failure**. An unemployed breadwinner and a failing student are examples of individuals in role failure.

2. *Status inconsistency*   When an individual holds two statuses that appear to be contradictory, she or he is experiencing **status inconsistency**. Having a nephew older than yourself, being old enough to marry without parental consent but being too young to drink at your wedding, or being highly educated yet working in a low-paying job are examples of status inconsistency.

3. *Role conflict*   When an individual's performance of one social role detracts from the proper performance of other roles, he or she is experiencing **role conflict**. Being a good student could conflict with being a good spouse or parent, for example.

Many people can cope with these role problems without too much difficulty. Others, however, suffer from **role strain**: they subjectively and stressfully feel that these problems are burdens, and this strain can affect their other social roles and obligations.

To deal with role strain, an individual can solve the problem, use escapist techniques to avoid the problem, or reduce the strain by subconsciously employing one of a number of defence mechanisms. Among the many different defence mechanisms are:

- **rationalization**   redefining the situation to make it seem less painful

- **projection**   rationalizing the problem by claiming that someone else is really responsible

- **compartmentalization**   separating the parts of one's life that are inconsistent or in conflict so that one does not have to deal with the two things simultaneously.

The relationship between a few of the many role-related problems and a few of the many defence mechanisms that people use to cope with them is illustrated in figure 3.3.

marginal persons
individuals who find themselves on the fringes of many groups but not fully immersed in any one group

role failure
the failure to meet the obligations of a clearly defined role that an individual is expected to perform

status inconsistency
the holding of two statuses that appear to be contradictory

role conflict
the performance of one social role that detracts from the proper performance of other roles

role strain
an individual's subjective and stressful feeling that role problems are burdens

rationalization
the redefining of a situation to make it seem less painful

projection
the rationalizing of a problem by claiming that someone else is really responsible

compartmentalization
the separation of the parts of one's life that are inconsistent or in conflict so that one does not have to deal with the two things simultaneously

FIGURE 3.3   Role Problems and Defence Mechanisms

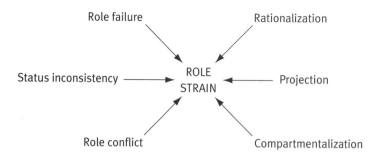

FORMAL ORGANIZATIONS

To manage the complexity of relationships, societies become formalized. Formal organizations replace informal relationships with rules, codes of conduct, laws, and other means of regulation. As labour is divided, the members of an organization take on a role — the behaviour expected of the person occupying a particular position. In a formal organization, the positions necessary in its division of labour are formally stated in the organization's documents, and the requirements of each role are specified in job descriptions. The organization's goals are continually met as individuals fill these positions, and when they leave, the organization continues with new individuals.

A **formal organization** is a secondary group in which roles, resources, and technology are coordinated to achieve a goal by means of a process that is formalized through written rules and procedures. Communication and leadership promote coordination, control, and problem solving.

One of the biggest problems faced by an organization is coordinating social behaviour to maintain social order and achieve common goals. Therefore, sociologists are interested in how organizations persuade people to cooperate. Essentially, people are motivated to work toward the organization's common goal through one or more of three procedures:

1. *The use of power*   **Power** is the ability to control the actions of others regardless of their wishes. Implicit in the idea of the exercise of power is the possible use of force.

2. *The use of influence*   **Influence** is the ability to affect the actions and decisions of others beyond one's authority to do so, or an indirect way of getting individuals to cooperate or conform to expectations. For example, a defence lawyer cannot decide a verdict, but she can influence it by the way she presents information to the jury.

3. *The use of authority*   **Authority** is the established right to make decisions about and to order the actions of others. We may not like getting a speeding ticket from a police officer, but we recognize his right to give us one.

Max Weber was one of the first scholars to emphasize the importance of formalization in organizations. He asked questions about why people obey orders from those in authority. He wondered whether it was a question of power or of discipline. Weber concluded that people obey the commands of others if they believe the order givers have legitimate authority.

formal organization
a secondary group in which roles, resources, and technology are coordinated to achieve a goal by means of a process that is formalized through written rules and procedures

power
the ability to control the actions of others regardless of their wishes

influence
the ability to affect the actions and decisions of others beyond one's authority to do so; an indirect way of getting individuals to cooperate or conform to expectations

authority
the established right to make decisions about and to order the actions of others

Bases of Legitimate Authority

Weber argued that there are three major bases of legitimate authority: traditional authority, charismatic authority, and legal–rational authority or bureaucracy.

TRADITIONAL AUTHORITY

Traditional authority rests on an established belief that certain traditions are sacred and that people who exercise authority on the basis of these traditions do so legitimately. This often implies the hereditary right of certain individuals to occupy positions of authority. The great advantages of traditional authority are that it provides historical continuity, which avoids continuous social upheaval, and it provides a base of previous knowledge and ways of doing things that set a precedent. An example of traditional authority is found in the nuclear family, where parents traditionally exercise authority over their children by virtue of the children's early dependence.

However, in a fast-changing society, tradition has some severe limitations as a way of getting things done. With change come new ideas and new activities, so traditional methods might not work for new practices.

CHARISMATIC AUTHORITY

Charismatic authority is the ability to motivate people to do things by the force of a strong, magnetic, overpowering personality. A person with this authority is believed to be special, and possesses some special ability or characteristic that inspires the loyalty of his or her followers. This kind of authority is perhaps the most efficient method of getting things done, but it does have drawbacks. Very few people possess charismatic personalities, so the problem of succession is particularly difficult, and the direction the authority takes his or her followers might not be beneficial (for example, Hitler and Nazi Germany).

LEGAL–RATIONAL AUTHORITY OR BUREAUCRACY

Legal–rational authority or bureaucracy is by far the most frequent type of authority in contemporary society. Legal–rational authority is based on the belief that specific patterns of rules, regulations, and procedures are legal and that those in authority have the right to give commands. This type of authority tends to be more systematic and impersonal than either traditional or charismatic authority and is therefore formalized. A **bureaucracy** is a highly structured secondary group that is governed by a detailed set of rules and that has a marked division of labour.

bureaucracy
a highly structured secondary group that is governed by a detailed set of rules and that has a marked division of labour

Bureaucracies

Organizations that are based on legal–rational authority tend to be bureaucracies. Weber described an "ideal-type" bureaucracy as one that would be a completely logical, rational system of organizing work. He identified six common features of bureaucratic organizations, each of which has inherent weaknesses:

1. *A bureaucracy is governed by a set of fixed and official rules and regulations.* These rules ensure fair and equitable running of the

bureaucracy. A policy or procedure governs every transaction, including transactions between different officers of the bureaucracy or between staff and clients. The more written procedures there are, the more likely the organization will be strangled in "red tape."

2. *There are levels of authority, an extensive chain of command to oversee operations.* The function of a hierarchy in a bureaucracy is to make certain that people and departments actually do what they are supposed to do and that they do it in the proper manner. The longer the chain of command is, the more susceptible this hierarchy of authority is to having a weak link. Information that is passed along the chain of command can be distorted or even lost.

   This becomes most apparent in a situation known as the supervisor's dilemma. In every organization, there is a level of positions known as the *supervisory level*, for which role performance requires some management skills (supervision, scheduling, work assignments, etc.) and some practical skills (law enforcement, machine operation, patient care, etc.). The supervisor's dilemma is "Am I management or am I worker?" If the supervisor "takes sides," then he creates a gap in the organizational communication chain. If he withdraws because the position of being the person in the middle is too stressful, he again creates a gap. The correct course of action is to act as a go-between, interpreting management's wishes to the workers and the workers' needs to management. This latter course of action is the most difficult to fulfill.

3. *The management of the organization is based on written documents* that are preserved in files for guidance and clarification (for example, memos, reports, letters, and computer printouts). Detailed documentation of every transaction is required. This documentation takes time, space, money, and labour. Forms need to be filled in, documentation needs to be approved, and decisions need to be authorized before action is taken. Furthermore, new rules and regulations have to be created for every new situation or case. Updating written documentation can be time-consuming and frustrating. As a result, organizations are often slow to change, even when change would be beneficial.

4. The written procedures and rules ensure that *everyone is treated in a consistent manner, without regard to personal considerations.* Bureaucratic principles require the maintenance of a detached approach. Everyone is to be treated objectively and equally. This rigidity in the hierarchy and the regulations does not account for individual needs and differences. As a result, the atmosphere of a bureaucracy is often impersonal. The individual employee may come to feel like a faceless, replaceable person and the client may feel objectified. For example, students often feel their student numbers are more significant to the organization than their names.

5. Because the rules that govern the operation of a bureaucracy are so specific in terms of responsibilities and duties, there tends to be a relatively *high degree of specialization in tasks.* Therefore, people in various positions often need specialized training.

When jobs are clearly delineated and people get locked into a job's original, narrow definition, it becomes easy to suggest that some tasks do not lie within one's job description. "It's not my job" becomes a common response to new problems that arise. This narrow thinking can stifle flexibility and creativity, and make it easy to clog up a bureaucracy. If every individual works to rule (that is, follows the job description to the smallest detail without using the various, effective shortcuts that most people create), then the whole process is slowed down considerably. And if a client chooses to make the organization dot every *i* and cross every *t*, the organization can come to a complete standstill.

6. *People are recruited or promoted in the organization on the basis of achievement criteria such as their competence, performance, knowledge, and ability.* People are chosen who are best qualified to fill the requirements of the position, which are outlined in the operating rules and duties of the bureaucracy. On the face of it, appointment to jobs on the basis of qualifications would seem to guarantee competence. However, this appointment approach blocks the promotion of people who are talented and who could be a valuable asset to the company. The problem is a Catch-22: they cannot develop skills without doing the job, but they cannot get a job without showing evidence of skills.

The use of merit as the only criterion for promotion also may create a problem. An organization that rewards an individual's successful performance at one level with promotion to the next level may promote the individual out of a job she can do into a job she cannot do. This process has been called "the Peter principle": employees eventually rise to their level of incompetence. The Peter principle can weaken an organization in two ways: first, it deprives the organization of an established and capable employee at one level, and second, it frustrates that employee by placing her in a job that she cannot do.

These six ideal components of bureaucracy are essential if an organization is to operate efficiently and to endure. The formalized rules and authority structures of bureaucracies enable them to operate predictably and consistently.

As we all have encountered, however, formal organizations can and do break down in their attempts to deliver service to clients. Bureaucracy is an unpleasant word to many people. It conjures up the idea of "red tape," strict adherence to cold-hearted and impersonal rules and regulations, inefficiency, and huge government departments that move at a snail's pace. Interestingly, the term **red tape** came from the tape commonly used to tie official papers. It is now recognized as the rigid application of regulations and routines, resulting in delays and exasperation in getting things done.

red tape
the rigid application of
regulations and routines

INFORMAL STRUCTURES

All the weaknesses of modern formal organizations have their source in one fundamental contradiction. This rational, efficient, logical structure is operated for and by human beings with their individual concerns, wants, needs, and prejudices. A perfect bureaucracy may meet theoretical demands while it denies human needs. In most bureaucracies that suffer from one or more of these built-in weaknesses, however, all is not lost. Where the formal organization fails, an informal organization typically sprouts to fill the gap. People get to know each other as individuals, not officers; they establish primary relationships; they break unnecessary and burdensome rules; they bypass the weak links in the hierarchy; secretaries perform functions that their bosses fail to do; senior workers are consulted instead of the supposed authority; and so on. This informal structure exists in all formal organizations and it is an important part of the "culture" of organizations that a new employee should explore as early as possible. As organizations increasingly face global competition, they need flexibility to give progressive employees more autonomy to develop creative business strategies with a more effective workforce.

Organizations are part of a larger social system; most are not self-contained units. They do not operate in a vacuum, but in an environment. They are affected by governments and their legislation, by customers and suppliers, by competitors, and by numerous other organizations and groups.

COLLECTIVE BEHAVIOUR

As we have seen, social behaviour usually follows a predictable and structured pattern. Group interaction is organized around established social norms and social roles. This makes much of social life quite routine. We spend a good part of our lives in organized groups. Fully organized groups are bureaucracies, with rigid, formal rules and regulations and a structured hierarchy of authority. This hierarchy has specific roles laid out in job descriptions and the organization has clearly defined goals and missions. If we hope to function in this type of social situation, we must adjust to its structure.

Most life events are also quite predictable. We have organized beliefs about the normal course of events in many familiar situations. Most of us have no difficulty knowing in advance what will happen when we go to the dentist, buy groceries, or attend classes. When students take an exam, they do not need to be told specifically to bring a pen rather than paper, because the teacher always provides paper but rarely supplies the pen.

However, not all group behaviour is routine behaviour. In unanticipated situations, social behaviour often is not guided by the accepted, everyday norms of conduct but becomes unstructured and unpredictable. No norms may exist or old ones may no longer be adequate. Extreme situations such as fires and earthquakes can lead to panic if cooperative behaviour breaks down. To better anticipate dangerous situations such as these and to know what to do to ensure safety, we are trained in emergency drills.

There is a wide range of group behaviour that is unstructured and unpredictable. **Collective behaviour** is a relatively unorganized pattern of mass social interaction. Collective behaviour is much more likely to take place under conditions of stress and circumstances in which groups are thwarted from achieving their goals. These unusual situations can be due to the natural or the social environment.

Some examples of collective behaviour are a crowd in panic due to an environmental disaster, mobs such as lynch mobs, riots, mass hysteria, protest rallies, political demonstrations, and constant changes in public opinion. Participants in these events generally have no clearly defined roles, goals, expectations, or definitions of

collective behaviour
a relatively unorganized pattern of mass social interaction

the situation, and they are often unresponsive to attempts at social control. A *social movement* is the most organized form of collective behaviour. Along with this kind of organization is a degree of leadership and ideological commitment to promote or resist social change.

THEORIES OF COLLECTIVE BEHAVIOUR

Collective behaviour is so diverse and lacking in predictability that it is difficult to come up with one explanation for its existence.

A macrosociological theory rooted in functionalism was developed by Neil Smelser in *Theory of Collective Behavior* (1962). His theory, called *value-added theory*, is regarded as one of the most comprehensive theories in the field. It explains collective behaviour as an attempt to change current social conditions. Smelser believed that when people are in a situation fraught with uncertainty, tension, or threat, they will attempt to change the stressful situation. Their definition of the situation will dictate the type of collective action they will take.

Smelser identified six conditions that are required for and that will lead to collective behaviour: structural conduciveness, structural strain, generalized beliefs, precipitating event, mobilization, and failure of social control.

1. Structural Conduciveness

Structural conduciveness refers to the basic conditions that make collective behaviour possible. The right circumstances, such as structural differences in society, must be present. For example, at the Oka standoff in Quebec in the summer of 1990, social conditions, such as the tension between the police and Mohawk warriors, precipitated the occurrence of a hostile outburst. The expansion of a golf course from 9 to 18 holes would have encroached on sacred native land. After a police officer was killed, more than 1000 police officers converged on Oka (population 1800). Other First Nation warriors, many of whom were US citizens armed with guns that they were not allowed by law to possess and carry in Canada, came to support the Mohawks. They blocked highways and closed bridges to Montreal. As another example, in the black ghetto riots of the 1960s, the existence of depressed black ghettos in US urban areas set the stage for collective behaviour.

2. Structural Strain

Circumstances such as discrimination, conflict, poverty, and uncertainty about the future place a strain on society. This strain encourages a collective effort to alleviate the situation. The aboriginals at Oka were fighting for land claims. US race riots stemmed from the ideal of equality and the reality of racism. In both cases, there was much tension and strain between groups.

3. Generalized Beliefs

For collective behaviour to develop, the group must believe both in the dangers of not acting on the intolerable situation and in the appropriate and effective actions that will change it. At Oka and in the black ghettos, the disadvantaged group had to recognize that discrimination was the problem and that peaceful protest had not changed anything. More drastic action was needed. In all episodes of collective behaviour, beliefs prepare participants for ensuing action.

4. Precipitating Event

Collective behaviour doesn't just happen; it is precipitated by particular conditions. When these conditions are recognized as problematic, a single incident, sometimes inflamed by rumour, can confirm suspicions and trigger the outbreak of collective behaviour. When a black person or an aboriginal is arrested, beaten, or killed by a police officer and the incident is perceived as unjustified, the tension of the situation may be brought to the boiling point.

5. Mobilization

When the group believes that the problem is serious and recognizes a need for group cohesion, it is ready to mobilize for collective action. This action could take the form of roadblocks and vandalism, attacks on police, marches on government buildings, and many other possibilities. Often the presence of a small militant group that has been waiting for mobilization will provide the organizing committee that is required to promote participation.

6. Failure of Social Control

When the foregoing conditions are met, whether collective action occurs or is suppressed depends on the success of social-control tactics, such as police action or action by other groups or individuals. Police and other agents can lose control and be unable to stop destructive collective action.

Critics of Smelser's theory believe that he left out an important element — namely, the emotional aspect of collective behaviour. Other theories emphasize psychological factors, contending that people undergo a dramatic change when they become part of a crowd. Rational people can turn into violent, deranged creatures capable of actions they would not consider under other circumstances. According to this theory, which is called the *contagion theory*, and theorists such as Gustave Le Bon (1841–1931), a crowd develops a collective mind. Members of a crowd have a sense of anonymity, which provides them with a feeling of power. They are susceptible to the spread of irrational suggestions and actions, and they can get caught up in the moment.

This type of theory may help explain the mass murder-suicide of the Jones cult in Guyana in 1978. Over 900 people killed their children and themselves by drinking Kool-Aid laced with cyanide. Jim Jones, head of the People's Temple, had charismatic appeal that aroused strong loyalty and enthusiasm in his followers. He promised them he would lead them into a better world. The US government suggested, however, that many who drank the Kool-Aid at Jonestown did so with a gun held to their heads.

The symbolic–interactionist theory suggests that collective behaviour emerges when there is social unrest or a breakdown of some sort in the social order. In these circumstances, people behave aimlessly and erratically, searching for some kind of solution. Because they are without direction, they are vulnerable to exaggerated opinions, rumour, and distorted perceptions.

KINDS OF COLLECTIVE BEHAVIOURS

Crowds

Crowd behaviour is a common form of collective action. It includes various forms of collective action: panics, mobs, riots, and disaster behaviour. A **crowd** is a temporary collection of people in close physical proximity. Physical closeness leads to social interaction. The kind of interaction that develops depends on the reasons for being there and the circumstances that are confronted. There are several characteristics that make the crowd a distinctive social situation:

crowd
a temporary collection of people in close physical proximity

1. *Members of a crowd are more open to suggestion.* The individual is easily influenced by the actions, opinions, and feelings of the rest of the crowd. It is difficult to remain sombre in a jubilant crowd.

2. *There is diffusion of responsibility for one's actions in a crowd.* People feel that they cannot be identified. It is then easier to forgo established social norms and roles and act in ways that are not routine.

3. *People in crowds are more spontaneous and give less thought to their actions.* They may do things they would never do alone.

4. People are less likely to follow established social norms because *they believe that they are invulnerable* and no one can single them out in the midst of the crowd.

In some crowds, crowd fear can build and lead to tragedy. The most familiar example of crowd fear is the kind of panic that occurs when people are trapped in a dangerous situation. **Fear** is the anticipation or actual experience of pain or severe distress. Fear can be expressed as a feeling of dread, horror, terror, and ultimately panic. In the aftermath of terrorist attacks in the United States and other targets with ties to the United States, the continued threat of terrorism has led to increased vigilance. In February 2003, millions of Americans rushed to obey the Homeland Security Department's counterterror advice to stock up on duct tape and plastic sheeting as part of a survival kit in case of attacks using nuclear, biological, or chemical weapons (Cernetig & Koring, 2003). If the goal of terrorism is to make victims feel less in control of their destinies, the attacks of September 11, 2001 succeeded. Constant alerts, usually unfounded, issued by the US government have served to increase the unease, thus doing the terrorists' job for them. **Terror** is an intense and enduring fear that emerges when an individual or a group is trapped in a dangerous situation for a period of time. Groups of people who are held hostage in banks or on hijacked planes experience overwhelming terror. **Collective panic** is a sudden, overwhelming terror experienced by a group of people who desperately attempt to flee when they believe there are not enough escape routes in a perilous situation. When this occurs, there is no cooperation that could lead to a plan of escape, and it is often the case that rumours of the impending disaster fan the terror. Sudden action by one person may trigger similar behaviour by others and cause a stampede, which often leads to injury and death by trampling. In Bhopal, India in 1984, more than 2000

fear
the anticipation or actual experience of pain or severe distress

terror
an intense and enduring fear that emerges when an individual or a group is trapped in a dangerous situation for a period of time

collective panic
a sudden, overwhelming terror experienced by a group of people who desperately attempt to flee when they believe there are not enough escape routes in a perilous situation

people died when toxic gas leaked from a Union Carbide plant. Tens of thousands of people panicked as they tried to escape the fumes and get to safety. Many people were trampled to death or run over by vehicles. The panic was heightened when police used loudspeakers to tell the crowd to run because poisonous gas was spreading.

Crowds can be emotionally aroused to act in very negative ways. An emotionally aroused crowd bent on violent and hostile action is called a **mob**. It cooperates, usually with the direction of leadership, to express a shared hostility through violence. A mob usually has a specific target, such as lynching a victim, attacking a police car, or burning down a foreign embassy. A striking example of this form of collective behaviour is the lynch mob. A **lynch mob** is a vigilante crowd intent on punishing others with its own version of law and order.

A less organized, less unified, and less goal-oriented crowd than a mob is a riot. A **riot** is an explosive crowd bent on destruction and violence. Many riots are politically oriented, with outbursts aimed at structural inequalities in society. There is usually initial confrontation with police and the destruction of property. Other riots can erupt in crowds such as rock concerts and soccer matches. In 1985, 37 soccer fans died and 300 were injured at the final game of the European Cup in Brussels during a clash between English and Italian fans. The English fans, using a metal fence as a source of weapons, forced the Italians backward. A number of fans were killed by falling masonry when a wall collapsed, and others were crushed in the ensuing panic.

mob
an emotionally aroused crowd bent on violent and hostile action

lynch mob
a vigilante crowd intent on punishing others with its own version of law and order

riot
an explosive crowd bent on destruction and violence

Masses

Not all collective behaviour involves face-to-face contact in crowds. People can be part of a mass. A **mass** is a group of people who share an idea or an objective or react in the same way to the same event, but who are not in close proximity to one another. When Marc Lepine killed 14 women in Montreal on December 6, 1989, there was a mass reaction of shock and outrage across Canada. Many parents shuddered when they realized that their daughters could have been among the victims. Each year, memorial services on the anniversary of the tragedy remind us of the horror of that day.

Masses are less emotionally intense than crowds, although emotions can escalate into widespread panic and mass hysteria. **Mass hysteria** is a frightening misunderstanding that is shared by a large number of people who become very anxious. A famous example of mass hysteria occurred in 1938 on Halloween night when Orson Welles produced a radio program based on H.G. Wells's novel *The War of the Worlds*. The program sounded like a regular newscast, but it was really a dramatization that reported the invasion of the East Coast of the United States by Martians. Millions of listeners believed the story and became very frightened. Some became panic-stricken, praying, crying, summoning ambulances and police cars, or fleeing frantically to escape death from the Martians. Telephone wires were jammed with warnings and farewells.

Masses can experience both fear and joy. These emotional responses can produce widespread changes in society. Changes in the method of packaging over-the-counter drugs have resulted from the intentional poisoning of products on drugstore and supermarket shelves. There have also been mass responses to environmental pollution and to crime and violence aimed at innocent victims, particularly women and children.

mass
a group of people who share an idea or an objective or react in the same way to the same event, but who are not in close proximity to one another

mass hysteria
a frightening misunderstanding that is shared by a large number of people who become very anxious

fad
an unusual piece of popular culture that is quickly and enthusiastically adopted by a small part of the population

fashion
the current, short-lived custom in dress, manners, speech, etc., that is adopted by large groups of people

craze
an excessive and unreasonable enthusiasm to rush toward something desired

public
a large number of people who share a common attitude on an issue

public opinion
the attitude about a particular issue that is held by the members of a public

Crazes, fashions, and fads are considered mass joys. All three are transitory and are quickly replaced by new ones. A **fad** is an unusual piece of popular culture that is quickly and enthusiastically adopted by a small part of the population. Fads can be quite bizarre, showing contempt for established patterns of behaviour. For example, unemployed lower-class youths in England began the punk hairstyle and clothing fad as an expression of their disgust with a political system that seemed to have betrayed a whole generation, depriving them of work. The various kinds of popular entertainment change quickly. Going to the roller-skating rink was a typical night of entertainment for many teenagers in the 1960s. In the 1970s, many North Americans became proud owners of pet rocks, complete with their own easy chairs, diplomas, and burial plots. (What is the definition of death for a rock?) In the mid-1980s, an evening of Trivial Pursuit was popular. In the 1990s, home videogame systems became widely popular.

A **fashion** is the current, short-lived custom in dress, manners, speech, etc., that is adopted by large groups of people. The Yuppies' concern for health in the 1980s led to the fashion of jogging. Minivans are the number one family car today. Hemlines go up and down and ties and lapels widen and narrow to the delight of the fashion industry. Diets come and go like the tides.

A **craze** is akin to an obsession with manic behaviour. A craze is excessive and unreasonable enthusiasm to rush toward something desired. The California and Yukon gold rushes were crazes that gave hope of fortune to many. Parents became frantic in the "Tickle-Me-Elmo" craze when these dolls could not be made fast enough. The videogame frenzy demonstrates how some people become so obsessed that they lose control of the emotional and mental processes that regulate behaviour.

Table 3.2 sets out these elementary forms of collective behaviour.

Publics

Through the exchange of information among Canadians, large numbers of people form collective opinions and attempt to influence others through the mass media. Mass communication is able to reach thousands or millions of people over a large geographic area with the same messages and suggestions. Many Canadians watch the same news on television or read the same news in newspapers. This often leads to formation of similar ideas. A large number of people who share a common attitude on an issue is called a **public**. Individuals can be part of many publics because, in a complex society such as Canada, there are numerous issues and problems. One public may be concerned with abortion, another with affirmative action, and another with environmental protection.

PUBLIC OPINION

The attitude about a particular issue that is held by the members of a public is called **public opinion**. It is a collective reaction to an issue. Public opinion develops from the exchange of information with others and from information accumulated from the mass media. There are many groups, as well as individuals, who attempt to influence and manipulate public opinion. People's attitudes often are influenced by their reference groups. There are also influential opinion leaders who use the mass media to sway opinions. They are usually well informed and can provide convincing arguments for accepting their views.

TABLE 3.2   Elementary Forms of Collective Behaviour

Organizational form	Dominant emotion		
	Fear	Hostility	Joy
Crowd (in proximity)	fear, terror, panic	mobs, lynch mob, riot	expressive crowds
Mass (geographically dispersed)	mass hysteria	mass rioting	fads, fashions, crazes

As social conditions change, public opinion often changes. However, the attitude of the public on any issue is often short-lived. To measure shifts in public opinion, there are numerous public opinion polls that tell the audience what others think. These polls survey a random sample of the Canadian population on a variety of subjects, from church attendance to capital punishment. When interpreting results from opinion polls, one must keep in mind that they reflect only transitory opinions. The results can also be distorted if pollsters ask loaded questions, if samples are not representative of the population, or if responses to questions are not truthful or are based on incompetent reasoning.

MANIPULATION OF PUBLIC OPINION

Ideally, mass media provide the vehicles by which Canadians can share information, attitudes, and ideas with one another. They are intended to convey the news, opinion, and debate necessary to make informed decisions. However, the impartiality of the media cannot be assured or even expected. There are several ways in which public opinion can be manipulated by the mass media and society.

When people are put into any collective experience where uncertainty prevails, this uncertainty makes people susceptible to rumour. **Rumours** are stories that have no basis in fact, but are powerful because they make an ambiguous situation meaningful.

Another way to manipulate public opinion is through **censorship**, which is the withholding of information released to the public that might influence public opinion. Testimony from the Paul Bernardo trial was censored to ensure a fair trial for Bernardo and to ensure that incriminating evidence was not made inadmissible by becoming too public.

Public opinion can also be manipulated through the presentation of distorted or incomplete information. **Propaganda** attempts to manipulate ideas or opinions by presenting limited, selective, or false information to induce the public to accept a particular view. It appears that the most effective propaganda does not play on public emotions, but provides the public with selective facts and allows them to come to their own conclusions. Advertising is a very common example of propaganda. In modern society with educated citizens, propagandists face obstacles to the easy manipulation of public opinion. There is competition among a variety of sources of information: for every group that presents one point of view, there are other groups with opposing or different ideas on the same issue. This plurality of views and sources of information encourages the public to use critical judgment when forming attitudes.

rumour
a story that has no basis in fact but that is powerful because it makes an ambiguous situation meaningful

censorship
the withholding of information released to the public that might influence public opinion

propaganda
the manipulation of ideas or opinions through the presentation of limited, selective, or false information to induce the public to accept a particular view

Despite the sophistication of modern citizens, propaganda can still be very effective. For example, in the mid-1970s, British Columbia's government had secured relatively full employment, the economy was booming, and the government itself showed a surplus of funds. However, the opposition party propagandized that the economy was weak and that there was a deficit. The opposition Social Credit party beat the NDP by using a technique known as the "big lie." That is, if you say something loud enough, long enough, and convincingly enough, people will accept it even if it is manifestly untrue.

CHAPTER SUMMARY

Human beings have always gathered together in social groups. There are two basic kinds of groups. Primary groups get together simply for the sake of getting together; secondary groups are externally organized and goal-oriented. A bureaucracy is a formally organized version of a secondary group with the specific goal of completing work. In any bureaucracy, there is constant and dynamic strife between the rule-governed formal structure and the parallel informal structure that is more suited to human needs. In some ways, the larger a human group grows, the more predictable its behaviour becomes. Large groups such as crowds, masses, and publics may well be more predictable than small friendship groups.

KEY TERMS

achieved status	mob
ascribed status	multiple roles
authority	out-grouping
bureaucracy	power
censorship	primary group
collective behaviour	projection
collective panic	propaganda
compartmentalization	public
craze	public opinion
crowd	rationalization
division of labour	red tape
fad	reference group
fashion	riot
fear	rite of passage
formal organization	role conflict
gender roles	role failure
group	role set
influence	role strain
in-grouping	rumour
lynch mob	secondary group
marginal persons	sex typing
mass	status inconsistency
mass hysteria	terror

REFERENCES

Le Bon, G. (1960). *The crowd*. New York: Viking.

Macionis, J., Jansson, M., & Benoit, C.A. (2004). *Society: The basics*. Toronto: Pearson Education Canada.

Smelser, N. (1962). *Theory of collective behavior*. New York: The Free Press.

Cernetig, M., & Koring, P. (2003, February 13). Fearful Americans gird for attack. *The Globe and Mail*, pp. 1, 19.

CHAPTER 4

Cultural Diversity

This chapter introduces you to the very essence of sociology, the concept of culture. Every society has accepted beliefs, values, rules, and patterns of behaviour. This chapter examines the uniformities and variations in these rules and beliefs. We have been systematically taught how to think and see things in prescribed cultural ways that we suppose are natural. This chapter also examines how cultures adapt and change and how newcomers attempt to fit into host societies. Finally, this chapter considers the concepts of race and ethnicity and the nature of prejudice and discrimination.

Chapter Objectives

After completing this chapter, you should be able to:

- Identify the distinguishing components of a cultural group.
- List examples of the shaping of individual behaviour by cultural forces.
- Assess impediments to acculturation faced by new Canadians.
- Track the diffusion process of a new cultural trait.
- Show how even very basic behaviour can be culturally relative.
- Demonstrate difficulties in clearly defining the term "race."
- Distinguish the major patterns of ethnic accommodation attempted by different societies.
- Outline the relationship between prejudice and discrimination.
- List the components of ethnic group identification.

Paul Henderson became Canada's hockey hero in 1972; Anson Carter became another Canadian hockey hero in 2003.

Anson Carter's story is truly a Canadian one. Anson's parents emigrated from Barbados in 1967. They arrived in Toronto just when the Maple Leafs won the Stanley Cup. At the time, they didn't know what everyone was celebrating. They knew all about cricket bats and nothing about hockey sticks. It didn't take long for the family to spend Saturday nights watching Hockey Night in Canada. They were hooked on hockey, and the coming years were filled with early morning practices, travel to tournaments, and thousands of dollars spent on equipment and ice-time fees. Twenty years after wobbling on the ice for the first time, the NHL star scored a heart-stopping overtime goal to win gold for Canada at the 2003 World Championships. Hockey and Canada go together.

DEFINING CULTURE

When asked what the term "culture" means, most people can think of several different meanings. Some might define culture in terms of personal refinement (being well mannered). Others may think that culture involves the finer things in life or highbrow activities (for example, good wine, classical music, attending opera and ballet performances, visiting art exhibitions, talking knowledgeably about philosophy). This is not the meaning of culture used in sociology. People who attend rock concerts or who are ardent fans of science fiction movies are no less part of a distinctive culture.

In sociology, we look to the commonplace to represent a society's culture more than we do the unusual. It is the everyday, taken-for-granted things that make up a culture. A simple but adequate definition of **culture** is everything we think, everything we do, and everything we possess because we belong to a particular society. This definition implies that culture is a group or shared thing, not something that an individual possesses. In order to understand what culture is, it is helpful to further describe the major components in the definition.

culture
everything people think, everything people do, and everything people possess because they belong to a particular society

COMPONENTS OF CULTURE

Language Is the Basis of Culture

In many ways, language is the cornerstone of culture. It is historically true that if a group loses its language, it tends also to lose its cultural distinctiveness. Awareness of these related losses has led many minority groups to perceive themselves as being swamped by a numerically dominant culture and thus to take stronger methods to preserve their language. The Welsh in the United Kingdom, the Basques in Spain, the Flems in Belgium, the Maori in New Zealand, and, of course, the Quebecois in Canada are just a few examples of linguistically threatened minority groups.

Every culture also has sayings that cannot be readily translated into other languages without considerable loss in meaning. Language is, therefore, **culture-bound** in that the meaning of concepts is lessened when they are removed from their cultural context. This effect can be witnessed even within a language. For example, the various forms of English (British, Canadian, American, Australian, Jamaican, etc.) have culture-bound concepts that do not translate, even within the framework of the same basic language.

culture-bound
meaningful within a cultural context and less meaningful when removed from that context

Of course, we do not have to speak to communicate with others. Much research has been done in the area of non-verbal communication. Examples of non-verbal communication are facial expression, body language (posture), gestures, paralanguage (for example, tone of voice, speed, stuttering, and hesitation), and touch. Non-verbal communication is harder to disguise than verbal communication. Therefore, it is much more likely to "leak" information about feelings.

Non-verbal communication is as culture-bound as language is; sometimes, an expression in one culture can have a different meaning in another culture. Westerners tend to look people straight in the eyes, but this is considered a challenge for many Asian people. A more appropriate gesture in Asian culture is to look down to show respect for the other person. Northern Europeans are often taught to "keep a stiff upper lip" and not to let emotions such as sorrow and grief show in their faces; in contrast, Southern Europeans are often taught to openly express their grief. This difference in expression does not indicate a difference in the depth of grief or sorrow that is felt. It is merely a culturally determined pattern of expression. Loudness of voice, speed of speaking, or pitch can also mean different things to different culture groups.

Everything We Think as a Member of a Specific Society

The common ideas and ideologies shared by members of a group are, of course, shaped and restricted by language. An **ideology** is a manner of thinking that is characteristic of a whole society or culture. Groups share symbolic meanings, such as the importance placed on pieces of printed cloth called national flags.

ideology
a manner of thinking characteristic of a whole society or culture

Beliefs are ideas that tell people what should exist or happen in a particular situation. For example, Westerners believe democracy can only be achieved in a system in which all citizens formally vote on a government. Beliefs also tell people how to respond in a situation in terms of feelings. In the past, we were expected to deal with grief by containing it. These days, we are increasingly being encouraged to express our grief. Beliefs shape the perceptions and actions of people who come to hold them. Mennonites, for example, believe that they should be more concerned with spiritual realities than with outward appearance. They dress alike in sombre clothing that de-emphasizes individualism and worldly concerns.

Societies also maintain shared **values**, which can be defined as the generally accepted standards of desirability of a society. For example, a value shared by most Canadians is good health. However, what precisely constitutes good health may differ from one society to another. At any one time, we hold many values and, inevitably, some values conflict with others. To resolve value conflicts, we rank our values in order of importance. Commonly shared values help hold society together while they simultaneously set it apart from other societies.

values
the generally accepted standards of desirability of a society

In 1990, our federal government commissioned the Citizens' Forum on Canada's Future (Report to the People and Government of Canada, 1991) to explore what it means to be Canadian and what we believe our core values to be. Over 400 000 Canadians participated along with 300 000 students in a separate students' forum. Seven important cultural values were identified:

- Belief in equality and fairness for all citizens in a democratic society.

- Belief in consultation and dialogue to promote peaceful solutions.

- Importance of accommodation and tolerance of all groups with the expectations that these groups also demonstrate these values.

- Support and celebration for Canada's regional, ethnic, cultural, and linguistic diversity.

- Compassion and generosity, which are demonstrated by "our universal and extensive social services, our health care system, our willingness to welcome refugees, and our commitment to regional economic equalization" (Report to the People and Government of Canada, 1991).

- Attachment to and protection of Canada's natural beauty.

- Commitment to our world image as a society that is peaceful, free, and nonviolent as it changes.

Everything We Do as a Member of a Society

People behave on a day-to-day basis in accordance with their belief systems. Thus, beliefs, attitudes, ideologies, etc., go a long way to shaping the everyday pattern of behaviour an individual follows. Every society has established patterns of behaviour that are called **norms**. Norms are standards of conduct and rules for behaviour that tell us how we should and should not behave. Norms provide order and predictability and a sense of social cohesion. They also serve as a basis for both self-evaluation and the evaluation of others, exerting pressure on people to conform.

norms
standards of conduct and rules for behaviour that tell us how we should and should not behave

In general, norms are usually derived from values. We value marriage and so we have prescribed appropriate behaviour patterns for couples. We also learn what is appropriate and inappropriate behaviour in terms of manners, politeness, citizenship, honesty, respect for belongings, etc. Many norms undergo **internalization** — that is, we learn them so well that we think of them not so much as culturally taught but as part of human nature. We might feel guilty if we violate these norms. Canadians are taught to respect authority as a means of maintaining law and order, while Americans are more likely to emphasize individual rights. Many Canadians would feel guilty if they were disrespectful in interactions with police, teachers, and parents. However, this guilt is not likely as strong as it once was, which may demonstrate the extent to which Canadians are becoming more Americanized.

internalization
a norm learned so well it is thought of, not as culturally taught, but as part of human nature

Another example of a norm is eating behaviour. Eating is a biological necessity: we need to eat to survive. Everything else about eating is culturally determined. This includes what we eat, the amounts we eat, when we eat, where we eat, how we eat, and so on. Many foodstuffs automatically conjure up a cultural connotation — fish and chips, lasagne, raw fish, maple syrup, apple pie, curried vegetables. Disorders such as anorexia nervosa, bulimia, and obesity are only known in some cultures. The size, numbers, and times of meals are determined by culture, as are appropriate seating postures and seating arrangements around a central food holder. Even the implements we use for eating (fingers, chopsticks, knives and forks, daggers) and the way we use them vary from culture to culture. An English person is taught to use a knife and fork very differently from a Canadian.

Everything We Have as a Member of a Society

As we follow normative behaviour patterns, we develop certain material possessions that help us perform these behaviours. Material possessions that are specific to a culture are called **artifacts**. As with ideas and behaviours, there are very few material possessions that are specific to only one culture in our multicultural world. We still, however, tie certain artifacts to certain societies. Baseball equipment and baseball diamonds are immediately seen as American, while ice hockey equipment and rinks are seen as Canadian. Even such everyday possessions as a car, a microwave oven, or a DVD player are seen by many cultures as part of a North American lifestyle.

artifacts
material possessions that are specific to a culture

Canada's passion for ice hockey (the worldwide meaning of "hockey" is specifically field hockey) may single us out in terms of material possessions and behaviour patterns more than any other activity. Many other countries play ice hockey, but in no other country is it the number one sport. In the whole of Finland, for example, there are fewer arenas than in Hamilton, Ontario. The sport defines many aspects of our material culture with ice skates, sticks, pucks, and other hockey equipment found in many Canadian households. A Canadian community, no matter how small, is not considered complete until its arena has been built. The arena has become the centre of much of the community's life. Canadians also possess one of the highest ratios per population of minivans, utility vehicles, and station wagons in the world, perhaps because so many families have to truck kids and equipment to and from the rink.

IMPACT OF CULTURE ON DAILY LIVING

Our culture has a significant impact on our daily lives. For example, our cultural lifestyle (for example, diet, fast-paced life, and transportation system) can lead to accidents and illness. Only in Western societies do we find the eating disorder anorexia nervosa. Our cultural obsession with thinness and dieting has led some young people to threaten their health through undernourishment. Conversely, the relative wealth of our society has led to the problem of obesity. And our fast-paced lifestyle has increased the probability that we might suffer from heart attacks, ulcers, or hypertension.

Often fads (discussed in chapter 3) and fashions (popular interest in certain material possessions) (discussed in chapter 3) can have negative social consequences. "Wedgie" shoes in the mid-1970s may have been to blame for a number of young women having difficult births with first-born children; the hypothesis is that the tilted sole of the shoes, if they were worn regularly, could have tilted the woman's womb. There is speculation that the fad of "teasing" one's hair may have caused a number of women who did this in the late 1950s and early '60s eventually to lose their hair. What are the long-term neurological effects of our fascination with videogames and home computers?

CHARACTERISTICS OF CULTURE

Culture is our social inheritance; it gives structure to our lives. There are four characteristics of culture:

1. *Culture is learned*   An individual is born into a culture that has existed and will continue to exist regardless of the existence of that individual. It is presented to the child as the social heritage of past generations. Each person is taught the values, beliefs, and rules of his or her culture. There are great differences between cultures, but there are also great differences between people within a culture.

2. *Culture is transmitted symbolically*   A culture is a shared set of symbols and their meanings. A **symbol** is anything taken by people to stand for something else. It may be an object, a sound, a word, a gesture, or an action

symbol
anything that is taken to stand for something else

that is useful for communicating with others. These symbols and their meanings include ideas about facts, ideas about desirable goals, and ideas about how people should or should not act. Flags, smiles, and words are symbols, and the meanings of these symbols are shared in a culture. Different cultures give symbols different meanings. For example, a cross means something different to Christians and to non-Christians.

3. *Culture is shared*   We learn our culture from others, such as parents, teachers, peers, and the mass media. People and institutions within a culture are designated to pass on certain values, skills, and ways of behaving. Each culture shares meanings and these meanings give order and pattern to life. Culture contains ideas and beliefs held in common. For example, almost all adult Canadians share an understanding of the rules of traffic by drivers and pedestrians.

4. *Culture is normative*   Each culture has a moral and social order. Each member of a culture learns what is right and what is wrong, good or bad, and what one should and ought to do in society. A businesswoman wears a suit to work because she knows what she should do.

SOCIOLOGICAL PERSPECTIVES ON CULTURE

Conflict Theory

Conflict theory sees culture as constantly in a state of flux or change due to unstable, powerful relationships. For the Marxist, economic variables are emphasized because they affect the norms and values of a culture. The dominant group promotes its norms and values to retain its power. Other types of conflict theorists also see culture in the context of powerful groups trying to impose their norms and values on the least powerful by persuasion or force. Control of technology is seen as an independent variable that affects the distribution of wealth, knowledge, and values.

Canada's treatment of its aboriginal population illustrates the conflict theory. The potlatch, an important social ceremony and social institution, was outlawed by the federal government along with many other cultural practices with the *Indian Act* of 1876. The residential school system was another example of the intent to wipe out aboriginal customs and language. Sociologists have stressed the importance of the link between language and cultural identity. The battle to protect the French language in Canada is another example of this theory.

Functionalist Theory

Functionalist theory sees shared norms and values as the glue that holds society together. We are born into a society with established norms and values, and through the process of socialization we systematically learn these values and internalize them. In this way, social order is possible because people have culture, a set of values and norms that are shared and that provide structure in the society. Shared values and norms serve a function and are relatively stable; they are not influenced by members of the culture. Shared values function to legitimize the institutions of society, and the norms derived from these values function to integrate society.

Symbolic–Interactionist Theory

Symbolic–interactionist theory holds that individual action can change culture as well as be influenced by it. People do not just passively accept the values and norms that make up the culture of a society. They change cultural meaning through creative actions, and they adapt the culture from the larger society to their everyday lives. While we learn many meanings that are common to the group, we also remain flexible and capable of developing and communicating new meanings when the established ones are obsolete or inappropriate.

Feminist Theory

In relation to the study of culture, feminists promote a greater emphasis on women and the female experience. The traditional, male-oriented view has emphasized that what is important about a culture are male activities and male concerns. **Feminists** study the important role of cultural definitions and belief systems and how they shape important aspects of group life for women and men. They focus on previously overlooked variables that lead to inequality (for example, gender relations). Margaret Conkey (1997) refuted the assumption that tasks assigned to members of prehistoric societies were gender-determined (that is, men were hunters and women were gatherers), and therefore she contended that present-day division of labour based on gender is not "natural." According to this view, changing the division of labour defined by gender becomes easier.

feminist
an advocate of the movement for women to have political, economic, and social rights equal to those of men

Both feminist theorists and conflict theorists give attention to the relationship between culture and inequality, particularly the ways in which cultural traits benefit men at the expense of women. They analyze the role of culture in supporting gender inequality, which leads to tensions and conflict between men and women. In societies where male culture dominates, popular culture in particular will reflect this domination. When examining "gangsta" rap music, it is evident that the singers, record makers, and distributors are mostly male. They make millions of dollars at the expense of women's dignity, and sometimes even safety (Scott, Schwartz, & VanderPlaat, 2000).

THE RELATIVITY OF CULTURE

There are a number of general cultural universals (features common to all cultures), such as the family, courtship, marriage, athletic sports, division of labour, education, and language, but there are no specific practices found in all societies. For example, every society may have the institution of the family, but family patterns differ among cultures. One of the most notable things about culture is the great diversity of different cultures and cultural traits. A **cultural trait** is the smallest unit of culture that can be identified (for example, one behaviour, one idea, and one object). Cultures vary widely in terms of beliefs, values, norms, and behaviours.

cultural trait
the smallest unit of culture that can be identified

Almost every behaviour that you can imagine has, at some place or time, been considered normal behaviour (normative), no matter how deviant, illegal, sinful, immoral, disgusting, weird, or unusual it might seem to you. Somewhere, at some time, any object has been worshipped, any sexual practice accepted, any food considered a delicacy, any behaviour considered moral or immoral.

ethnocentrism
the evaluation of other cultures in terms of one's own cultural values and standards

People have a strong tendency to be **ethnocentric** — that is, to evaluate other cultures in terms of one's own cultural values and standards. Most people are overly hasty in judging certain cultural traits of other people as being wrong instead of being simply different. To be ethnocentric is perfectly understandable, because each of us is brought up in a certain culture and we internalize the beliefs of that culture, and accept them without question as the right way of doing things. Consequently, we assume that if our way is the right way, then everything that is different, especially if it is opposite, is, by definition, wrong. However, this error in reasoning can have serious consequences. It can lead to prejudice and discrimination, which can produce intergroup hostility and conflict. It also hinders the possibility of growing and changing through exposure to different ideas and lifestyles.

cultural relativity
the idea that every cultural trait can only be fully understood and evaluated by the standards of right and wrong of the society in which it originated

The overcoming of prejudice leaves room for greater flexibility and breadth of outlook. To aid in this process, it is essential to understand the concept of **cultural relativity**, the idea that every cultural trait can only be fully understood and evaluated by the standards of right and wrong of the society in which it originated. Consequently, an idea that seems strange, silly, or repulsive to us may have an important function to perform in the culture in which it is accepted.

An example of this is found among the Azande of West Central Africa. They prescribe that a girl's first sexual intercourse should always be with her father. The minimum jail term for such activity is five years in Canada. The Azande are not, however, an immoral, promiscuous, or decadent society; in fact, their moral code is in many ways more rigid than any Western country. Premarital sex is punishable by death. The punishments are usually only applied to women. The Azande's average age at marriage is similar to that of most primitive societies — about 13 or 14 years.

Eons ago, some wise Azande must have figured out the possible technical and emotional difficulties that two 13-year-old virgins may encounter on their wedding night. It was therefore seen as being necessary to educate one of the novice partners prior to the nuptials. First sexual intercourse can be a frightening and painful experience, so it must have been deemed necessary to find an instructor whom the girl trusted and with whom she already had a warm relationship. In many primitive societies, a maternal uncle carries out this same educational ritual, but the Azande chose the girl's father as the "logical" educator. Notice that there is no connotation of sex and loss of virginity here that corresponds with Western concepts of sex and loss of virginity. This sex act is not performed for pleasure, and especially not for procreation. No one is supposed to have fun from this encounter; it is purely educational.

Most Westerners would be repulsed by this method of being introduced to sex. However, our method would make no sense to an Azande. The Azande would look in disbelief at the frantic, furtive, and ignorant ways in which most young people in our society drift into their first sexual experience.

All cultures are different, and no culture is "better" than another. Values and norms that work well in one culture may be rejected by another culture. This view encourages us to have a tolerant attitude and to make a greater effort in understanding and interpreting other cultures.

CULTURAL DIVERSITY

A society may be unified in its culture and share the same set of beliefs, values, and norms. However, most modern societies are not culturally integrated but are quite diverse, containing clashing cultural components. Many doubt, for example, that a unified Canadian culture really exists. Instead, a variety of ethnic, religious, linguistic, interest, and regional groups coexist in Canadian society, such as the Hasidic Jews of Toronto, the Chinese community in Vancouver, and the Friends of the Earth Society across Canada.

However, people who belong to these distinctive cultural groups may still share a great deal with other Canadians. Therefore, they are referred to as subcultures that coexist within Canadian society. **Subcultures** are small groups within society that share most of the ways of the main society but that have some distinctive values and ideas of their own.

Members of a subculture may share a common age, religion, ethnic heritage, belief system, occupation, or hobby. They may also share exclusion from the larger society — for example, prison inmates. Many subcultures have a unique language with specialized vocabulary and idioms, or **argot**. Argots are found among those in the same occupational group, social group, or way of life. Many medical patients are in the dark about their condition because the technical terms used by medical staff have no meaning for them. The purpose of an argot can be to disguise from outsiders the meaning of what is said and therefore to exclude them from the group.

subculture
a small group within society that shares most of the ways of the main society but that has some distinctive values and ideas of its own

argot
a unique language of a subculture with specialized vocabulary and idioms

CULTURAL CHANGE

Cultures are not static; they are continually changing through innovation and diffusion. People invent and introduce new ideas, objects, or methods of doing things into a culture. New technologies for sharing information and ideas play an important role in this process of cultural change. Changes in the balance of regional and ethnic groups, between young and old, rich and poor, rural and urban, all make a difference. A vivid example of changes in our values and behaviours is evident in our realization of the danger to human survival that is posed by our continuous assault on the fragile environment. We are developing an environmental conscience and we feel guilty when we don't reduce, reuse, and recycle.

Cultures also change when they adopt ideas, technologies, and customs from other cultures. These cultural exchanges have increased dramatically with the spread of mass communications.

Trade, military conquest, exploration, tourism, and missionary work have also encouraged cultural exchanges. The North American diet of hamburgers, french fries, and Coke has spread to the Far East and the new independent countries of the former USSR, taking with it negative health consequences. The process by which cultural elements spread from group to group within a society, or from one society to another is called **cultural diffusion.**

cultural diffusion
the process by which cultural elements spread from group to group within a society, or from one society to another

We must also consider people who leave the comfort of their own culture and move to a foreign society. Knowledge of concepts like ethnocentrism and cultural relativity become especially important when dealing with immigrants into a society, especially those people who did not make a conscious choice to come to this country but were forced by circumstances to leave their home. War, repression, genocide, or famine may have been their only way of life at home. Every immigrant, no matter what their reasons for entry into our society, undergoes a period of adjustment to the ways of the new society. This process of adjustment is called **acculturation.** The degree to which an immigrant acculturates to the host society depends on a number of things:

acculturation
the process of adjusting to the ways of a new society

1. *Does the immigrant have the ability to acculturate?* Acculturation is obviously much easier for someone whose language is the same as the language in the host country, and whose "old country" requires similar cultural and technical skills of its population, than it is for someone whose language is different or whose technical skill is not as advanced.

2. *Does the immigrant possess the desire to acculturate?* Some immigrants become "ingratiated immigrants" and constantly talk about how wonderful their new experience is. Others refuse to adjust; they live their lives as if they were simply in a different place at a different point in time and they ignore Canadian institutions, rights, duties, and obligations. Most immigrants, however, fall somewhere between these extremes. They cling to what is familiar and what is an integral, ingrained part of their being, and at the same time they strive to get along in their new cultural surroundings. The degree to which an immigrant acculturates depends in large part on his or her reasons for coming here. If someone makes a conscious choice to come to Canada because it offers certain, specific advantages, she is much more likely to acculturate than is someone who was forced from a home that he never wanted to leave.

3. *Will the host society accommodate the immigrant?* Different groups and different individuals find different levels of acceptance from the host society. The degree to which an immigrant is accommodated depends on factors like race, religion, and language. The closer an immigrant's characteristics are to those of the host society, the more likely he or she will be accommodated.

culture shock
a feeling of being bombarded by so many new stimuli (ideas, activities, lifestyles, etc.) that adjustment seems impossible

Many immigrants go through a stage of **culture shock**, a feeling of being bombarded by so many new stimuli (ideas, activities, lifestyles, etc.) that adjustment seems impossible. Culture shock can be manifested as depression, confusion and disorientation, severe homesickness, a vague and blank expression, inappropriate responses, and so on. Chronic culture shock can afflict sufferers on a relatively mild but somewhat inhibiting level for long periods of time or even, in extreme cases, for the rest of their lives. Acute culture shock often precipitates a crisis for the sufferer, and can result in a meaningful solution such as a permanent return home, a temporary return that cures homesickness for the time being, or simply a determination to adjust.

temprocentrism
the belief that one era in time is superior to all others and should be used as the standard by which other periods of time are judged

Because cultures change with time, cultural problems can be exacerbated by temporal (time-related) ones. For example, it is possible for an individual to be **temprocentric** — that is, to maintain the belief that one era in time is superior to all others and should be used as the standard by which other periods of time are judged. The aging hippie who thinks that 1968 was the high point of civilization, the music lover who thinks that Buddy Holly's death was the day the music died, and the student who thinks that only the here and now counts all exhibit a temprocentric attitude.

future shock
a feeling that society is changing so rapidly in technological terms, and new stimuli arise so quickly, that it is difficult or impossible to adapt to the changes

Alvin Toffler, in **Future Shock** (1970), describes a condition of the same name in which people feel that society is changing so rapidly in technological terms, and new stimuli arise so quickly, that it is difficult or impossible to adapt to the changes.

The relationship between time and culture can also be seen in those things that continue to exist in society even though they no longer serve any useful purpose.

Areas of society that do not change as quickly as the rest of society are said to be examples of **cultural lag**. Many examples of cultural lag can be drawn from the law, because the law typically changes at a slower pace than public opinion. There are two kinds of cultural lag in the law. One kind, often a source of comedy in movies and TV shows, includes antiquated laws that cover practices that once were considered contrary to the social good but that are not of concern to people now. A law prohibiting the emptying of spittoons in the street is an example of an antiquated law. The other kind of cultural lag in the law is more serious — the lack or inadequacy of laws covering practices that are very much of concern to people today. Examples include equal rights legislation, sexual assault laws, abortion laws, and delinquency laws. The fact that the law is a laggard is not necessarily a bad thing. It gives law makers time to ensure that public opinion has not gone temporarily further than the society will eventually want the law to go. Another example of lagging law is environmental protection legislation. In the time between industrial and technological advancement and changes in social values, we failed to handle the problems caused by development with appropriate laws and, by our inaction, seriously harmed the environment.

cultural lag
a process in which some areas of society do not change as quickly as the rest of society

MULTICULTURALISM

In the last few centuries, the world has seen many large-scale population movements. People have moved for a variety of reasons:

- Ukrainians and Lithuanians fled Russian imperialism.

- Poles, Czechs, and Hungarians fled repressive communist regimes.

- Chileans, Salvadorans, and Filipinos fled American-supported dictatorships.

- Sicilians, Irish, and East Indians escaped from poverty and famine.

- Jamaicans, Bajans, and Trinidadians sought outlets for their talents unavailable to them in the West Indies.

- Ugandan Asians, Vietnamese, and Yugoslavs wanted to avoid internal civil strife.

- British, Dutch, Spanish, Portuguese, and French just seem to have a historical tendency to want to roam the earth.

Sometimes it appears that the whole world is on the move.

One of the outcomes of this massive population movement is that the populations of previously homogeneous societies are now increasingly diverse, with a wide variety of national origins and distinctive physiological characteristics. The majority of people in Canadian society find this multiethnic, multiracial, multireligious mix to be beneficial, vital, and stimulating. However, some members of society still refuse to accept or acknowledge this modern social fact. A small element oppose this mosaic society as vigorously as possible and, sometimes, vent their displeasure on the more socially visible representatives of this process. In this section, we will look at the historical process by which Canada has become increasingly multicultural. We will examine the ideas of race and ethnicity, and the various ways in which society can adapt to this diversity. Finally, we will examine the lingering effects of prejudice and discrimination.

Civil Rights: The Historic Struggle

civil rights
the rights of individuals to not be treated as second-class citizens, especially the right of freedom from servitude

Civil rights are the rights of individuals to not be treated as second-class citizens, especially the right of freedom from servitude. When most people think of the term civil rights, they tend to think of the struggles of black Americans in the 1960s, but the history of the term and the concept goes back much further. The establishment of a senatorial government in ancient Rome and its continuous strife with the imperialistic Caesars was an ongoing battle for the rights of ordinary Roman citizens (though not for the rights of Roman slaves). The signing of the *Magna Carta* at Runnymede in England in 1215 transferred powers away from autocrats and into the hands of a greater number of people. On November 5, 1605, Guy Fawkes and a number of co-conspirators attempted to blow up the British House of Parliament, in large part because the government was not representative of the needs of the majority of citizens, but just a tool of James I. The Red River uprising of 1869–70 in Manitoba was an attempt to entrench certain rights in the agreement of the West to be incorporated into the Dominion of Canada. The Fabian socialists of the 19th century fought for legislative control over child labour laws and of working conditions in general. The women's suffragette movement of the early 20th century recognized the disadvantaged position of women in Western society and sought to rectify it.

The recent history of civil rights activity is often traced to 1954 when the US Supreme Court ruled, in the case of *Brown v. Board of Education*, that racially segregated schools were inherently unequal. The court ordered that the United States undertake desegregation of schools with "deliberate speed." In the early 1960s, northern US cities became the focus for a powerful black civil rights movement. The movement produced beneficial outcomes, such as the 1964 *Civil Rights Act*, but also degenerated into large-scale riots in the middle and late '60s. Another positive outcome of this movement was the alteration of black peoples' self-images; instead of hoping for acceptance as quasi whites, they accepted and approved themselves through the black power and "black is beautiful" movements.

The concern for civil rights and the increased democratization of society spread to young whites in the United States and fanned out across the world. The political actions at American universities were mirrored in Canada at the Sir George William campus of Concordia University and in the streets of London, Paris, and Berlin. Unfortunately, this action also degenerated into the riots in Watts and Detroit, the "merry month of May" barricading of Paris, and the setting up of quasi-military terrorist organizations such as the Red Brigades of Italy, the Baader-Meinhof gang in Germany, and the Minutemen in the United States. The culmination of this activity was the Kent State University massacre of peacefully demonstrating students by the National Guard.

In the 1970s, the women's liberation/feminist/women's movement gained impetus and began speaking out about the institutionalized discriminations that women had to suffer, even in modern society. As a result of this action, every Western society, with the exception of the United States, has in the past 20 years enacted legislation that expressly forbids any discrimination based on gender.

In Canada in recent years, we have witnessed the enactment of a considerable amount of legislation that is intended to ensure the equality of all people under the law. In October 1971, the Liberal government of Pierre Trudeau initiated its policy of "multiculturalism within a bilingual framework" to encourage the expression of non-English, non-French culture. This policy arose from one of the conclusions of the

Royal Commission on Bilingualism and Biculturalism (1967–1970) that other cultures were being overshadowed by the emphasis on biculturalism. It was thought that a policy of multiculturalism would more accurately depict the Canadian reality.

There were two main aspects to multiculturalism:

1. the encouragement of selected minority/ethnic activities within the mainstream of Canadian society, for example, the introduction of ethnic language classes and support of festivities and holidays; and

2. a set of values that opposed prejudice and discrimination and that supported equality of opportunity.

The repatriation of the Canadian constitution in 1982 included the drawing up of the *Canadian Charter of Rights and Freedoms*. The Charter included provisions guaranteeing freedom of conscience and religion; freedom of thought, belief, opinion, and expression; mobility rights; and equality rights. The Charter also endorsed the principle of affirmative action programs; guaranteed that English and French would retain equal status as the official languages of Canada; and affirmed aboriginal treaty rights.

In 1981, the Ontario *Human Rights Code* was introduced, guaranteeing freedom from discrimination in the provision of services, occupancy of accommodation, employment opportunity, the signing of contracts and freedom from harassment. All of these guarantees ensured freedom from discrimination on the basis of race, ancestry, place of origin, colour, ethnic affiliation, citizenship, creed, age, sex, marital status, family status, or handicap. Ontario also established the Human Rights Commission and, subsequently, the Ombudsman's Office to enforce the Code and to investigate possible violations of it.

Prejudice and Discrimination

Many of the policies and laws cited above were implemented and enacted to decrease the levels of prejudice and discrimination that existed in society. A **prejudice** is a preconceived idea that the behaviours and personality traits of an individual can be predicted on the basis of the human categories to which the individual belongs, and any action that is taken on the basis of a prejudice is **discrimination**. Many people believe that they can know something about a people's characters and behaviour patterns by knowing their racial origin, ethnic identification, religious affiliation, sexual preference, gender, age, or any number of other such categorizations. Although it is often true that you can tell something about a person because of these associations, it is only a small proportion of the individual's total being.

In general, the relationship between prejudice and discrimination is that prejudicial attitudes are the basis for discriminatory action. It is possible, however, to conceive of four relationships between the two concepts:

1. *Unprejudiced non-discrimination*   In this state, a person has no preconceived notions about other groups and never acts in a discriminatory way. In practice, it is hard to imagine this state really existing.

2. *Unprejudiced discrimination*   In this state, a person behaves in a discriminatory way toward a group but holds no discernible prejudices about the group. A person may perform a discriminatory act in order to go

prejudice
a preconceived idea that the behaviours and personality traits of an individual can be predicted on the basis of the human categories to which the individual belongs

discrimination
any action that is taken on the basis of a prejudice

along with his or her neighbours or peers. For example, a landlord might refuse to rent an apartment to a representative of a certain group, not because he holds any animosity toward the group, but because he's afraid of upsetting his neighbours.

3. *Prejudiced non-discrimination*   In this state, a person holds prejudicial beliefs and attitudes but realizes that it is morally or legally (or morally *and* legally) wrong to act on them. Prejudiced non-discrimination is much more likely to occur than unprejudiced discrimination.

4. *Prejudiced discrimination*   In this state, a person both holds preconceived notions about a group and acts upon them.

minority group
a collection of people who share common traits and hold significantly less power than society's dominant groups

Most prejudice, but not all, is directed toward members of **minority groups** — that is, collections of people who share common traits and hold significantly less power than society's dominant groups. This definition of a minority group can include situations where the denoted people are actually numerically superior (women in North America, blacks in South Africa) but lack power.

stereotype
a generalized and exaggerated picture of an entire category of people

The simplest form of prejudice is the **stereotype**, a generalized and exaggerated picture used to describe entire categories of people. These pictures are usually wrong in predicting how an individual member of the group will react, and contribute to the spreading of myths and caricatures. Although stereotypes are usually negative, they can just as easily be positive — for example, the perception that all Asians are highly intelligent.

There are a number of different theories of how people develop prejudices. Some of the leading psychological theories are:

- *Learning theory*   Prejudice is either directly taught to young people by their caretakers or indirectly communicated to them by avoidance behaviour or body language.

- *Persistent stranger anxiety theory*   Young children often go through a stage in which they cling to one parent, usually the mother, and become hysterical if they are approached by anybody else, sometimes even the other parent. Some psychologists suggest that many of us never fully get over our agitation around strangers and thus are more likely to judge people who are very different from us in an overly negative way.

- *Theory of harsh, physical discipline*   This theory suggests that children who are harshly, physically disciplined tend to grow up viewing the world in very simplistic terms of right and wrong, black and white, correct and incorrect. If someone or something is not like they are, then that someone or something must be wrong, deviant, or incorrect. Adults who were physically disciplined as children tend to transfer their pent-up hostility and learned aggression to other people.

Discrimination can take many forms. It can be mild or severe; it can be negative (refusing to rent an apartment to someone because he or she is a student) or positive (setting aside a quota of jobs for some previously disadvantaged groups). In any guise, though, discrimination is still an action based on a non-rational, preconceived notion. The act of giving a person a position or an opportunity as a way of partially correcting previous wrongs, but not a way of rewarding the person's merits, is called **tokenism**. Some job-quota programs are tokenist. Also tokenist is the deliberate showing off of a member of a minority group as a way of demonstrating that an organization is "doing its bit."

There are six types of discrimination, presented here in ascending order of severity:

1. *bad-mouthing*   the use of slurs and insulting names to represent and put down a minority group, or the telling of jokes deliberately meant to demean the subjects of the jokes

2. *avoidance behaviour*   the refusal to attend functions, live in residential areas, work in offices, stay at hotels, or, in general, go to places that are frequented by members of distinctive minority groups

3. *active discrimination*   the committing of acts such as damaging the property of disadvantaged groups, or refusing to rent houses or give jobs to members of minority groups

4. *physical violence*   the assaulting of individuals because they belong to certain minority groups

5. *homicide*   the killing of individuals simply because they are identifiable members of a minority group and are unfortunate enough to be around at an inopportune time

6. *genocide*   the deliberate attempt to annihilate a minority group.

    The most publicized example of genocide is the Holocaust, the mass extermination of Jews by the Nazis, but there have been more recent examples of genocide: the "ethnic cleansings" in southeastern Europe and the Rwandan massacres, both of which occurred in this decade. There have also been examples of genocide in North America. In Southern Ontario, at least two aboriginal nations, the Tionontati (also known as the "Petun" or Tobacco Indians) and the Neutrals, were wiped out largely as a result of the military efforts of other aboriginal nations. And in the United States, many aboriginals were massacred in pursuit of the American policy of **manifest destiny**, the belief that white people were given dominion over North America as a result of divine intervention, and were thus justified in removing the aboriginal nations.

Social Distance

The degree of social acceptance of a newcomer will often depend on the degree of social distance an individual from the host society wishes to maintain from the members of a given group. **Social distance** is the point at which an individual thinks that another group should be prohibited from any further integration into society. Social-distance scales try to measure the social acceptability of different groups to the host society. The scales are constructed as a series of increasingly personalized questions. A group is named and then the respondent is asked the questions, which usually are phrased somewhat more subtly than the following:

1. Do you think we should allow these people to set foot on Canadian soil?

2. Do you think that we should allow them in as visitors?

tokenism
the act of giving a person a position or an opportunity as a way of partially correcting previous wrongs, but not as a way of rewarding the person's merits

manifest destiny
the belief that white people were given dominion over North America as a result of divine intervention, and were thus justified in removing the aboriginal nations

social distance
the point at which an individual thinks that another group should be prohibited from any further integration into society

3. Do you think we should allow them to take up residence here?

4. Do you think that they should be able to become citizens?

5. Could you see yourself having a member of this group as a speaking acquaintance?

6. Would you be comfortable with a member of this group being employed at your place of work?

7. Would you be comfortable with a family living in your neighbourhood?

8. How about as a next-door neighbour?

9. Could you see yourself ever making friends with a member of this group?

10. Would you be comfortable if a member of your family were to marry a member of this group?

11. Would you be comfortable if this marriage produced offspring who would then be direct members of your family?

Notice that the questions are structured so that they hit closer and closer to home. The degree of social distance is the point at which the respondent says no. This point can and does vary as different groups become the subject of the scale.

Race and Racism

race
a large category of people distinguished from others by inherited physiological differences

A **race** is a large category of people distinguished from others by inherited physiological differences. These physiological differences include such things as skin colour, hair texture, general stature, and facial structure. The most prominent of these features tends to be skin colour. The colour of a person's skin depends on the balance of certain chemicals present in the skin. This balance has been adjusted through evolution over the millennia by the intensity and directness of the sun's rays in the geographical areas in which groups originated.

This simple biological defence mechanism has, unfortunately, taken on a social significance far above anything warranted by scientific evidence. A major result has been **racism**, which is systematic prejudice and/or discrimination on the basis of physiological differences. There is no anatomical, physiological, philosophical, spiritual, psychological, anthropological, or sociological backing for racist ideologies. Nevertheless, racism persists as a significant and growing social blemish.

racism
systematic prejudice and/ or discrimination on the basis of physiological differences

The term race tends to defy adequate definition for a number of reasons:

1. It is hard to determine just how many races there are. Sociological and anthropological tradition holds that there are three races: caucasian (white), negroid (black), and mongoloid (oriental). This classification subsumes many varied physiologically distinctive peoples, such as Melanesian, Arab, Australian, Aboriginal, and North American Indian.

2. The classification does not take into account the vast differences among subgroups within the main groups: Slavs and Celts, Latinos and Scandinavians, Chinese and East Indians, Bushmen and Zulus, and so on.

3. People often confuse the idea of race with other social facts:

a. The most common confusion is that between race and ethnicity. People often refer to the British or French races. These are not examples of race; they are examples of **ethnicity**, a shared cultural heritage and a sense of peoplehood.

b. Race and religion are also often confused. There is no Jewish race or Moslem race, for example: Judaism and Islam are religions that people of any racial origin are free to adopt.

c. Language groups are also confused with racial groups. Adolf Hitler spoke of Aryan and Semitic races. However, Aryan is an adjective that is correctly applied to a set of languages native to Northern Europe, while Semitic languages are found in the Middle East.

ethnicity
a shared cultural heritage and a sense of peoplehood

In many ways, the concept of race has become quite meaningless. There are probably as many classifications of races as there are people doing the classifying. Racism is still, however, a socially significant force. Two aspects of racism often get lost in people's thinking about race. First, many apply the epithet "racist" only to white people, and ignore racism directed toward whites by other groups. Second, people often think of racial conflict as occurring only between white and black people or between white and oriental people; they forget that oriental and black people have a whole set of relationships totally independent of white influence or involvement.

Attempts To Justify Racism

Throughout history, racists have searched for any "evidence" that may in any way support their claims:

- One source that has been used to justify racist claims is the Bible. In the story of Noah, it was suggested that, after the ark came to rest on Mount Ararat, Noah's three sons and their wives became the progenitors of the three major races. Noah cursed one son, Ham. The nature of the curse was that all of Ham's children (descendants) would be servants. Ham was thought to be the progenitor of the black race, and so the Hamitic curse was taken as a justification for the enslavement of black people. It was suggested that Noah was passing on what God had ordained. It is difficult to believe, however, that every outburst by Noah was a reiteration of God's word, or that one simple passage could be a justification of centuries of servitude.

- When Charles Darwin published his *Origin of Species* in 1859, it immediately became the focus of almost as much convenient interpretation as the Bible has suffered. Many social Darwinists argued that black people were lower on the evolutionary scale than whites. It was suggested that blacks lacked the capacity for feeling and understanding that whites possessed. This was a convenient rationalization for treating black people like stock animals to be bought and sold and prodded, poked, and examined for infirmities. In the light of modern research, this supposition is obvious nonsense and, furthermore, was never even hinted about by Darwin himself.

- In the 1960s, a South African psychologist, Jensen, suggested that the IQ testing he performed on white and black people demonstrated that white people are intellectually superior to black people. Jensen's procedures were extremely culture-bound. The tests were generated in Western Europe, using language, symbolism, and mathematics geared toward survival in Western European culture. The prejudicial belief that one race is collectively more intelligent than another has come to be termed **Jensenism**.

Jensenism
the prejudicial belief that one race is collectively more intelligent than another

Racism is based on a succession of fallacies. There are no pure races; there is no evidence that one group is intellectually or emotionally superior to another. Suppression of information about minority achievements is often followed up by attempts to point out a lack of minority achievement, thus providing a nice piece of circular reasoning.

Ethnic Differences

The words race and ethnicity have their roots in substantially different domains. Race belongs in the realm of the physical sciences, of physiology and anatomy. Ethnicity, in contrast, which is derived from the Greek word *ethnos*, meaning peoplehood, belongs to the realm of the social sciences. The term ethnicity can be briefly defined as having a shared cultural heritage. This definition implies a degree of recognition by the people involved that they share a historical association and that they retain an identification with each other. In the past 20 years, many citizens of North America have become interested in their "roots" or ethnic heritage. This *ethnic revival* appears to be driven by two factors:

1. Changing times, harsh economies, increased uncertainty, and stressful lifestyles combine to leave people searching for something stable and dependable to provide them with a solid sense of identity. Many people have found this sense of identity in their ethnic heritage, and others have found it in religion. The revival of interest in ethnic heritage and in religion often go hand in hand.

2. The media have often concentrated on ethnically based material in the last 20 years, sometimes in a positive light, sometimes in a negative. This attention has raised people's consciousness about their ethnic origins.

Ethnicity can be a positive, integrative force that brings together people with common interests and provides them with a social network and a system of social support. However, ethnicity can also be divisive when one or more ethnic groups cling too closely to hostilities that belong to another place and time.

Patterns of Accommodation

Throughout history, countries have accommodated new ethnic groups in their midst in a number of ways.

ASSIMILATION

assimilation
a process of cultural accommodation in which one group is completely absorbed by another

Assimilation is the complete absorption of one group by another. The culture of an assimilated group will completely disappear. British immigrants to Canada tend to be totally assimilated by the second generation.

THE MELTING POT

In a **melting pot**, the host society expects new groups to assimilate almost completely but also to contribute something distinctive to the society. Thus, German brewing techniques, Cantonese food, and British constitutional democracy are commonplace in all of the countries that have been settled in the last 200 years. The melting pot concept is usually associated with the United States.

melting pot
a process of cultural accommodation in which one group is almost completely absorbed by another but contributes something distinctive to the whole

CULTURAL PLURALISM

In **cultural pluralism**, the host society expects new groups to contribute to the society, but also encourages new groups to retain much of their cultural heritage and practices. In Canada, this approach to accommodation is a government policy called **multiculturalism**, or government-assisted cultural pluralism. In many ways, multiculturalism is a more realistic social policy than the US policy of the melting pot society because it reflects the reality that has come to pass in both countries.

cultural pluralism
a process of cultural accommodation in which one group is added to another and retains much of its cultural heritage and practices

multiculturalism
government-assisted cultural pluralism

SEGREGATION

In a segregated society, different social groups live, socialize, and play completely separately. In some countries, there is voluntary segregation, but in others this segregation is mandated. Until recently, **apartheid** was South Africa's government-enforced policy of segregation. Under apartheid, all South Africans were racially classified at birth, and this classification, documented on identity cards, governed where people could and could not live, whom people could and could not marry, in what jobs people could and could not work, and where people could and could not dine, swim, and play.

apartheid
South Africa's government-enforced policy of segregation from 1948 to 1990

Measuring Ethnic Identification

Whether or not an ethnic group is closely knit can be measured by readily observable factors. These factors can be established through a series of questions.

GROUP IDENTIFICATION

- Do people label themselves as belonging to the group?
- Do they pay regular visits to their homeland?
- Do they socialize mostly with people of the same ethnicity?

LANGUAGE RETENTION

- Do they still speak their mother tongue?
- What language do they use around their household?
- Do they send their children to language school?

ENDOGAMY

- Do they seek out marital partners from their own group?
- Do they attempt to influence their children's dating patterns?

RESIDENTIAL SEGREGATION

- Do they buy houses and lease apartments in specific sectors of the city in order to be close together?

- Are there small urban villages made up of just one ethnicity?

CULTURAL INSTITUTIONS

- Are there places where they can worship in their mother tongue?

- Are traditional forms of weddings and funerals still adhered to?

- Are there specialized schools to transmit the culture and language?

- Are there social and sports clubs specifically for the group?

Canada is one of the most ethnically diverse countries in the world. This fact can be demonstrated most clearly in a listing of the most common languages spoken: English (over 21 million); French (over 7 million); Italian and Cantonese (over 300 000 each); Punjabi, Spanish, and German (about a quarter million each) (Statistics Canada, 2001).

This linguistic diversity, coupled with the diversity of culinary expertise and religions and social ceremonies and practices, makes Canada a rich society indeed.

CHAPTER SUMMARY

Culture is the glue that holds society together. It consists of behaviour patterns, value systems, material possessions, and language. Although these components are the same from one culture to another, their expression can vary widely. Something that is highly valued in one culture may well be looked down upon in another culture. Adjustment to a new culture is one of the most difficult life changes that an individual can go through. The way that a culture changes and the pace of that change can cause difficulty for some of the members of the culture. A group that shares a cultural heritage is called an ethnic group. Sometimes people confuse ethnicity with the physiologically based concept of race. Although racism has no scientific backing, it persists in modern society.

KEY TERMS

acculturation	ideology
apartheid	internalization
argot	Jensenism
artifacts	manifest destiny
assimilation	melting pot
civil rights	minority group
cultural diffusion	multiculturalism
cultural lag	norms
cultural pluralism	prejudice
cultural relativity	race
cultural trait	racism
culture	social distance
culture shock	stereotype
culture-bound	subculture
discrimination	symbol
ethnocentrism	temprocentrism
feminist	tokenism
future shock	values

REFERENCES

Brown v. Board of Education. (1954). 347 US 483; 74 S Ct. 686.

Canada, Royal Commission on Bilingualism and Biculturalism. (1967–1970). *Report of the Royal Commission on Bilingualism and Biculturalism.* Ottawa: Queen's Printer.

Canadian Charter of Rights and Freedoms. (1982). Part I of the *Constitution Act, 1982*, RSC 1985, app. II, no. 44.

Citizens' Forum on Canada's Future. (1991). *Report to the people and government of Canada.* Ottawa: Supply and Services Canada.

Conkey, M. (1997). Men and women in prehistory: An archaeological challenge. In C.B. Brettell & C.F. Sargent (Eds.), *Gender in cross-cultural perspective* (pp. 57-68). Upper Saddle River, NJ: Prentice Hall.

Darwin, C. (1859). *On the origin of species by means of natural selection.* London.

Human Rights Code (Ontario). (1981). SO 1981, c. 53; RSO 1990, c. H.19.

Jensen, A. (1969, Winter). How much can we boost IQ and scholastic achievement? *Harvard Education Review*, 1-123.

Scott, B., Schwartz, M., & VanderPlaat, M. (2000). *Sociology: Making sense of the social world.* Toronto: Pearson Education Canada.

Statistics Canada. (2001). Language composition of Canada: Detailed language spoken at home. *2001 census*. Catalogue no. 97F0007XCB01004.

Toffler, A. (1970). *Future shock.* New York: Random House.

CHAPTER 5

Socialization

This chapter looks at the lifelong process of learning the cultural requirements of our society. It explores the development of a self-concept, and analyzes the ways in which we acquire the skills, knowledge, and motivations required for participation in social activity. It also examines the preconditions and major agents of socialization, and how we acquire gender identity.

Chapter Objectives

After completing this chapter, you should be able to:

- Distinguish among the different dimensions along which human development takes place, and show how social development shapes the other dimensions.

- Formulate your own position on the balance between nature and nurture in shaping human behaviour.

- Analyze the social forces that shape an individual's self-perception.

- Describe the role of the major agents of socialization in shaping personality development.

- Describe the complex process of acquiring gender identity and assuming gender roles.

- Identify persistent elements of gender-based discrimination in the allocation of social roles in Canada.

As humans, we have an astounding ability to absorb the culture into which we are immersed. There is, however, striking evidence of limitations to our receptivity to our social environment. The sad case of a girl named Genie supports this evidence. Genie was discovered in 1970 by California authorities. From the age of 2 to 13, she was severely mistreated by her abusive father and partially blind mother, who was completely dominated by her husband. Genie was isolated in the back room of her parents' home, harnessed to a potty chair, able to move only her hands and feet. At night, she was laced into a kind of straitjacket and put into a wire cage. She was fed sparingly by her brother, who was not allowed to talk to her. She heard only her father's doglike barking when he beat her for crying or making noise. When she was found, she had no bowel or bladder control and could not stand erect or chew solid food. She could not speak or under-stand language. With intensive treatment, Genie became physically healthy. Attempts were made to socialize her but with limited progress. She did not fully acquire a language and at the age of 24 lacked some of the language skills of 5-year-olds. She developed a fairly large vocabulary and could comprehend everyday conversation. However, she had limited knowledge of grammar and couldn't use pronouns or use intonation to express meaning. This case gives support to the view that unless a child learns a language at an early age, this ability is permanently hindered. It demonstrates that social isolation and neglect are extremely detrimental to young children. Genie never was fully socialized and was eventually institutionalized.

THE INTERNALIZATION OF CULTURE

For a culture to survive, its patterns of thinking and acting must be passed from one generation to the next. This process of transmission is called socialization. It involves training the young in the ways of society so that they can function in that society.

socialization
a complex, lifelong learning process in which an individual develops selfhood and acquires the knowledge, skills, and motivations that are needed to be a member of society

Socialization is a complex, lifelong learning process in which an individual develops selfhood and acquires the knowledge, skills, and motivations that are needed to be a member of society. In this process, a carefree infant is transformed into a disciplined adult. An infant has no self-awareness, is utterly helpless, and is completely dependent on others for her every need. Gradually, a sense of self is developed. A young child is attuned only to her own needs, but, gradually, she learns by example and by reward and punishment to conform to the expectations of others. She learns language, control of impulses, and skills.

internalization
learning that is so efficient that social responses are automatic and the individual is not aware that they are learned or patterned

She takes on social roles and internalizes the norms and values of the family and, later, the wider society. These norms and values become part of her nature, and feelings of guilt may arise if she does not conform to them. This **internalization** of society's ways is subtle. The learning becomes so efficient that social responses are automatic and the individual is not aware that they are learned or patterned. Hence, it is difficult for an individual to point out cultural traits of her own group, because she takes them for granted. Through socialization, we acquire the knowledge, skills, and motivations that we need in order to participate in social life. The process of socialization, according to functionalists, performs vital functions that maintain the structure of society from one generation to the next.

Socialization is only one of four dimensions of a child's general development. The social dimension clearly affects the other dimensions.

Physical Development

Although the process of maturation means that people generally grow bigger and taller and refine their motor skills as they get older, this process is helped, hindered, or otherwise constrained by such factors as culture. A lack of appropriate social contact can lead to the physical underdevelopment of children.

Intellectual Development

As children get older, they become increasingly capable of handling symbols and abstractions. Original learning potential is probably determined by a combination of physiological and psychological factors, but everything else about learning is de-termined by social factors. Our opportunities to learn, the subjects we cover, the surroundings we use, the materials available to us, and the time period in which we learn are all culturally determined and therefore may inhibit or enhance learning potential.

Personality Development

The development of a consistent personality structure takes place in an orderly, psychological process, but this process can be enhanced or disrupted depending on social processes such as family integration, occupational status, and ethnic origin.

Social Development

The fourth dimension of a child's development is the main focus of attention in this chapter. It involves the social relationships that the child establishes, his or her growing ability to operate in a social setting, and his or her learning of the norms, values, statuses, and roles of the society. As we have seen, the social development dimension clearly affects the other dimensions.

PRECONDITIONS FOR SOCIALIZATION

Frederick Elkin, in *The Child and Society: The Process of Socialization* (1960), de-scribed the preconditions of socialization. Before we can begin to discuss the ways in which a child learns the ways of society, we first must be aware of those things that have to be present before the process can begin. Elkin identified three preconditions.

An Ongoing Society

A child is born into a society that already exists and has already developed a set of norms, values, statuses, and roles. It is the child's duty to learn them and the par-ents' duty to transmit them. Therefore, the focus of socialization is the transmission of an existing culture and an attempt to motivate the young to participate in it. Transmission and motivation can become problematic in adolescence and young adulthood. The young will often question their need to abide by a set of rules laid down by previous generations in previous times that seem to have little direct rel-evance to their current situation. As a result of this questioning, social norms, values, statuses, and roles do not remain fixed but are modified as society changes.

An Adequate Biological Inheritance

Elkin argued that an individual, to be able to play a full social role, has to be "free of damage to brain and body." This assertion provoked a strong social response from those involved with and concerned about the rights of the physically and mentally challenged, because they thought that his view could lead to discrimination against these groups. People could use a scientific treatise on the need for adequate bio-logical inheritance as an excuse for underemployment or other discrimination against the handicapped. However, Elkin never intended this result; he was merely pointing out that the closer one is to society's norms of "adequacy," the better chance one has of "fitting in" with society.

A Distinctly Human Nature

Elkin maintained than an individual, to be fully capable of socialization, had to be born with a distinctly human nature. "Human nature" implies possession of all the basic sentiments of humanity: love, shame, aggression, ambition, envy, sympathy, cruelty, and especially **empathy**. For Elkin, it is empathy, the ability to imaginatively place oneself in the situation of another individual, that distinguishes humans from other species.

empathy
the ability to imaginatively place oneself in the situation of another individual

Elkin's assertion about human nature goes to the heart of the ongoing nature–nurture debate. How much of our personalities, capabilities, and behavioural patterns are innate and how much are traits we learn in our constant interactions with others? Social scientists are not in agreement that there is such a thing as human nature, let alone what its components might be. Even if we are born with these basic sentiments, we are not sure whether they are unique to humans or whether other species possess them too. Is a cat that is taking its time with a mouse being cruel? Does it understand what it is like to be on the other end of the claw? Is a psychopath, defined as an individual who is incapable of empathy, fully human? Think of a time in your own life when you shocked yourself by a display of raw emotion that you didn't think yourself capable of. Was it an instinctive response? Was it a response that you had learned over time and that was simply exaggerated by the circumstances?

SOCIALIZATION THROUGH THE LIFE CYCLE

There are four basic types of socialization that permit us to learn and change throughout life: primary socialization, adult socialization, anticipatory socialization, and resocialization.

Primary Socialization

Primary socialization occurs in childhood. It involves the development of language and individual identity, the learning of cognitive skills and self-control, the internalization of moral standards and appropriate attitudes and motivations, and the gaining of some understanding of societal roles.

Early childhood experience is very significant in shaping future intellectual, social, and emotional health. The first five years set the foundation for the rest of life. The experiences and opportunities at this stage determine whether or not a child will grow into a caring, competent, and flexible adult.

At birth, an infant's brain is only a quarter developed. Billions of neural connections still have to be made. As the child relates to and interacts with her social world, these connections are formed, strengthened, and permanently wired. Different parts of the brain develop at different times. There appear to be optimal or critical periods for development of various functions. Most functions develop in the first five years. Some windows of opportunity are open until the age of 10. The single most important factor that affects healthy development is a secure attachment to at least one caregiver.

Adult Socialization

Adult socialization occurs beyond the childhood years. Primary socialization lays the foundation for later learning, but it cannot completely prepare us for adulthood. Our society confronts us with new role expectations as we move through life. For example:

- We move beyond the family into the neighbourhood, we enter school, become an adolescent, choose an occupation, marry, have children, and encounter middle age, retire, then die. Each new stage in life involves new lessons.

- Society changes and we must equip ourselves to cope with new situations.

- We must deal with specialized situations such as geographic and social mobility, physical handicaps, and marital breakdown. Each of these situations requires further socialization.

Anticipatory Socialization

Anticipatory socialization occurs in advance of the actual playing of roles. We rehearse for the future by learning something about role requirements (behaviour and attitudes) and visualize ourselves in the role. For example, children practise being students before they go to school. We may practise being married, being parents, or being retired before we actually assume these roles. College students in field placements, clinical experiences, internships, or co-operative programs are engaging in anticipatory socialization for future occupations.

Resocialization

Resocialization occurs when a new role or a new situation requires us to replace established patterns of behaviour and thought with new patterns. This is more difficult than the original socialization, because established habits interfere with new learning. However, we are capable of changing throughout life. An example of resocialization is the process that alcoholics go through when they break their addiction in Alcoholics Anonymous.

Although the learning that occurs in childhood lays the foundation for future development and is crucial, socialization is a lifelong process. Every time we enter a new group or assume a new role (become a college student, start a new job, get married), we undergo a stage of preparation. Adult socialization is particularly necessary in Canada's complex, changing society. As children, we learn general knowledge, values, skills, and behaviour relevant to many roles. As adults, we acquire information specific to particular roles, often voluntarily (we choose to go to college, get a job, have a family). With the tremendous changes occurring that require adjustment, we continue to be socialized into new roles and situations.

SOCIALIZATION AND THE INDIVIDUAL

Most of the early work on how an individual develops a self-concept came from studies of children's playgroups that were carried out by Charles Cooley (1909) and George Mead (1934). One of the first things that they noticed was that each child

significant other
a person who is extremely important to an individual's development

seemed to have a central person who was extremely important to their development. Cooley and Mead called this person a **significant other**. The significant other was identifiable by the fact that he or she was the person from whom the child most wanted to seek out attention and affection and by whom the child least wanted to be punished. This led to the realization that socialization is essentially a process of responding to rewards by repeating approved behaviours, and of avoiding negative reactions by not performing disapproved behaviours. Another way to measure the significant other is to observe to whom the child turns at key emotional times. As one gets older, one's significant other may change: a lover, a spouse, a religious leader, a teacher. However, the idea of having one central person to provide a sense of self and security remains relevant.

The effect of the absence of a significant other may be more far-reaching than Cooley and Mead ever believed. One example could be a child's failure to thrive, where the only contributing factor to the child's unusually slow physical development seems to be a social environment that is lacking in affection, attention, and discipline from a significant other. Other historical evidence of the failure-to-thrive syndrome is the reportedly small stature of children who were brought up in orphanages. This size difference cannot be simply explained in nutritional terms.

In our daily living, the people around us continually react to our actions, behaviours, statements, and so on. We assess the reactions of others and interpret what these reactions tell us about our personality. The **looking-glass self** is the picture that we get of ourselves from the reactions of other people to us. We must be very cautious about these "looking-glass incidents," however, because we often get a false reading of other people's judgments about ourselves. For example, we may think a person laughing nearby is laughing at us when, in fact, the person is oblivious to our existence. Nevertheless, we often try to adjust our behaviour patterns to alter what we think are traits that looking-glass incidents have shown to be negative, and to reinforce traits that other incidents have shown to be positive.

looking-glass self
the picture that we get of ourselves from the reactions of other people to us

Part of the looking-glass process in young children is the process of "taking the role of the other." Children learn how others perceive the world by putting themselves in their roles. Children put themselves in other roles by playing made-up roles in games, by playing the role of fictional hero figures, by interacting with an imaginary friend, or by playing alone but playing two roles simultaneously. Children develop a number of skills during this process. First, they develop the ability to interact socially with other human beings. Second, they develop imaginative creativity. Third, they develop the rudiments of the ability to empathize by trying to see the world from a different perspective.

Cooley and Mead also believed that at some time in the early socialization process, we all step back from this activity and try to get an overall picture of ourselves among the community of people with whom we interact. We add up the impressions gathered from our significant others, the self-concept and insights gained from thousands of looking-glass incidents, the pictures of ourselves that we think each of our group memberships has, and so on, and summarize them to get one comprehensive view of ourselves. Through this process, we establish our **generalized other** — the concept of ourselves that we think exists in the community. Most of us retain the belief that this social construction of ourselves (Mead called this the "ME") differs somewhat from our real self (the "I"). This belief leads to other attempts to restructure our personalities or, at least, our patterns of behaviour, as we try to

generalized other
the concept of ourselves that we think exists in the community

close the gap between the "I" and the "ME." We go through a process of changing our behaviour so that people can glimpse "the real me."

The work of Mead and Cooley is consistent with the symbolic–interactionist approach due to their emphasis on human interaction and symbolic communication. Our interactions are based on our interpretive understanding of our social involvement. We communicate symbolically using language. Without language, and the communication that makes it possible, we would be unable to learn and pass on our culture (Knuttila, 2002).

AGENTS OF SOCIALIZATION

There are many agents that contribute to the socialization process. **Agents of socialization** are large-scale settings or institutions that help to shape our norms and values alongside our significant others. These agents affect every Canadian and exert a powerful influence during the impressionable childhood years. Some agents that help shape our personality and behavioural patterns are the family, religion, peer groups, the education system, and the mass media. Social contexts such as gender, one's racial/ethnic ties, and one's social class standing also have an impact on the socialization process.

agents of socialization
large-scale settings or institutions that help to shape our norms and values

The Family

Society has charged two agents, the family and the school, with the socialization of children. Although the contemporary family now shares some functions with other agents, its impact on the child is the most significant. Learning occurs rapidly during the years of early childhood when the family has almost exclusive control over and close emotional bonds with the child. The family touches every sphere of the child's existence. The family lays the foundation for other socialization agents.

The study of child development has demonstrated clearly that, for most of us, by the age of five our fundamental characteristics are permanently set: our basic behavioural patterns, our intellectual quotient, our basic personality structure, our pattern of coping with stress, and our problem-solving techniques. The family is responsible for our maintenance and socialization during this significant time. Most of us accept the family as an enduring, reliable source of support, and most of us usually select our first significant others from the family.

The specific family situation affects the child in specific ways. Growing up in a one-parent, same-sex, or blended family is different from growing up in a more conventional family. Sibling interaction plays an important role in socialization; it provides practice in cooperation and competition.

The family's role in socialization has changed dramatically in the last 40 to 50 years. Increasing numbers of mothers of young children have returned to work, and a widespread system of day care has evolved. More people move away from the area where they were raised, separating them from their extended family. The number of single-parent, same-sex, and blended families continues to increase. But despite cynicism about the "diminishing" role of the family, it remains the most significant agent of socialization.

The family is not the only agent of socialization. It can only present to us a narrow segment of the culture, and we tend to take the values, roles, norms, and statuses of our family group as the only correct ones. We need other agents to give us a wider picture of the possible experiences, choices, and lifestyles that are available to us.

Religion

Like the family, religion is a universal institution. There are vast differences in the forms of religious rituals and the content of the belief systems, but sociologists and historians have no knowledge of any group that does not have some form of religion. Sociologists are not concerned with teaching religion — they leave that up to theologians. Their interest lies in the relationships between people's beliefs and the way they live, and in the functions and consequences of religion for society.

Religion has several definitions, depending whether it is defined for theological or scientific study. When most people think of religion, they think of a belief in a divine or supernatural power. Religion involves a code of conduct, a code of ethics, and a philosophy. Social scientists define religion in terms of humans developing systems of meaning to interpret the world.

Some systems (commonly called religions) take into account the supernatural (for example, Christianity, Judaism, and Islam). Other systems, called humanistic perspectives, do not. **Religion** can be defined as a system of beliefs and practices surrounding a supernatural order of beings, places, and forces.

Religion concerns the meaning of life. It implies that our existence has meaning beyond what we give, and that meaning lies in some supernatural reality. The world we know through our senses is only part of a greater reality, and this greater reality can only be known through faith. Sociology, as a science, is unable to assess the faith claims of religion (for example, that there is a God). It does, however, explore the social aspects of religion — the beliefs people have, the factors influencing the inclination to be religious, the impact that religious commitment has on one's attitudes and behaviour, and religion's impact on social life.

religion
a system of beliefs and practices surrounding a supernatural order of beings, places, and forces

THEORETICAL PERSPECTIVES

CONFLICT THEORY   Karl Marx (Marx & Engels, 1964) believed that established religion legitimized a given social system. According to Marx, religion helped to contain potentially explosive forces. It taught that acceptance of one's fate and faithful performance of religious obligations is pleasing to God. For the oppressed masses, religion became an "opiate" that pacifies present deprivation with the hope of future glory. He argued that religion was a tool that the dominant group uses to coax oppressed groups into complacency.

Modern sociologists may use this argument and describe how the psychic relief of religion may facilitate survival in a dehumanizing environment. Like a narcotic, religion eases the pain but does not remove the cause. It often retards the struggle for change. For example, the traditional religion of American blacks has made their subordinate status more bearable. The religious services provide tension release and escape, and the focus on the afterlife has promised a hope of a better life to come.

FUNCTIONALIST THEORY   As with Marx, Émile Durkheim (1954) saw religion as a basis for social stability. Marx argued that it seduced the oppressed into passivity regarding injustice, knowing that it would be corrected in the afterlife. For Durkheim, social order was a prerequisite for human happiness and creative endeavour. His focus was on the contribution that religion made to social order by fostering cohesion among group members. Humans conceptualized the idea of a god to create a collective conscience and find mutual support. Durkheim saw religion as performing an important function in providing explanations for life's troublesome mysteries and a foundation of morals and ethics.

SYMBOLIC INTERACTIONISM   Max Weber (1961) maintained that ideas, whether they are objectively true or not, represent one's definition of reality. He viewed religious behaviour and thought as a part of everyday conduct. Religion, he recognized, had a social dimension that can be studied according to its nature and relationship to the rest of life. He believed that ideas about religion have the potential to influence behaviour. Weber stressed that religion is not so much an "external social fact" as an internal and personal motivating force (Knuttila, 2002). Religion represented a reference group from which an individual could develop identity.

SOCIAL FUNCTIONS OF RELIGION

Many members of society use religion to meet a wide variety of needs:

- Religion *enhances solidarity* among the members of the group and supports its values and norms. This effect is expressed by the aphorism "a family that prays together, stays together." Even in societies in which several religious groups coexist, religion in general buttresses such institutions as the family, promotes the keeping of the law, and condemns drug and alcohol abuse and cruelty. To the extent that individuals identify with a religion, its ethical content may deter them from engaging in anti-social acts. In this way, social control is reinforced. **Social control** is the process by which members of a group encourage desired forms of behaviour and discourage undesired forms. Because societies depend on the willing cooperation of their members, this kind of reinforcement becomes especially important, since it is based primarily on the internalization of values rather than on external surveillance.

- *Membership* in a religious group may be an integral part of individual identity. For the Old Order Mennonites in southern Ontario, every facet of life is pervaded by religion. Distinctive clothing identifies them with their religion. Belonging to such all-embracing religious groups permits little variation in personal commitment. Non-conformers are expelled. For many people in Canada today, religion has less impact on identity. A man may identify himself as a doctor, a husband, a father, or a Canadian before identifying himself as a member of the United Church, for example.

- Religion *makes the world more comprehensible* by providing explanations of the mysteries of life. It requires the individual to accept certain phenomena on faith.

- The **prescriptions** (the rules and directions of behaviour that are set down and recommended) and **proscriptions** (the banning or condemnation of certain behaviour) that underpin religion's social control provide the individual with *a guide for everyday conduct*. Attitudes, opinions, and actions

social control
the process by which members of a group encourage desired forms of behaviour and discourage undesired forms

prescriptions
the rules and directions of behaviour that are set down and recommended

proscriptions
the banning or condemnation of certain behaviour

are justified in terms of the religious code, which establishes what is right and wrong. For example, a Catholic physician would probably refuse to perform abortions.

- Everyone must *cope with fear and anxiety*, and with the inevitability of death. The belief in a life after death of many religions makes bearable present injustices. Members accept that there are happenings in the universe that are beyond human understanding, and they hope for a better afterlife and eventual reunion with loved ones. The persistence of religion in societies in which it is suppressed by the state shows that religion meets fundamental human needs that are not fully eased by secular belief systems such as communism.

  ❑ The number of Canadians who attend religious ceremonies is difficult to quantify exactly, though poll results provide a good estimation. It appears from recent statistics that attendance has fallen significantly for both Protestants and Catholics, but Protestant attendance is on the rise again. Even though a majority of Canadians no longer attend religious services on a regular basis, an overwhelming majority continue to identify with historically dominant groups. The ties with religion continue to remain strong as a result of the fusion of religion, family, and culture. Many return to their places of worship for religious holidays, baptisms, weddings, and funerals. According to Statistics Canada (2001), the two biggest influences on religious attendance are age and immigration status. Older people have the highest attendance rate; those aged 25 to 34 have the lowest. The increase in attendance in Toronto in the 1990s was entirely because of the city's immigrant population.

Peer Groups

peers
other people of approximately the same age and social status

After the family, **peers** — other people of approximately the same age and social status — constitute the second most powerful socialization agency. One of the first experiences that a child has outside the family is with a peer group. The peer group then becomes the first place the child encounters the idea that there are different ways of doing things from their parents' way of doing things — and even, perhaps, the idea that their parents' values or beliefs might be wrong for them. From early childhood throughout life, people attach a great deal of importance to peer relationships. Parents realize that their children need companions and take pains to help them find friends, and they worry if they don't relate well to other children. Adolescent peer groups are highly gratifying for teenagers, and very influential in current lifestyle matters such as fashion and music. For issues concerning future life goals and educational aspirations, however, parents are often a more important influence than peers are.

The peer group is the child's first experience of independence from authority. The group is usually a self-generating group without enforced membership, and the leadership role is usually based on personal qualities, not on a status such as parent, teacher, or religious leader. There is a great deal of input into decision making by all of the group members. Internal relationships are largely egalitarian. Consequently, the child first experiences the democratic process in action. If disagreements within this group are fundamental, the child can opt out.

Children learn from one another. Peer contact provides opportunities to practise social roles, to develop interaction skills, to cooperate, and to compete. Peers are a source of information. Children interpret the world for one another in ways that adults cannot duplicate. Adults are unaware of some matters that are important to their children (such as the latest trends). Some sensitive subjects are often more easily discussed with peers.

Adolescence is the peak of peer-group influence. The teenager reaches out for the companionship, opinions, and tastes of age mates. This process helps bridge the gulf between childhood dependence on family and adulthood. Peer relations remain very important throughout life. Adults may have more inner resources than children do, but they remain sensitive to the opinions of their friends. Peer experiences with give-and-take interaction influence one's values and attitudes — for example, in such ethical abstractions as rules, fair play, and honesty.

The Education System

Education is an institution that affects all of us. The law requires us to attend school for at least 10 years, although most Canadians stay in school longer than that. Going to school is such a regular part of growing up, it seems difficult to imagine how we would be fully socialized without it.

In sociological terms, education is not synonymous with either learning or socialization. Although it involves both, not all learning or socialization takes the form of education. **Education** is the deliberate and organized transmission of values, knowledge, and skills. Teachers and students meet at a designated time, in an appropriate setting, to pursue systematically a defined learning objective. Schools are educational organizations and the passage to adulthood of children in Canada is channelled through these organizations.

education
the deliberate and organized transmission of values, knowledge, and skills

FUNCTIONS OF EDUCATION

The most widely recognized function of the educational system is to facilitate the transition from participation in family relationships to involvement in relationships in the larger society. Participation in society involves membership in four key institutional areas: the economy, the social stratification system, the political order, and the culture of society. Preparation in these areas is so essential that the educational system fulfills a specific function with regard to each of these areas. Over time, the perceived relative importance of these different functions can change quite radically, but they always persist.

THE ECONOMY   Preparing children for adulthood involves training in the practical skills required to become productive members of society. In the past, except for highly specialized occupations, a great deal of this training took place on the job. Today, school has taken over the central role of occupational learning. Education has become the major agency for **occupational socialization**, or the preparation of students for entering the job market. The economy depends on an adequate supply of efficient and motivated workers for its operation. The education system must meet this task.

occupational socialization
the preparation of students for entering the job market

SOCIAL STRATIFICATION   Social stratification (social inequality in terms of property, power, and prestige) is a prevalent aspect of social life. Occupations carry unequal amounts of prestige and benefits of income, and people will tend to avoid the less-rewarded positions in favour of the more attractive ones. Therefore, social stratification introduces an element of status competition. In other words, inequality presents an allocation problem. **Status allocation** is the process of distributing individuals among the different positions in society.

Societies have dealt with the problem of status allocation by developing strategies for regulating the process of status acquisition. In today's society, many statuses are acquired through open competition on the basis of an individual's effort and ability. This open competition is in contrast to closed competition on the basis of gender, class of origin, and racial or ethnic background. In an open society, education plays an active role in the process of allocation. Ideally, its task is to provide everyone with an equal chance to compete and to assess a student's class of destination on the basis of talent and ability. School is the place where students are tested, where their academic achievement is evaluated and compared with that of their peers, and where, on the basis of comparative assessment of their performances, they are channelled in appropriate directions. Students leave school with a certificate, a diploma, or a degree that qualifies them for a specific level of social stratification.

It is not enough, however, to be taught where one fits into society; acceptance of that decision is also important. Therefore, as a major social selection agency, the education system not only is involved in the screening process, but also functions as an agent of **status socialization**, or the process of teaching people to accept their position in the social stratification system. Compliance with the outcome of the selection process is accomplished through guidance counselling, in which students' aspirations are aligned with the school's estimation of their abilities. Students are taught to be realistic about their mobility prospects. Social inequality is warranted as long as people have an equal chance to prove themselves. People are more likely to accept this if they believe the assessment procedures are fair and accurate.

THE POLITICAL ORDER   Learning to participate in social life also includes preparing for membership in the political order. Our first encounter with authority and the political order takes place in the family. We learn to accept parental authority because it is for our own good, and we learn to follow rules, knowing that their violation will result in sanctions. However, the education system is needed to prepare us for the formally organized and uniform public authority structure in the larger society.

In Canada, public authority is organized along democratic lines. Our system of government attempts to make authority accountable to the people. As citizens, we are called upon to become politically involved, by speaking up for our interests and by monitoring the performance of our elected politicians. The education system has the task of preparing us for this type of active participation. Courses in history and political science are aimed at achieving this goal.

CULTURE   The three functions of education already discussed all have the goal of preparing students to fit into a particular niche in the division of labour in a socially differentiated society. Another important function is to teach children to become members of the same community, to create a common cultural identity. The cultural function attempts to foster a sense of collective identity and purpose. We learn that

---

status allocation
the process of distributing individuals among the different positions in society

status socialization
the process of teaching people to accept their position in the social stratification system

we are bound together by common traditions and values, and from this awareness ideally follows self-identification and pride.

HUMAN ENLIGHTENMENT   Although role socialization is a very important function of education, moulding our personality to serve the demands of society is not its sole function. Personality development, reaching one's potential, and learning moral and aesthetic sensitivity are also prized. Self-enrichment, self-realization, and autonomy are encouraged and promoted. The education system not only tries to pass on collective wisdom of the past, but also functions as a source of innovations. New scientific ideas, new interpretations of culture, and critical examination of existing knowledge are also highly valued. It may well be that the importance of this function of education has been diminished in the last 20 years. Fostering critical analysis can be seen to be contradictory to the more conservative function of producing happy, productive, consuming workers.

Education in Canada is under provincial rather than federal control, except for the education of aboriginal people and military personnel. This allocation of responsibility has produced a great deal of diversity among the education systems of the various provinces, in terms of what students are taught, how they are taught, and how long they are taught. For example, more citizens of Ontario (per capita) have degrees, certificates, or diplomas and spend more years in school than do Newfoundlanders. Provincial wealth, availability of employment, and rural residence are some of the complex reasons for the differences. Even within provinces there are variations. Most decisions concerning elementary and secondary education are made at the local community level by elected school boards. Therefore, in most cases, the community in which you live will determine what education system is available.

Universal schooling came into existence in Ontario in 1871 with the introduction of a state-supported system of compulsory education. This marked education as being socially significant and having important public functions to perform. The family delegated part of its responsibility for the socialization process to the schools. The education system was transformed into a bureaucracy, with regulatory power centralized at the top. The government had the authority over important areas, such as teacher certification, curricula, and textbooks.

Countries such as Canada assign the education system a major role in preparing children for adulthood. The knowledge and skills needed in our industrialized society are too extensive and complex for most parents to convey to their children. Nonetheless, a small but increasing number of families are opting for home schooling for at least a portion of their children's formal education. They have questioned the quality of education in the public system. These ambitious people must provide a curriculum of study that is regulated by the school system.

For many children, enrolling in school is their first encounter with a formal institution. The child is treated as a member of a group and continues to learn that the demands of organizations often take priority over the individual's own wishes.

The socialization process involves teaching children four types of knowledge:

1. *Formal knowledge*   Formal knowledge provides children with information and skills that they need to function in society.

2. *Values*   The education system attempts to transmit societal values and goals, such as motivation to achieve, individual responsibility, and respect

for other people's rights. The system also plays a vital role in orienting the child to Canadian society, a society that contains strong ethnic and regional identities and that consumes US mass media.

3. *Interpersonal skills*   Children learn new social skills as they cope with the demands of a formal organization. They are confronted with impersonal rules for behaviour, such as cooperating, being on time, and waiting your turn.

4. *Self-evaluation*   Throughout childhood and adolescence, a child's interaction at school provides reflections for the looking-glass self. It is necessary for the child to know what sort of person he or she is, relative to his or her peers. The education system attempts to evaluate children according to universal standards. The system is made up of teachers, principals, curricula, textbooks, and other students.

Teachers are powerful agents of socialization because they are the human contact between students and the formal organization of the school. There are several important ways in which the teacher exercises influence on the child. The teacher acts as the major vehicle for transmitting the school curriculum and related values. The teacher establishes the rules of expected behaviour as well as methods that attempt to correct inappropriate behaviour. The teacher is also a potential role model.

manifest function
the designed and evident purpose of a social institution

latent function
the underlying or hidden purposes that evolve in a social institution

Thus, the socialization role is played on two levels. One is the overt or **manifest function** of the school system — that is, the system's designed and evident purpose, which is to pass on to the young the skills and knowledge of the culture. The other is the **latent function**, the underlying or hidden purposes that evolve in a social institution. These hidden purposes include the school system's role in reinforcing prevalent middle-class values, a method of social control by ensuring that the young are occupied rather than roaming the streets, and a means of reducing potential unemployment and welfare dependence.

The Mass Media

The mass media are impersonal communication sources that reach large audiences. They transmit information to the public on a large scale. They include television, radio, movies, DVDs, CDs, and print media. The media act as direct agencies of socialization. They reflect nearly every facet of society; however, these reflections are not necessarily accurate. Situation comedies picture what happens in other people's families. Advertisements entice children and adults with all the regalia supposedly necessary for them to be healthy, happy, and respectable. Many television programs and DVDs present us with an astonishing number of violent crimes in one evening. The American Psychological Association (APA) released a study involving five experiments with 500 college students in the May 2003 issue of the *Journal of Personality and Social Psychology*. The result of the study contradicts a popular view that listening to angry, violent music serves as a positive catharsis for people. The study examined the effects of seven violent songs by seven artists and eight non-violent songs by seven artists. The study concluded that violent lyrics in songs increase aggression-related thoughts and emotions and could indirectly create a more hostile social environment ("Study shows violent lyrics create hostility," 2003).

The effects of mass media appear not to initiate certain acts of behaviour, but subtly influence general values and attitudes. For example, if a child watches an abundance of murders and other violent crimes on television, he or she is not likely to go out and murder someone as a result of this bombardment. The more likely result is that the child, on hearings of or even witnessing a violent crime, will have a less emotional reaction than someone not exposed to this violence. The value of life may seem somewhat meaningless to a generation that has witnessed numerous simulated and real deaths in the media.

The impact of television as a socialization agent has been of particular concern to child development experts. The average television set is on five to six hours a day. Many children watch anything and everything. This activity takes away time from other activities, replacing hours of playtime through which children learn society's norms and social skills. Reading, a skill that requires practice, is not often a priority.

Parental monitoring of television can reduce its negative effects. Children's interpretation of media content is moulded by the opinions of parents, teachers, and friends. Parents may forbid watching violent television shows or can recommend educational shows. They can offer advice on what toys are worthwhile, and on ways in which problems can be solved without violence.

Researchers have also looked for beneficial effects of the media. For example, television has been studied as an agent of anticipatory socialization for work roles. They have concluded that although television does provide a wide perspective on work roles, it also oversimplifies what the real world is like. It does not reflect the true job market when it frequently portrays occupations with high prestige. It also shows stereotypical behaviour that is often misleading and superficial.

While they are being entertained, children are also absorbing a lot of incidental information about their society. We anticipate that shows with single-parents, same-sex, or blended families, or families with adopted or handicapped children, might help children with similar experiences to feel comfortable. Research has demonstrated that frequent watchers of shows such as *Sesame Street* are better prepared for school than infrequent watchers.

As children mature into adults, they encounter an increasing diversity of socialization agents. These people and institutions help them learn more specialized roles. A great deal of occupational socialization occurs on the job. Newly divorced adults often learn the single role through self-help groups such as Parents Without Partners. Many courses are offered in the community on topics such as effective parenting, coping with widowhood and divorce, stay-at-home parents' re-entry into the labour market, and those designed to help immigrants acculturate to Canadian culture.

OVERSOCIALIZATION

When realizing how powerful the socialization process can be, we might mistakenly believe that we often become oversocialized. People are not completely moulded by the values and norms of their society. If this happened, there would be no free will, and people would not be responsible for their actions. Although people brought up in the same society usually speak the same language, value many of the same things, and behave in a similar way, there is not absolute conformity. People are born, it seems, with different temperaments and aptitudes, and are unique individuals. They are capable of questioning norms and values, and of making changes. Individuals also create new roles as they modify situations to suit themselves, as well as taking on roles.

Although nearly everyone is socialized within the family, every family is unique. Socialization is also carried out by a variety of agencies and people, all with different interpretations of society's norms and values, and with different perspectives. Evidence of deviant behaviour in every society demonstrates that no system of socialization is perfectly efficient.

GENDER SOCIALIZATION

Gender roles are learned in the course of socialization. In all families, boys and girls are treated differently. Peer-group activities of boys and girls also differ. Gender role stereotypes are reinforced in the media and in advertising.

Our concept of who we are and the pattern of behaviours that reflects our personality are greatly influenced by our sex, gender, gender identity, and gender roles. Each of these concepts has distinct differences that help us to understand the complexities of social behaviour.

sex
the fact of being male or female as determined by chromosomes, hormones, anatomy, and physiology

gender
recognition of maleness or femaleness as designated by society

gender identity
one's sense of being male or female

gender socialization
a complex learning process in which people learn to be masculine and feminine according to society's expectations

Sex is a biological term — the fact of being male or female as determined by chromosomes, hormones, anatomy, and physiology. Sex is an *ascribed status* with culturally defined rights and obligations.

Gender is recognition of maleness or femaleness as designated by society. It is an *achieved status* that refers to social, psychological, and cultural characteristics of prescribed behaviours, attitudes, feelings, and traits. These are culturally associated with and assumed to be appropriate to the status of maleness and femaleness. Within the last few decades, there have been remarkable cultural changes in opinion concerning what behaviours are "natural" for males and females. Today, it is a generally held belief that distinctions between male and female social roles reflect one's culture more than biological differences between the sexes.

Gender identity refers to one's sense of being male or female. In most cases, one's gender identity will match one's sex. However, a *transsexual* is a person who has the gender identity of the opposite sex, for example, a male transsexual has a female gender identity. Transsexuals may have sex reassignment surgery to have a body that matches the sex they feel they are. Surgical reassignment is a decreasing practice. Increasingly, those who were thought of as transsexual are being seen as gender confused, a condition that requires counselling rather than surgery.

Gender socialization is a complex learning process in which people learn to be masculine and feminine according to society's expectations.

CULTURE, SEX, AND GENDER

Our culture shapes our behaviour. It defines appropriate behaviour patterns for each sex. Traditionally, it had been assumed that biological differences between males and females give rise to behaviours that are "natural" for each sex. However, this view is now being refuted. For example, mothers were once thought of as being the only natural nurturers, but fathers are now recognized as being capable of fulfill-ing the nurturing role as well.

Gender roles are the culturally defined set of behaviours that are considered appropriate for each sex in society. Many people believe that these roles are not usually based on activities in which the particular sex is "naturally" good. Therefore, many argue that gender roles are probably not determined by nature or biology, but rather defined by culture and social agreement. Sex is natural, gender is social. It is important to note that since people are often ethnocentric, they may think their gen-der roles are appropriate and natural, when they may simply be social agreements that are open to change.

Many social scientists have been intrigued by the trend among many men and women of sharing long-established gender roles. This is a significant change because all of human social life has been built around the relationships between the sexes. In fact, changes in gender relationships are likely to affect our entire social structure.

Some people have put considerable effort into socializing children in ways that are non-traditional. Many are encouraging these changes by making de-sexed or androgy-nous roles more acceptable and even preferred over traditional sex roles. **Androgyny** refers to the presence of both traditional feminine and masculine traits within indi-viduals of both sexes.

androgyny
the presence of both traditional feminine and masculine traits within individuals of both sexes

In the past, we assumed that masculinity and femininity were opposite person-ality traits, and that the more masculine a person was, the less feminine he (or she) could be, and vice versa. Men who possessed traditional female traits such as nur-turing, tenderness, and emotionality would have been considered unmanly. Women who worked hard to get ahead in the business world would have been seen as too masculine and not very feminine. Today, however, many social scientists assert that an individual can possess both masculine and feminine traits because they are in-dependent of one another. Therefore, an androgynous person could be described as being understanding and compassionate as well as assertive, self-reliant, and ambitious.

In many families and communities in Canada, there is less emphasis on the so-cialization of traditional sex roles for males and females and more emphasis on the socialization of androgynous sex roles. Individuals are being encouraged to draw on their "feminine side" in social relationships with others (for example, parenting roles, friendships, and love relationships) and on their "masculine side" in other relationships and situations (for example, competition, work, and sports).

There is a great deal of evidence to show that androgynous people are rela-tively well adjusted and can handle many of life's difficult experiences because of their ability to draw on both personality dimensions. The socialization processes needed to encourage an individual to establish an androgynous role are becoming more common. In many families, the parents have become androgynous role mod-els for their children. Many mothers are in the workforce, where they need to be competent, confident, and assertive to succeed. Fathers are taking a more active role in nurturing and caring for their children. Single parents have to assume both parenting roles. Same-sex parents are able to fit into these androgynous roles.

Parents and educators are attempting to create a more gender-free environ-ment. This is evident in the purchasing pattern of toys for boys and girls. It is more acceptable for boys to play house and express their feelings, and for girls to build things and be rough and tough. The rapid growth rate of female involvement in contact sports is another indicator of this trend. There has been a concerted effort to make educational material as gender-free as possible. Both boys and girls participate in family studies and industrial arts in the school curriculum. Non-traditional occupational roles for men and women are more acceptable today, although there is still room for improvement in this area.

CROSS-CULTURAL COMPARISONS OF GENDER ROLES

Although biology provides two universal and distinct sexes, cultures provide almost infinitely varied gender roles. Behaviour that is appropriate for males and females differs widely among cultures. Norms appropriate for a Canadian man or woman are quite different from those of a Chinese man or woman. Margaret Mead (1935) gave a dramatic description of the cultural influence on behaviour when she studied three societies in New Guinea. In two, there was considerable similarity in the behaviour of men and women. Both Arapesh men and women were unassertive, cooperative, and emotionally kind. In contrast, both Mundugumor men and women were aggressive, selfish, and insensitive to others. They were also headhunters and cannibals. In the Tchambuli society, there were distinct differences. The gender roles were reversed from stereotypical gender roles in our society. Men were submissive, emotional, and nurturing with children and women were dominant, unemotional, and wore no jewellery. These cultures are somewhat unusual. The most common pattern in societies is one in which the male is dominant over women and children. Even when equality between sexes does exist, it is usually limited to certain areas of life, such as in home or work situations. However, since gender roles are social agreements, it is possible to continue to erase the distinctions between masculine and feminine behaviour patterns. This is evident in the apparent change in the occupations that are considered appropriate for each sex. It is now much more acceptable to pursue non-traditional occupations (for example, women in the military).

Despite many changes in Canadian gender roles, boys and girls still tend to go through largely traditional gender socialization. As well, biological differences in size, strength, and childbearing capabilities cannot but have consequences for social behaviour.

EXPLAINING GENDER DIFFERENTIATION

The biological differences between males and females provide the basis for different social roles for men and women in all societies. Traditionally, society has tied together the reproductive function and the nurturing role. However, some researchers are now questioning the supposed biological urge to nurture by raising the possibility that the nurturing role is socially defined. Women are no longer necessarily expected to devote their life only to their family.

There are many beliefs about the differences between males and females — for example, that girls are more social than boys, and that girls are more suggestible and less analytic. These beliefs remain largely unsupported, although, according to Maccoby and Jacklin (1974), some beliefs have been supported by evidence. It appears there are small differences in some areas of cognitive ability. Girls tend to have greater verbal ability than boys, whereas boys have greater visual–spatial ability. Possibly as a result of this superior visual–spatial ability, boys appear to have superior mathematical ability too, particularly in algebra. It also appears that in virtually all societies males are more aggressive.

We cannot automatically assume that these differences are due solely to nature. It may be that biological factors such as hormones and brain differentiation play a role; however, it is unclear how much weight should be attributed to these forces. Biology and learning are so intertwined that it is almost impossible to disentangle them. Social learning — that is, positive reinforcement and the imitating of role models — can also have a profound effect in these areas. Children identify themselves as male or female quite early, even before they realize that sex is permanent. They develop definite ideas about what males and females do. Other theorists explain these differences as part of a child's cognitive development. They believe that children organize the world and interpret it through sex roles. One point to consider is that if gender differences are solely a function of biological sex differences, there should be no variation across cultures in gender roles. Since there *is* variation across cultures, it appears that differences are caused more by culture than by biology. However, research into sex differences raises more questions than it answers.

There are also many views concerning the sociological significance of gender differentiation. Functionalists view gender differentiation as the most effective way to raise and support a family. It lays the framework for the division of labour, and men and women have distinct roles that help maintain family stability. Conflict theorists see gender differentiation as creating conflict in the relationships between men and women. Two factors, economic dependency and physical strength, are believed to be at the root of this conflict in which women are exploited. These theorists did predict that the sexes would become more socially equal as soon as women became economically self-sufficient and had alternatives in caring for children if they decided to enter the workforce.

GENDER AND SOCIAL INEQUALITY

A basic assumption, common to nearly all societies, is that men and women are unequal in some sociocultural way. Conflict theorists and feminist sociologists study social inequalities and ways in which to modify socialization processes to help address the inequalities. Feminist sociologists are particularly concerned with gender socialization as children learn how to become masculine and feminine according to society's expectations. They examine the process of internalizing norms that specify gender inequality and gender division of labour (Teevan & Hewitt, 2001).

An excellent example of societal influence is in the media. Although legal reforms and social constraints may point to increasing equality between the sexes in Canada, widespread beliefs and attitudes change very slowly. Children and adults continue to be exposed to negative attitudes about gender issues. The media convey gender socialization messages with some video games and popular music promoting anti-female and pro-violence themes. Tracy Dietz (1998) analyzed 33 popular Nintendo and Sega Genesis games and found that when females do appear, they are often presented as sex objects. Aggression is part of the strategy or object of the game in the majority of games, with nearly a quarter depicting violence directed at women.

Gender roles are more flexible today than they were in the past. More women are in the workforce, and the word "househusband" is gaining acceptance. "Parental"

sexism
the act of prejudging a
person in a negative way
on the basis of gender

leave for childbirth and initial child care is a Canadian employment insurance (EI) benefit. However, children learn gender stereotypes early, and changing these traditional gender roles requires ongoing effort. **Sexism**, the act of prejudging a person in a negative way on the basis of gender, continues to be a problem. It restricts the social and economic opportunities of individuals, and primarily those of women.

Sexism particularly influences opportunities in the workforce, where women experience lower wages, fewer fringe benefits, less security, and lower status. Women who have families and who work outside the home often carry a double burden. The responsibilities of a two-career family are borne more by women than by men. Although some men are becoming more cooperative in sharing household chores, for the most part women do more. Changing gender roles through socialization will alter this division of labour. Even though there has been a dramatic increase in the percentage of women in the workforce, men and women continue to show differences in the type of jobs they hold. Women still predominate in clerical, sales, and service positions, and men are more likely to be in the professions, managerial positions, and the skilled trades. This situation is changing, but slowly.

Society is becoming more aware of sex discrimination and more attention is given to the socialization process to reduce it. Governmental affirmative action programs are attempting to remedy the results of sexist hiring practices. Education concerning sexual harassment and violence against women, including date rape, is aimed at protecting women from these destructive practices. Attention is also focused on the sexist practices that disadvantage men — for example, the frequent presumption that custody of children of divorced parents should be awarded to the mother. With greater understanding of social behaviour and cultural influences, sociologists may help to reduce sexual inequality.

RACIAL/ETHNIC AND SOCIAL CLASS SOCIALIZATION

Conflict theorists argue that the attitudes and behaviours people learn through socialization vary, not only by gender, but by social class and race/ethnicity. For example, compare aboriginal and dominant Canadian cultures. Aboriginal traditions stress teamwork and commitment to the good of the community, while the dominant Canadian culture emphasizes competition and personal achievement (Scott, Schwartz, & VanderPlaat, 1999). People within various social classes and ethnic groups tend to learn ways of thinking that perpetuate these groups. They tend to be taught to accept their position in the social structure of the larger society (Côté, 2001).

Conflict theorists point out that socializing into social class and ethnic groups could lead to prejudice and discrimination. Aboriginal students in public schools may be perceived as less cooperative and intelligent when not showing the competitive spirit. Most middle-class children are given many educational advantages and socialized to accept the importance of an education, while lower-class children may not have the same opportunities or be taught the same values.

Symbolic interactionists point out that we are not born with prejudiced attitudes or the tendency to discriminate; we learn them along with dominant/subordinate patterns of interactions. Parents in the subordinate social groups often prepare their children to live in an environment in which they are likely to encounter prejudice and discrimination (Scott, Schwartz, & VanderPlaat, 1999).

CHAPTER SUMMARY

We learn how to operate in the society we are born into through the process of socialization. Socialization not only affects our social development, but also has a profound effect on our physical, intellectual, and personality development. We are shaped by interactions with key individuals in our lives and by the incidents and interactions of everyday life. The family, religion, education system, peers, and ethnic and social class group have significant roles to play in this developmental process. The role of the media seems to be increasing. There is greater awareness that many of our gender roles are predominantly socially taught and, therefore, that inequities in these roles can be eliminated over time.

KEY TERMS

agents of socialization	occupational socialization
androgyny	peers
education	prescriptions
empathy	proscriptions
gender	religion
gender identity	sex
gender socialization	sexism
generalized other	significant other
internalization	social control
latent function	socialization
looking-glass self	status allocation
manifest function	status socialization

REFERENCES

Cooley, H. (1909). *Social organization*. New York: Scribners.

Côté, J. (2001). Socialization. In J. Teevan & W.E. Hewitt (Eds.), *Introduction to sociology: A Canadian focus* (pp. 69-98). Toronto: Prentice Hall.

Dietz, T.L. (1998). An examination of violence and gender role portrayals in video games: Implications for gender socialization and aggressive behaviour. *Sex Roles*, *38*, 425-442.

Durkheim, É. (1954). *The elementary forms of religious life* (J.W. Swain, Trans.). Glencoe, IL: The Free Press.

Elkin, F. (1960). *The child and society: The process of socialization*. Toronto: Random House of Canada.

Knuttila, M. (2002). *Introducing sociology: A critical perspective* (2nd ed.). Toronto: Oxford University Press.

Maccoby, E.E., & Jacklin, C.N. (1974). *The psychology of sex differences*. Stanford, CA: Stanford University Press.

Marx, K., & Engels, F. (1964). *On religion*. New York: Schocken.

Mead, G.H. (1934). *Mind, self and society* (C.W. Morris, Ed.). Chicago: University of Chicago Press.

Mead, M. (1935). *Sex and temperament in three primitive societies*. New York: Dell.

Scott, B.M., Schwartz, M., & VanderPlaat, M. (1999). *Sociology: Making sense of the social world*. Toronto: Pearson Education Canada.

Statistics Canada. (2001). *2001 census*. http://www12.statcan.ca/english/census01/home/index.cfm.

Teevan, J., & Hewitt, W.E. (Eds.). (2001). *Introduction to sociology: A Canadian focus*. Toronto: Prentice Hall.

Weber, M. (1961). *The Protestant ethic and the spirit of capitalism* (T. Parsons, Trans.). New York: The Free Press.

Study shows violent lyrics create hostility. (2003, May 7). *The Globe and Mail*, p. B13.

CHAPTER 6

Deviant Behaviour

In any society, most of the citizens adhere to the society's rules most of the time. Some citizens habitually break those rules. Most of us break a rule or two from time to time. This chapter examines the different types of deviant behaviour. It also considers the available data on deviance, some explanations of why some people deviate and others conform, and the options available to society for dealing with deviance.

Chapter Objectives

After completing this chapter, you should be able to:

- Recognize that your perception of normative and deviant behaviour is a judgment bound by cultural and temporal restrictions.

- Evaluate the validity of commonly published statistics about criminality and deviance.

- Evaluate the validity of commonly held assertions about criminal and deviant behaviour.

- Categorize deviant behaviours according to their levels of social acceptance and functions.

- Assess the balance of physiological, psychological, and sociocultural factors in an individual's becoming deviant.

- Assess the roles of various elements of the judicial and penal system in the control and management of deviance and criminality.

- Assess the efficacy of various methods of prevention, punishment, and rehabilitation of crime and deviance.

During a National Hockey League game on March 8, 2004, a Colorado Avalanche player, Steve Moore, was removed from the ice on a stretcher after being struck from behind by a Vancouver Canuck player, Todd Bertuzzi. Bertuzzi grabbed Moore from behind, "sucker punched" him, and then drove him into the ice face first. The assault was said to be in retaliation for Moore's hit on another Canuck player — a hit that drew no penalty and was deemed within the rules by the governing body.

Should Bertuzzi's offence be dealt with in the same manner as if it took place on the street? Is it acceptable for a professional sport to have a subculture of violence?

Have these type of offences in arenas been increasing in number and seriousness, while crime statistics in the rest of society have continually decreased? What socialization factors might contribute to an otherwise law-abiding citizen neutralizing his own set of ethics? Have hockey players learned to live up to a label that requires them to avenge perceived wrongs, thus bypassing the enforcement and justice system set up by the league to deal with offences? How can and should such incidents be managed to reduce the probability of their recurrence? These are the types of questions that the sociological study of deviant behaviour can shed light on.

BACKGROUND

From childhood, we all have experiences of people who are different from the general population. Some of these people are different by accident or fate; some are different by design. That is, to a certain extent, they are different by choice. Deviant behaviour, which is behaviour that is outside socially accepted boundaries, usually falls into the latter category, although sometimes people who are different by accident are designated deviant by the main society. A deviant, then, is usually someone who deliberately defies the norms and values of his society. However, there are no hard and fast rules as to just what constitutes a deviance.

Some people would argue that only behaviours that contravene Canada's *Criminal Code* (1985, as amended) should truly be considered deviant, but there are behaviours that are not illegal, such as alcoholism, drug addiction, and mental illness, that obviously disturb the social well-being of our society. Other people would point out that the most frequently performed behaviours are usually normative while infrequent behaviours are designated deviant. Although this observation is accurate for the most part, there are some very important exceptions to the rule. Saintly acts — the ministrations of Mother Teresa, for example — are by definition uncommon, but nobody would designate them deviant. Likewise, the most frequently performed sexual act is masturbation, yet we are a long way from accepting the behaviour as normative.

Yet another approach to deviance involves examining many cultures for commonalities to find some cultural universals of behaviour — that is, behaviours that are accepted or rejected worldwide. Those rejected worldwide would then be considered deviant. This approach has two major difficulties. First, every behaviour except mother–son incest has been deemed acceptable in some society at some time, so little is left to be designated deviant. Second, some behaviours that are considered fairly normal in some societies are considered extremely inappropriate in others, which makes nonsense of an attempt to discover a pattern of cultural universality.

THE RELATIVITY OF DEVIANCE

Deviance is not an absolute concept, but a concept that is relative along a number of different dimensions:

- Deviance is relative to culture. Something that is unacceptable behaviour in one culture may well be considered acceptable or even desirable in another culture. Male homosexuality, for example, is considered horrific in some cultures, and is treated with mixed feelings in most others. Still, other societies expect young men to go through a period of homosexual activity as a prelude to settling down to a heterosexual relationship.

- Within one society, behaviour considered deviant to the main society may well be the norm within one of the society's subcultures. Carrying a weapon is a criminal offence in Canada, yet in at least one subculture it is the norm. People of the Sikh faith, who have lived in Canada for nearly 200 years, carry a kirpan, a short, ceremonial sword, as a symbol of their willingness to defend their faith. Multicultural societies — that is, just about every modern society — are full of these kinds of cultural conflicts.

- Deviance is also relative to historical era. A behaviour that is acceptable at one point in history may be considered deviant at another. In the 19th century, cocaine use was considered normal among the middle and upper classes; in fact, a good host was expected to provide a mixture of snuff and cocaine for his or her guests. There was nothing illegal or improper about this custom, nor was there any knowledge that cocaine use might be physically damaging. It was not until the 1930s that it started to become apparent that there were medical difficulties associated with snorting cocaine. Only then was controlling legislation passed in most Western countries.

  - Some deviance may simply be behaviour that is ahead of its time. As recently as the late 1960s, the feminist movement (then labelled Women's Lib) was depicted as deviant and unnecessary, even by usually progressive elements of society. Today, equal rights, equal opportunity, pay equity, and anti-discrimination provisions are written into the laws or constitutions of all industrialized nations except the United States.

- One's age may also determine whether an action that one is performing is considered deviant or not. For example, it is an offence in Ontario to consume alcoholic beverages on licensed premises if you are under the age of 19. On the eve of your 19th birthday, you can be charged if you are caught drinking in a bar. One day later, though, that behaviour is virtually expected in many sectors of our society.

- Whether behaviour is considered appropriate or not may also depend on one's social standing. Traditionally, a certain degree of wild, uninhibited, bizarre, and often seemingly self-destructive behaviour has been tolerated among students in postsecondary institutions. Similar behaviour by faculty members would probably result in disciplinary action. Even words used to designate some behaviours reflect these distinctions. "Eccentric" behaviour suggests offbeat activities of someone from the professional classes, but the same behaviour by a lower-class person would be considered evidence of psychological disturbance. Sentencing in our courts often seems to depend as much on social standing as on the severity of the crime. Robbing someone at knifepoint of $100 will carry a heavier sentence than defrauding a company by means of a computer of $1000, which in turn will be treated more severely than income tax evasion of $10 000. How much of this difference is due to the threat of harm to the victim, and how much is a matter of the socioeconomic status of the perpetrator?

- People tend to deviate from social norms along only one dimension of their lives. For example, there is a popular misconception that if a male is a transvestite, then he is in the preliminary stages of being a transsexual, and he will probably also be homosexual, and he may be a child molester, and he might have extremist political views. However, the vast majority of male transvestites are heterosexual; their gender identity is very clearly male and they prefer to wear women's clothing for sexual stimulation. The incidence of child sexual abuse among transvestites is minimal, certainly much lower than that among "straight" males. And there is no known sociological link between sexual behaviour and political beliefs.

THEORETICAL PERSPECTIVES ON DEVIANCE

Functionalist Theory

The functionalist school of thought suggests that deviance, rather than being harmful to society, may play a necessary role in social life. Émile Durkheim pointed out that deviance is sometimes simply an expression of the great diversity of humankind. Many behaviours that we might bring sanctions against (for example, group sex, drug usage, exhibitionism) are really just different forms of expression and recreational behaviour, and should be left to individuals to decide on their participation. We have already noted that deviance may well be behaviour that is simply ahead of its time. While the behaviour may currently be condemned, at a later date we may see how this activity has helped the society to change. Deviance may also perform the function of increasing the solidarity of the non-deviating majority of the society. The population may draw together to resist the outrage that they believe is being perpetrated by the presence of the deviant group. For example, the activist group Mothers Against Drunk Driving (MADD) was formed in response to deaths and injuries caused by intoxicated drivers.

Finally, deviance may be an economic stimulant. Part of the attraction of Times Square, Soho, St. Catherine Street, Hollywood Boulevard, and Yonge Street is the "unusual" people that occupy these areas. Their pressure thus creates a tourist attraction. The paraphernalia, costumes, and artifacts that surround various deviant lifestyles have to be created, manufactured, and sold, which creates jobs. And to a certain extent the continued employment of police officers, social workers, nurses, and others is ensured by deviant behaviour.

bourgeoisie
owners of the means of production

proletariat
workers for the bourgeoisie

lumpenproletariat
people who live outside the economic system imposed by the bourgeoisie

Conflict Theory

Karl Marx postulated that there were three significant social groups. The **bourgeoisie** owned the means of production. The **proletariat** could make a living only by working for the bourgeoisie, who would exploit them but never appropriately reward them for their work. The **lumpenproletariat** were people who were in the same dilemma as the proletariat but who chose, instead of becoming wage-slaves of the bourgeoisie, to live outside the economic system imposed by the bourgeoisie. The lumpenproletariat existed by participating in activities frowned upon by the bourgeoisie such as begging, stealing, and subsisting. To Marx, the lumpen-proletariat were deviant only because they were forced into a position of opposing a system set up by the wealthy designed to keep them rich and to keep others down. Any behaviour that resisted this oppression and exploitation was justifiable, even if it involved activities that were deviant and criminal.

From the perspective of conflict theory, deviants have their status imposed on them by legislation drawn up to protect the interests of privileged groups. Under this system, people and institutions such as police officers, the armed forces, social service workers, and the judiciary are seen as puppets of the people in power, employed to ensure that the oppressed are kept in their place and that the privileged position of those in power is not threatened.

To conflict theorists, deviance naturally arises when wealth and power are unequally distributed in a world where the individual's goal is to ensure material survival. Those acts that threaten the existing social structure are designated deviant, while those acts that supported the existing distribution of wealth and power are considered normative. The development of laws surrounding drugs and intoxicants offers a good example of how, according to conflict theory, deviance is constructed. It is very clear that the shaping of these laws during the 20th century was not particularly related to any assessment of the medical and social consequences of their use. One of the most powerfully addictive substances known to us is also one of the most deadly and debilitating, yet tobacco is readily available at any corner store. Alcohol is the cause of a great proportion of our social and family upheavals, yet is available with only minor restrictions. At the same time, substances that have a much less debilitating effect (for example, marijuana, ecstasy, LSD, and peyote) are illegal. The legally available drugs have for centuries been the drugs-of-choice of white, middle-class society, while the illegal intoxicants are historically linked with blacks, Hispanics, Indians, and other minority groups.

In summary, conflict theorists see the crimes of the underclass as being forced on them by the miserable conditions that they have to endure. Other crimes, including crime committed by the controlling classes, are a natural consequence of the greed and self-centredness that are an inevitable outcome of a capitalist economy.

Symbolic Interactionism

The symbolic–interactionist perspective on deviance is best seen in the notion of labelling theory, which will be covered at greater length later in this chapter. In brief, the interactionist would want to ask the question "What does the deviant act mean to the individual performing the action?" If the individual perceives the act as an attack against the basic injustice of the society, that is what it symbolizes to her or him, but it cannot then be interpreted to mean that there is objective evidence that society as a whole is intrinsically unjust.

EXPLANATIONS OF DEVIANT BEHAVIOUR

Before we can explain why some people engage in deviant behaviour, we must explain why most people conform to society's rules most of the time. **Conformity** is

conformity
the tendency of people to behave within society's norms

the tendency of people to behave within society's norms. Norms, as we know already, are routine patterns of behaviour that most people adhere to as a matter of course. So why do people stick to the rules?

1. The main reason people don't routinely kill, rob, maim, or deprive others of liberty has nothing to do with fear of punishment. Rather, it has been ingrained into us that these behaviours are inherently wrong. Through the process of socialization, we learn and internalize appropriate social behaviour and learn not to behave in socially inappropriate ways. Conforming to society's norms becomes habitual and belief that these norms are correct is automatic. As a result, engaging in any behaviour that contradicts this socialization would affect our social conscience and cause us psychological difficulties.

vested interest
benefits that people receive from the society in exchange for fulfilling their obligations to that society

2. Citizens of a society have a **vested interest** in obeying society's rules — they receive benefits from the society in exchange for fulfilling their obligations to that society. If we abide by the laws, customs, norms, and values of our culture, we increase the likelihood that we will obtain a fair share of our culture's material rewards and social prestige. If we stray from these boundaries, our rewards will decrease or even be forfeited.

social control
the forces that encourage individuals to abide by society's rules and that invoke sanctions against them if they break the rules

sanctions
negative and coercive techniques to ensure conformity

3. People conform in response to agents of social control. **Social control** refers to the forces that encourage individuals to abide by society's rules and that invoke sanctions against them if they break the rules. **Sanctions** are negative and coercive techniques to ensure conformity. Social control is often backed by the implicit threat that force can and will be used if the person does not toe the line. The obvious agents of social control are the police, the justice system, the armed forces, and other government bodies. Other agents of social control that use sanctions include education ("How do you expect to get a good job if you don't go to school?") and religion ("You'll never get to heaven if you don't do this"). In *gemeinschaft*-like communities (see chapter 9), something as relatively simple as gossip serves as a powerful means of ensuring conformity.

There are a variety of theoretical explanations of why people break society's rules, some of which are discussed below. No single theory can completely explain any one deviant behaviour. Deviance of any sort is the result of a complex interaction of many contributing factors. These theoretical explanations of deviance fall into two categories. In one, we ask why it is that people will break rules, norms, and laws in which they fundamentally believe. In the other type of theory, we see people engaging in deviant behaviour because they believe that society's rules are outdated, inadequate, unfair, or discriminatory, and thus more honoured in the breach than in the observance.

Simplistic explanations suggest that deviants are just crazy or sinful or evil, but it is clear that becoming deviant is the end product of a long and complex process and that many things that people think are the "cause" of deviance are, in fact, just one small step in this process. Figure 6.1 shows a "map" of the possible contributions to an individual perpetrating a deviant or criminal act; this diagram is especially apropos in looking at violent acts.

FIGURE 6.1   POSSIBLE CONTRIBUTION TO A DEVIANT ACT, AND THE CYCLE OF PERFORMANCE OF THE DEVIANT ACT

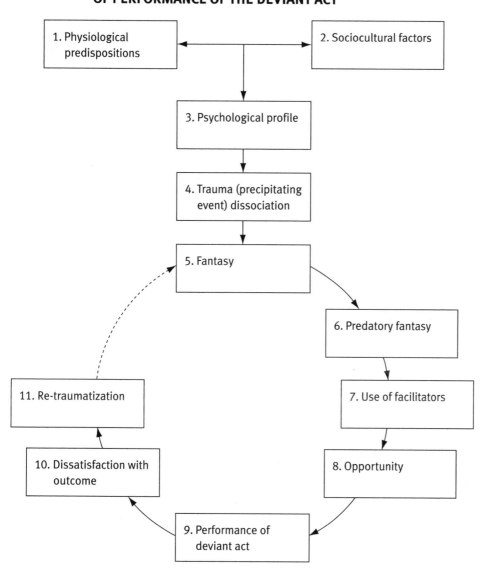

1. Physiological Predispositions

In the social sciences that study socially unacceptable and abnormal behaviours, there is an increasing tendency to look for physiological factors that may play some role in causing such behaviour. Hormonal, chromosomal, enzymal, and other bio-chemical and genetic factors have been explored.

CHROMOSOMES AND CRIME

Every human cell contains 46 chromosomes, arranged in pairs. Each parent donates 23 chromosomes. The mother always donates X chromosomes, which, as a result, are called the female chromosome. The father can donate either X chromosomes or Y chromosomes; the latter produce male children, and so the Y chromosome is called the male chromosome. If the 23rd pair of chromosomes is XX, the child is female; if it is XY, the child is male. In 1961, there was a report of a man with a configuration of XYY, or an extra Y. Real interest in XYY men was not aroused until 1965, when a study in a maximum security mental institution showed that 3 percent of its male inmates were XYY. It was later established that the incidence of extra Y males in the general population is only about 0.06 percent. These inmates had a number of things in common: they were tall, heavy, mentally dull, and aggressive. Almost all of them had been institutionalized because of incidents of extremely violent outbursts.

There seems to be evidence, then, that an extra Y chromosome contributes in some way to anti-social or even criminal behaviour. This conclusion is by no means universally accepted. Important questions arise: If a man has inborn criminal tendencies, can he be held accountable for his behaviour? Is there any hope of rehabilitation? What should be done with XYY children? Should we test everybody at birth and track them, or would this be an infringement of civil rights? So far, no male has been able to successfully claim diminished responsibility because of an extra Y chromosome, but it is at least theoretically feasible to do so.

PMS AND VIOLENT OUTBURSTS

For centuries, women have known that emotional outbursts, which may or may not become violent, are closely related to the rhythms of the menstrual cycle. For nearly as long, doctors, mostly men, have diagnosed these symptoms as being *psychosomatic*, or related to the emotional state of the patient. It is only in the last 20 years that premenstrual syndrome (PMS), a cluster of symptoms that seem to peak in the four or five days immediately prior to menstruation, has been recognized as a disorder. PMS can have such a traumatic effect on some women as to render them incapable of controlling their actions.

Four unusual legal decisions have forced the medical profession to look anew at PMS. In one British case involving the stabbing of one barmaid by another, the offender was put on probation rather than in jail because the judge accepted her defence of PMS as a mitigating circumstance. In another British case, a woman was allowed to plead guilty to manslaughter rather than murder when she deliberately drove her car over her estranged husband. In New York City, a Brooklyn judge accepted the PMS defence in a case of child battering where the mother-defendant had no previous history of abusive behaviour. And in Sydney, Australia, a woman was acquitted on a murder charge after killing her husband with a kitchen knife in a domestic altercation.

The PMS defence is a double-edged sword for women. On the one hand, it is recognized that PMS is a real biological event that can have severe emotional outcomes and that methods of control must be sought. On the other hand, this knowledge can become a prejudice if, for example, potential employers have preconceived notions about this "weakness" of women.

HORMONAL RATIOS AND SEXUAL PREFERENCE

A misadventure in laboratory experiments on rats has led to some speculative research into the role that different balances of sex hormones may play in determining an individual's sexuality. A pregnant female rat was inadvertently given an excessive dose of female hormones (estrogen and progesterone). The male offspring in the subsequent litter showed very early signs of homosexual behaviour. Studies of hormone levels in humans have since been done, with wildly varying results. Some studies have shown female homosexuals to have higher levels of testosterone and androgen (the so-called male hormones) than female heterosexuals; other studies have concluded that male homosexuals have higher levels of progesterone and estrogen than male heterosexuals; a significant number of studies have shown no such relationship at all.

The meaning of these assorted findings is difficult to determine. Even if hormone balance is a factor in sexual preference, it is but one item in a complex, predominantly psychosocial process. And, as with extra Y chromosomes, a number of questions are left unanswered. If the difference in hormonal levels is the cause of homosexuality, is this difference an imbalance (that is, unnatural) or simply a natural, differential distribution of hormones? If it is seen as an imbalance, will homosexuals be browbeaten into "cures"? Are our notions of "normal" hormonal ranges short-sighted and self-serving?

2. Sociocultural Factors

MALSOCIALIZATION

In the chapter on socialization, we saw how individuals are integrated into an ongoing society by a subtle process of learning and internalizing the norms and values of that society. We also saw that it is possible for the socialization process to be disrupted. **Malsocialization** is poor integration of a culture's norms and values. The socialization process can fail in a number of ways:

malsocialization
poor integration of a
culture's norms and values

- Children may be deliberately socialized into deviant behaviours for the parents' profit. Parents have been known to teach their daughters to become prostitutes or their sons to break and enter.

- The role models available to children may be deviant ones. Over 70 percent of abusive parents were themselves abused as children (Strauss, Gelles, & Steinmetz, 1981). In other words, the only way they learned to deal with child discipline was through the inadequate models that their parents provided. When times are stressful, some people resort to this type of early learning.

- Some homes are not conducive to the development of appropriate social standards. If discipline is overly harsh and erratically enforced, if there is a general lack of affection between parents and between parents and children, if supervision is lacking, and if the family lacks togetherness, then the probability that a child will get in trouble with the law in his or her teens is 95 percent. The amazing thing is that 5 percent of such families do not produce delinquents.

The vast majority of perpetrators of criminal acts were at one time victims, probably of abusive behaviour. The media darling of abuse is sexual abuse, because it creates the most sickening social reaction. Physical abuse comes a close second, because the breaks, bruises, and contusions can be easily displayed. Regardless of this, it may be emotional abuse that has the most far-reaching effect on the victim. Sexual and physical abuse may well be regularly coupled with emotional abuse. Research on post-traumatic stress disorder shows remarkable similarities between the victims of abuse and the condition of armed forces personnel serving in a combat zone. War has been defined as 95 percent boredom and 5 percent pure hell. In the 95 percent boredom, however, the victim is mentally anticipating the pure hell. The terror continues even when the terrorist action is not present. Thus, the soldier in the trench waits for the fire-fight or bombardment and the abused child waits for the next assault.

Abuse can take a number of forms. Neglect in the form of lack of attention, lack of affection, or lack of appropriate supervision can mean that the child does not develop the ability to empathize and sympathize with other human beings. Increasingly, the role of social rejection in triggering anti-social outbursts is being investigated. The Columbine massacre is thought to have been precipitated by the severe social ostracism and taunting of the two perpetrators by the "cool kids" and "jocks" at their high school.

ANOMIE THEORY

Durkheim

The first person to attempt to give a sociological explanation of deviant behaviour was Émile Durkheim. Durkheim introduced the concept of anomie as a basis of deviant behaviour. **Anomie** is a state of confusion that arises when an individual is faced with a conflict of choices in a society that provides no clear guidelines. The more complex society becomes, the less clear it is what distinguishes appropriate from inappropriate behaviour, what constitutes a correct moral decision, and which set of values is right. As a result, an individual can become chronically stuck between two equally desirable choices, or, more painfully, between two equally undesirable choices. Once the individual makes a choice, the anomic state lifts. Even if the individual eventually comes to believe that he or she made the wrong choice, the mental torment is gone. If, however, the individual remains in anomie, then the possibility of a deviant outcome increases.

In chapter 1, we outlined how Durkheim's (1951) notion of anomie played a role in suicide, one possible deviant outcome. Anomie may also lead to deviance through psychiatric disorder. Unable to cope with the demands of choosing between alternate realities, the individual escapes from reality. Escapist behaviours such as alcohol abuse, drug usage, and chronic daydreaming are deviancies that may be precipitated by anomie.

Merton

Robert K. Merton, an American sociologist, extended Durkheim's concept of anomie to include many more behavioural patterns. Merton (1957) maintained that anomie referred especially to a faulty relationship between society's accepted goals and the access (or, specifically, lack of access) to the legitimate means of attaining those goals. In our society, success goals are very clearly defined; they surround property ownership, material possessions, conspicuous consumption, occupational prestige, and expensive leisure-time activities. Only those who are regularly employed in a well-paying job, usually with postsecondary education, have the minimum requirements to attain this lifestyle. Nearly all citizens have "bought into" society's notion of the good life, yet many do not have access to the legitimized ways of achieving

anomie
a state of confusion that arises when an individual is faced with a conflict of choices in a society that provides no clear guidelines

these goals — a good education and a job. Given this built-in anomie between society's goals and access to the means to achieve these goals, Merton suggested that some people will "innovate" ways to attain these goals. Some "innovations" will be criminal or deviant.

Most people in society desire these goals and have access to the means to achieve them. These people, Merton suggested, have a vested interest in conformity. Other people reject society's goals and the established ways of achieving them, and "retreat" from mainstream society. Some retreatists may be seen as societal drop-outs, such as vagrants, psychotics, or addicts. Other retreatists, however, productively and constructively set up their own isolated and semi-isolated communities. Others reject society's goals and the means to achieve them, and want society to adopt different goals and different ways of achieving them. These retreatists display some form of "rebellion." And others adjust to society's goals and means of achieving them through "ritualism." The ritualist has forgone all hopes of successfully achieving societal goals, but still clings compulsively to the society's way of doing things — the ritualist is an obsessive rule follower.

DIFFERENTIAL ASSOCIATION

According to the theory of **differential association** (Sutherland & Cressey, 1960), any person can be trained to adopt and follow a pattern of deviant or criminal behaviour. Whether an individual adopts a deviant lifestyle depends on whether the positive outcomes of the deviant behaviour outweigh the negative outcomes, in the form of sanctions against the behaviour imposed by the main society. Gradually, the deviant behaviour may seem more and more acceptable. This shift in attitude often occurs as the individual becomes more and more isolated from the influences that would reinforce the idea that the behaviour is unacceptable. Thus, the individual comes to define certain situations as appropriate occasions for deviant behaviour. The individual learns to master the techniques of deviant activity and picks up motives, attitudes, and rationalizations that seem to justify the behaviour. This process is facilitated by intimate personal groups. The crucial step comes when the individual sees more factors in favour of the deviance than against it.

According to the theory of differential association, then, an individual drifts from a behaviour pattern of conformity to one of deviance as the deviant behaviour receives more positive reinforcements from a close intimate group. Deviance is a behaviour that is learned in these groups. The groups teach or model attitudes, techniques, and motives to which the newcomer adapts. In *Oliver Twist*, for example, Fagin's boys seem increasingly attractive to Oliver, so much so that he is eventually able to participate in their criminal activities. The individual in the group comes to see as normal what others see as deviant. A great deal of white-collar crime is rationalized by the very principles of business milieu. When "business is business" and it's a "dog eat dog" world, a lot of shady operations can be explained away.

NEUTRALIZATION THEORY

Closely allied to differential association is neutralization theory, which attempts to explain how individuals can break rules in which they believe (Sykes & Matza, 1957). **Neutralization** is the process of excusing deviant behaviour on the grounds of

differential association
a theory that any person can be trained to adopt and follow a pattern of deviant or criminal behaviour

neutralization
the process of excusing deviant behaviour on the grounds of mitigating circumstances

mitigating circumstances. The individual says, in effect, "I know this behaviour is wrong but this situation, at this time, calls for me to act in this way." That is, the individual would find the behaviour unacceptable if it were performed under different circumstances, at a different point in time, or by somebody else.

An individual's ethics are neutralized through rationalization. For the most part, these rationalizations are intended to protect the individual's self-esteem rather than to convince others. There are a variety of ways of rationalizing deviant behaviour:

- *Denial of responsibility*   The individual suggests that the behaviour is not his own fault. He may suggest that circumstances conspired against him: "I was left with no option." He may see himself as helpless in the face of social forces: "I had a very bad childhood." He may excuse a social problem by giving it a medical label: "I'm sorry I hit those people with my car, but I'm an alcoholic and sometimes my disease becomes uncontrollable."

- *Denial of injury*   The individual suggests that her behaviour, though wrong, can be excused because no harm was done. Car theft is called "joy riding" if the thief "only" intends to use the car to ride in for a while, not to sell it. Vandalizing buildings with spray paint is called graffiti or, sometimes, an "urban art form."

- *Denial of a victim*   The individual suggests that the victim in some way had it coming or doesn't really care about the victimization. The individual sees the victim as a rightful target: "So I stole from the school cafeteria — they've been ripping off students for years." Sometimes the individual sees the victim as benefiting from the event: "The insurance is worth more to them." The individual may not see a company or an institution as a victim: "The office supplies I took will be used mostly to do company work at home." The government is rarely seen as a victim. The individual who evades taxes often also complains about government deficits.

- *Condemning the condemners*   The individual turns accusations against him onto his condemners. The individual who defends his behaviour on the grounds that "business is business," when accused of being unethical and criminal, may accuse his accusers of being "communists" or "socialists." A terrorist who massacres bystanders may claim that no one is innocent; those who do not share his beliefs are against him. Perhaps the most common example of this type of rationalization in modern society is the attempt by men accused of rape to imply that responsibility lies with the victims of rape because of the way they dressed or their sexual history.

- *Appeal to higher loyalty*   The individual admits the deviance of her behaviour but suggests that she had an unselfish motive. The individual may claim to have performed the act to help her friends, family, or group, or to have done it on behalf of her god or government. Deviant behaviour is defended on the ground that higher loyalties can and do excuse baser acts. Even governments have excused break-ins, infiltration of minority groups, assassination, and even invasion of other countries on the basis of "national security."

LABELLING THEORY

According to labelling theory (Becker, 1963), some individuals deviate or continue to deviate after being caught, simply because society affixes the label "deviant" on them. It becomes easier for the individual to live up to the label than to fight it. The impact of the label can be traced through a cycle of social responses to a deviant act that make it more and more difficult for the individual to shake off the deviant designation. There are six steps in this social response cycle:

1. The individual commits a **deviant act** — that is, a single behaviour that is contrary to society's norms. This act could be a single, isolated occurrence or it could be a part of a previously undetected pattern. This action is often called **primary deviation**, which is deviant behaviour that occurs prior to the society's knowledge of the individual's behaviour.

2. The individual is detected in the deviant act. The detection may be official, involving (say) police intervention, or it may simply be that friends, neighbours, or colleagues come to know about it. In any event, a **stigma**, or widespread and very strong disapproval, is attached to the behaviour and, by extension, the individual.

3. The individual is now given a label, usually a derogatory one, such as "thief," "pervert," or "criminal." Although it is possible that the individual only experimented with the activity a few times, the label comes to dominate society's perception of him. Henceforth, thoughts of him, conversations about him, and encounters with him automatically include references to the label. This will remain the case even if other elements of the person's life are unrelated to the label.

4. The labelled individual may lose a lot of her old friends and acquaintances and have some difficulty acquiring new ones. Most people who are aware of the label will, at least, treat her with suspicion, be reserved, or avoid her company.

5. The vast majority of people need some degree of social acceptance and social support. If previously open social networks are closed off to the individual, he will attempt to find or form new ones. He may turn to the company of people who have acquired a label like his. For these people, the label is not a deterrent and social acceptance will be granted.

6. To remain a member of any group, a person has to conform to its norms, even if those norms are contrary to the norms of the mainstream society. Thus, the individual conforms to the norms of a deviant group by continuing to practise that deviance. This behavioural pattern is known as **secondary deviation** — the individual behaves in a deviant way in part because of a socially acquired self-image of deviance. The individual has thus progressed from a single deviant act to a **deviant career**, a lifestyle based on involvement in a deviant activity.

It must be pointed out that labelling theory does not explain the origins of deviant behaviour so much as the process by which people become entrenched in a deviant lifestyle after experimenting with a deviant behaviour. The classic example

deviant act
a single behaviour that is contrary to society's norms

primary deviation
deviant behaviour that occurs prior to the society's knowledge of the individual's behaviour

stigma
widespread and very strong disapproval of a behaviour or an individual

secondary deviation
deviant behaviour that occurs in part because of an individual's socially acquired self-image of deviance

deviant career
a lifestyle based on involvement in a deviant activity

of labelling is the ex-con who finds it hard to re-establish a niche in society after parole from prison. The acquired label should not be seen as absolutely binding. At any step in the process, the individual can, in theory, exercise free will to avoid its downward spiral and reject the labelling process. However, it is very difficult for most people to fight the overwhelming social forces at work in the process.

3. Psychological Profile

While people who deviate consistently from society's norms and rules cannot be stereotyped into hard and fast personality types, they do tend to have a few traits in common. Many display low self-esteem and are poor at establishing normal social relationships. When suspects for major crimes are caught, members of the public often remark on how normal they look or people who lived in their locality will comment on what nice, ordinary neighbours they were. This normalcy surprises people so often that it is almost a defining trait. The vast majority of perpetrators of crimes and major deviances are in fact quite ordinary and conventional in both their appearance and thinking. While many might think that the deviant or criminal is likely to condone any behaviour by others, they are usually quite punishment-oriented toward other transgressors, while still showing a remarkable ability to neutralize their own values.

Early behavioural signals that a child may be on the path to a delinquent career include serial fire setting and regular abuse of animals.

4. Trauma

The combined effects of physiological predispositions, underlying sociocultural factors, and a personality conducive to perpetrating criminal and/or deviant acts may lie dormant unless a precipitating traumatic event forces them to the surface. The cannibal serial killer Jeffrey Dahmer, for example, maintained that his mother's refusal to take him when she had won a custody battle from his father (she took his brother) was the crucial event in his downward slide. His mother's refusal was the ultimate rejection for a young boy. Dahmer maintained that that was the day he started to close down emotionally. If feelings hurt too much, then stop feeling. This emotional vacuum is usually referred to as **dissociation**, a feeling of inner numbness. Often perpetrators of horrendous crimes, when caught, seem to have a small sardonic grin that infuriates the public; closer scrutiny will often show that the rest of the face is blank and that there is no laughter in the eyes. These latter can be the outward manifestation of an inner emptiness.

Victims of abuse and veterans of the battlefield will often display a lack of the emotional highs and lows that is symptomatic of the normal human condition. The person appears to be coping, but inside the emotional numbness is eating away. Some people carry this burden around with them for decades; to others they may appear to be operating effectively, but close perusal shows a lack of normal emotional ups and downs.

dissociation
a feeling of inner numbness

5. Fantasy

Nature abhors a vacuum and for some people what will come along to fill this emotional vacuum caused by dissociation is excessive and increasing **fantasizing**. The fantasizing becomes obsessive. There are very clear signals that a person has reached

fantasy
imagination unrestrained by reality

this stage in the cycle. An individual may constantly tell self-aggrandizing stories that are manifestly untrue. He could be prone to inappropriate and often immature outbursts. He has a tendency to be continuously and extremely manipulative in dealings with others, especially those he is supposed to be close to. Obsession with self or obsession with material possessions are common; this can be displayed in perfection in dress, a constant desire to have all the latest things, or an over-concentration on body image. A person displaying these symptoms is potentially dangerous.

6. Predatory Fantasy

The obsessive fantasizing can escalate in some people and become increasingly predatory, involving a victim or victims. This stems from a desire to control others. Early experience of being dominated by others plus poor social skills result in the individual only knowing one way to interact with other people. As the fantasies become increasingly predatory, more danger signals arise. The person wants to control the activities, fashion choices, entertainment patterns, socializing circles, etc. of partners and is prone to fits of jealousy. His partner's perceived signalling of interest in others, or reception of interest from others, will result in verbal threats; these may be coupled with name calling or attempts to unfairly label the third person. The predatory fantasy escalates until a clear plan emerges, a plan that includes a victim.

7. Use of Facilitators

Although there is now a plan in place to commit the deviant act, lingering doubts, conscience, or conditioning may hold the person back. This is the point in the cycle that alcohol, drugs, pornography, or violent media can play a role in precipitating the deviant act. These are simply facilitators; the deep-seated plan and desire to carry out the act is already present. Alcohol and drugs can provide the individual with the diminished sense of responsibility, through the removal of inhibitions, that the individual needs to carry out the act. Media depictions can suggest methodologies for pursuing these desires. Note that these things are not the causes of the deviance, as is often supposed; the contributing factors are already extensive before the facilitators play a role.

8. Opportunity

Another factor that has to fall into place is that the circumstances of the predatory fantasy have to arise at the same time as the presence of facilitators. The individual may spurn a number of such opportunities as he struggles against his impulses.

9. Performance of the Deviant Act

Eventually opportunity will knock, the facilitators will be present, and the individual will succumb and perform the deviant act.

10. Dissatisfaction with the Outcome

Performing the deviant act is often unsatisfactory. The individual may well have a residual sense that he is doing wrong, but this may be misinterpreted as a sense that he did not plan it quite right. Acting out any fantasy is of course a recipe for disaster. In the fantasy, you are in the director's role. All the actors do what you want when you want it. You decide on location, costume, setting, etc. The timing of everything is perfect because you have complete script control. If you act out the fantasy, however, reality will intrude, people will have their own wants, needs, and desires, or something will go wrong.

A negative feeling remains; the gnawing doubt that if you only changed a few details you could get it right next time.

11. Re-traumatization

Effectively, the person has re-traumatized himself. He has lowered his self-esteem because he could not get the act right. He has also begun to fantasize about doing it bigger and better. Thus, the cycle has begun again.

CLASSIFICATION OF DEVIANCE

There are various ways of classifying the seriousness of a deviant act along a continuum ranging from the most serious (for example, first-degree murder) to the least serious (for example, adolescent sexual experimentation). There is, however, no common agreement on the relative seriousness or degree of wrongfulness of many deviant acts (for example, pornography or drunkenness) or even if some acts should be classified as deviant at all (for example, homosexual behaviour).

There are two common ways of classifying deviance.

Measures of Seriousness of a Deviant Act

- The level of seriousness of a deviant act depends on the degree of agreement in society about the wrongfulness of the act. The more people there are who agree that an act is wrong, the more serious the act is seen to be. Thus, you can describe a continuum with different degrees of perceived wrongfulness:

0%	50%	100%
Indifference (Tax evasion)	Controversy (Pornography)	Total agreement (Mass murder)

- The level of seriousness of a deviant act also depends on the severity of the society's response to that act:

0%	50%	100%
Polite avoidance (Bizarre clothing)	Minor jail sentence (Breaking and entering)	Capital punishment (Planned murder)

- Finally, the level of seriousness of a deviant act depends on the society's estimation of the degree of harm done by the act:

0%	50%	100%
Victimless vices (Petty gambling)	Property crime (Auto theft)	Violent crime (Terrorist acts)

The most serious acts, then, are ones that elicit

- broad social agreement that they are very wrong,

- a severe social response that usually wants to see severe punishment inflicted on the perpetrators, and

- a view that a great degree of harm has been inflicted on the society.

Criminal and Non-Criminal Deviance

The other common way of classifying deviance is to determine whether or not the act contravenes Canada's *Criminal Code*. Some acts that are clearly contrary to the Code are often not felt to be as deviant as other acts that are in no way illegal. Most people in our society would agree that chronic alcoholism is more socially damaging than occasional use of marijuana.

CRIMINAL DEVIANCE

Criminal deviance comprises acts that contravene the *Criminal Code*. This category can be subdivided further.

CONSENSUS CRIMES   Consensus crimes are those for which there is widespread agreement that they are wrong. They are seen as being socially harmful and the general opinion is that they should be punished. Such acts as murder, rape, kidnapping, armed robbery, arson, and breaking and entering bring an almost uniform social response. For the most part, these are predatory crimes. Even though these acts are seen almost universally as being socially damaging, the category is not unchanging. Many people believe that incest, for example, should be decriminalized. **Decriminalization** does not mean legalization; it simply means that the act is no longer covered by the *Criminal Code*. The act could still be covered by the civil code and those who commit the act could be subject to retribution, such as mandatory psychiatric treatment. Similarly, although many governments are waging a "war on drugs" with "zero tolerance," the medical and social science communities have forcefully informed governments that this approach is counterproductive, and is more likely to drive drug use even further underground and increase the dangers. Instead, these communities recommend that the problem be seen as a health care problem and that the physical and psychosocial malaise be treated through the health care system.

decriminalization
removing an act from coverage by the *Criminal Code*

CONFLICT CRIMES   Conflict crimes are offences (that is, they contravene the *Criminal Code*) about which there is debate whether they should even be termed crimes. Some people claim that they are victimless vices, such as gambling or prostitution, but one can argue that in fact there are victims involved — for example, families that lose resources to gambling or women who are being exploited through prostitution. Some crimes seem to be on the books only to protect those in power at the expense of others — for example, mischief, vagrancy, and public disturbance laws seem to be selectively enforced. Other laws seem to interfere with individuals' rights to choose for themselves — for example, drug and abortion laws and restrictions on euthanasia.

NON-CRIMINAL DEVIANCE

Responses to non-criminal deviant acts depend more on informal social controls than on laws. These acts are not illegal but they do, to a greater or lesser degree, disturb the population.

SOCIAL DEVIATIONS   Social deviations are serious enough to attract public attention and are usually held to need controlling or treating. Individuals who are defined as belonging to one of these categories or as needing the intervention of an agency that has been set up to deal with the issue are usually stigmatized. Psychiatric illnesses, alcoholism, drug dependency, and delinquency are examples of social deviations. Common to all of these problems is a vagueness surrounding their definition. For example, at what point is someone an alcoholic, or what degree of aberrant behaviour is needed to classify someone as mentally ill?

SOCIAL DIVERSIONS   Social diversions are acts that are out of the ordinary or unusual and that may mildly discomfort the ordinary citizen, but that are not considered serious enough to warrant any type of official intervention. The acts are usually treated with polite avoidance or uncomfortable amusement. Unusual forms of dress, mannerisms, hairstyles, and speech patterns are examples of social diversions. Many sexual diversions like transvestism and fetishism are also in this category, as are faddish activities, such as keeping pet rocks.

As we have seen, attitudes toward certain behaviours change over time. What is considered criminal at one point in history may be decriminalized and considered a social deviation at another point. For example, homosexuality was a criminal offence prior to 1968, but is increasingly accepted and legitimated as a type of sexual behaviour, especially with recent changes in laws regarding same-sex unions. Previously acceptable behaviours can, over time, become less and less acceptable — for example, cigarette smoking. Other behaviours can simultaneously occupy different points on the acceptable–unacceptable spectrum for different, and often large, portions of the population — for example, abortion and euthanasia.

RATES OF DEVIANCE

A *rate* is a type of ratio, a way of relating one number to another — for example, the percentage of people within a population who take part in a certain activity. Rates of deviance are notoriously difficult to estimate. Because of the nature of the activities being studied, there is a loss of information, or *data loss*: a certain degree of deviance goes undetected, a certain amount more goes unreported, and even more goes "untreated." This data loss can be seen clearly in the variation in crime statistics between the actual crimes that are committed and the proportion of crimes that are punished. Some estimates suggest that only 1 in 20 rapes are reported and that less than 4 percent of rapists are ever punished for their crimes.

crime funnel
a depiction of how an increasing amount of crime goes unresolved the further one progresses through the justice system

The fullest illustration of data loss can be seen in a process called the **crime funnel** — a depiction of how an increasing amount of crime goes unresolved the further one progresses through the justice system. Not all criminal acts that are committed are even noticed. Of those that are noticed, not all are reported. Of reported acts, not all are recorded and even fewer are investigated. Investigated acts do not necessarily lead to a suspect, and not all suspects are charged. Not all suspects who are charged are brought to trial, and not all trials are completed. A percentage of those who are tried are found not guilty, and a percentage of those who are found guilty are not necessarily sentenced.

Figure 6.2 is a graphical representation of this data loss.

DIFFERENT TYPES OF RATES

The sociology of deviant behaviour has borrowed some terminology from the health care field to calculate various types of rates of disorders. One basic concept is social epidemiology — the study of the differential distribution of disease among various social groups. Social epidemiology attempts to establish whether a certain disorder (for example, alcoholism, psychiatric illness, criminal activity, or faddish behaviour) affects different segments of the population at different rates. The population can be segmented by age, social class, ethnic group, gender difference, etc. An epidemiologist asks questions such as:

- Are different age groups prone to different types of psychiatric illness?

- Are rates of alcoholism unevenly distributed among different social classes?

- Do different ethnic groups perpetrate different amounts and types of crime?

- Are males or females more likely to take part in deviant sexual behaviour?

There are two distinctly different types of rates. The **incidence** of a disorder is the number of new cases of the disorder that arise in a given year. The **prevalence** of a disorder is the total number of cases that now exist. One way of estimating the prevalence of a disorder is to add the new cases to the old cases and then to subtract the solved, cured, or controlled cases. Both types of rates are necessary so that we can establish whether a problem is growing, shrinking, or remaining stable.

incidence
the number of new cases of a disorder that arise in a given year

prevalence
the total number of cases of a disorder that exist

SOURCES OF DATA ON DEVIANCE

Measurements of levels of deviant behaviour will always be imprecise; however, within these measurements there are different levels of reliability and validity of data. Even the "softest" sources are useful, because they may shed new light on a problem or, in some cases, may be the only available source of data.

Official Agency Data

Official agency data are taken from the monthly, quarterly, and annual reports produced by agencies specifically designed to deal with a certain type of deviance or criminality. The police, the criminal and civil courts, correctional institutions, the Addiction Research Foundation, and the Canadian Mental Health Association are just a few of the organizations in our society whose primary function is to monitor certain behaviour patterns and to publish statistics related to the activity. As we have noted, an indeterminate amount of deviance and criminality goes undetected or unreported, and thus the statistics of these agencies will always be incomplete. Furthermore, some agencies' categorizations of data can be vague or misleading.

FIGURE 6.2   THE CRIME FUNNEL

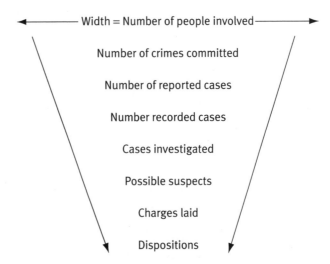

For example, some reports on sexual abuse have grossly overestimated the amounts of abuse in society by asking people to report on actions that have happened to them. The agency then decides whether or not to categorize actions as abuse, instead of allowing "victims" the opportunity to state for themselves whether they thought the actions were abusive.

Non-Official Agencies

Some agencies come by data on deviance inadvertently. For example, insurance companies get data on criminal activity as a result of claims made by victims. The mortality rates published by hospitals can provide us with data on self-destructive behaviour such as alcohol and drug abuse. These data are not as reliable as those from official agencies, but they do offer different perspectives on a problem.

Self-Report Accounts

Self-report accounts are "confessions" made to researchers in field surveys. A researcher may have a questionnaire with a list of disreputable activities and the respondent is asked to list which of the following activities he or she has taken part in. Although self-report accounts present much interesting information on minor crimes and deviations, the more serious an activity is viewed as being, the more likely a respondent is to hide involvement in it.

Victimization Surveys

Probably more valuable than self-report questionnaires in terms of data generated are surveys in which respondents are asked to list the crimes they have suffered. The researcher can also ask questions about the impact of the crime on the individual's life. Another type of information that can be elicited is the person's perception of the level of criminality and deviance that exists in the society and how safe the average citizen is. Canadians tend to overestimate the level of criminality in society because of the attention paid by the media to crime and deviance and the ready availability of American images, coupled with people's inability to see that, at least in terms of crime, Canada and the United States are very different cultures. Television can bring images of violent acts from anywhere in the world into living rooms almost instantaneously. All of these factors combine to create a higher level of fear than is warranted. Many people believe that they are living in a high crime society but, at the same time, ignore the fact that they themselves have seldom if ever been victimized.

Victimization surveys can produce information that is not otherwise available. People will acknowledge having been the victims of crimes that they thought were not worth reporting to the police. In cases in which the victims know the criminal, they may not have reported the offenders out of fear of reprisal or because they did not want to get the offender into trouble. Sometimes, victims have not reported crimes because they thought official agencies would be ineffectual in dealing with the problem. Some activities are simply tolerated by the populace even though they are crimes — spouse abuse and teenage drinking are two good examples. All of these activities and avoidance behaviours are more likely to show up on victimization surveys than on official agency surveys. It is through victimization surveys that we know such information as only 1 in 20 sexual assaults are likely to be officially reported.

Observational Studies

As we explain in the appendix, there are two kinds of observational studies. In **participant observation**, the researcher plays an active role in the group being studied. In **non-participant observation**, the researcher observes the activities of the group being studied as an outsider. These observational methods can be used in either an open format — that is, the subjects know that your purpose is to study them — or a closed format — that is, the subjects are unaware of your research activities. One of the major difficulties of the open-format method is that groups defined as deviant or criminal are understandably reluctant to have their activities observed and reported on. Despite this reluctance, social scientists have managed to produce very informative study data on groups such as prisoners, psychiatric patients, street gangs, and heroin users, usually with their knowledge and cooperation.

participant observation
a research method in which the researcher plays an active role in the group being studied

non-participant observation
a research method in which the researcher observes the activities of the group being studied as an outsider

SOME COMMON QUESTIONS ABOUT CRIME AND DEVIANCY RATES

1. *How do Canadian rates of crime and deviance compare with those of other countries?*

In general, Canadian rates of crime and deviance are far lower than those of the United States and on a par with those of other Western countries. Table 6.1 shows relative rates for various crimes in Canada, the United States, and the United Kingdom. The United States always outstrips Canada and the United Kingdom in all types of crime, but the relative Canadian and UK rates fluctuate depending on the type of crime.

2. *Are rates of criminality and deviance changing?*

Many people think that crime and deviance rates are constantly increasing. The picture, however, is not that simplistic. Sometimes the answer to this question depends on the period with which you compare the present statistics. Murder rates provide an interesting example of this. If we compare current rates with those of the

TABLE 6.1   Relative Rates of Crime in Canada, the United States, and the United Kingdom

Crime	Canada	United States	United Kingdom
Murder	1.0	4.0	3.0
Violent crime	1.0	5.0	0.5
Rape	1.0	3.0	2.0
Armed robbery	1.0	2.0	4.0
Wounding	1.0	18.0	0.5

1950s, it is clear that the murder rate has approximately doubled. Some people might suggest that murder rates were lower in the 1950s because capital punishment was enforced. However, the relation between murder rates and capital punishment is not so direct; in fact, the relation between murder rates and general social conditions appears to be more significant. Murder rates rose steadily from the 1950s to the 1970s, when the death penalty was abolished, and since abolition the rates have gradually declined, with only slight increases in times of severe economic deprivation. Murder rates are certainly well below levels from the last century, and, significantly, the benign period of the 1950s coincided with a period of full employment and widespread prosperity.

Other factors produce increases in crime statistics but may not indicate a real increase in criminal activity. Nowadays, people are more likely to report crimes than to ignore them. Increases in the human and technological resources of police forces also increase official ability and vigilance in detecting crime. Most of the actual increase in crime statistics can be attributed to the increased vigilance of our burgeoning police forces in terms of traffic and other minor violations. The public's perception of crime is also distorted. Almost all incidences of violent crime are reported in the media, while other crimes tend to go unreported. As a result, many Canadians believe that the rate of violent crime is increasing and represents over half of all crimes committed. The statistical evidence, however, contradicts this belief: levels of violent crime have not significantly changed in the 20th century, and violent crime represents less than 13 percent of all *Criminal Code* offences (Statistics Canada, 2002).

With some forms of deviant behaviour, the rates of participation may not have changed as much as people's willingness to acknowledge their participation in the behaviour. For example, 30 years ago acknowledgment of one's homosexuality would likely have resulted in loss of job, public disgrace, and perhaps even physical violence. Today, even though homosexuality is not accepted by all groups in society, these outcomes are much less likely and, therefore, more and more gays and lesbians openly acknowledge their homosexuality. Rates of homosexuality are not increasing; rather, previously hidden statistics are now more available. Rates of deviant behaviour probably do not fluctuate greatly from one generation to another. In contrast, rates of crime seem to depend on the state of the economy — specifically, the level of unemployment — and on the percentage of people within a population who are in the "crime-prone" years of 15 to 25.

   3. *Do some social groups commit more crimes than others?*

Deviant and criminal behaviours are often viewed as the predominant domain of the lower classes and certain minority groups. Two opposing theories attempt to account for this view. One theory suggests that the underprivileged have unequal access to society's resources and that they resort to crime and deviance to offset some of this disadvantage. The other theory suggests that the underprivileged are the victims of institutionalized prejudice and discrimination. They are more thoroughly policed and thus are more frequently detected in their criminal activities. When they are caught they are more often prosecuted, more frequently convicted, and more often imprisoned. Therefore, the underprivileged seem more crime-prone than they really are. At the same time, the crime funnel is working more to the advantage of the middle and upper classes. To a certain extent, both theories are true; the problem is determining how much deviance and criminality can be accounted for by each theory. Another factor that boosts lower-class crime rates is their visibility: lower-class crimes and deviancies tend to be more visible and more easily detected than middle- and upper-class crimes such as fraud, embezzlement, and insider trading. These sorts of crimes are hard to figure out, let alone detect and prosecute.

SOCIAL RESPONSE TO CRIME

The question of how society should respond to crime and deviance is actually two separate questions:

1. *How can society best respond to criminal and deviant behaviour?* In other words, what methods will work best in minimizing the behaviour? Such questions as whether or not capital punishment deters people from committing crimes can be answered empirically.

2. *How should society respond to behaviour that is considered deviant or criminal?* First, is the behaviour in any way society's business? For example, gambling for monetary reward is illegal in Ontario except if it is directly run by and to the advantage of the provincial government. Second, is it morally right to employ certain techniques even if they can be shown to work? It is important to question whether capital punishment can be morally justified even if it could be shown to have a deterrent effect.

There are seven different, sometimes complementary, sometimes contradictory, purposes for employing sanctions such as fines or imprisonment against deviant and criminal behaviour:

1. *restraint*　to prevent the behaviour from happening;

2. *individual deterrence*　to inhibit the possibility that the individual will repeat the behaviour;

3. *general deterrence*　by punishing one person for the behaviour, to set an example to others and to dissuade them from misbehaving;

4. *rehabilitation*　to correct what went wrong in the individual who committed the act;

5. *moral affirmation*　to reinforce in the rest of society that its beliefs are correct;

6. *retribution*　to exact revenge — the principle of "an eye for an eye" or punishment for its own sake; and

7. *compensation* to make the individual, in some material or behavioural way, pay for the damage caused by the behaviour.

These goals are not necessarily consistent, and in fact they are often in conflict. How can we achieve retribution and rehabilitation at the same time? Nor do they necessarily work in practice. There is a popular belief in the deterrent effect of punishment, yet most psychologists believe that individual deterrence has some limited application, while general deterrence has no validity at all.

TECHNIQUES FOR MANAGING DEVIANCE

Attempts to manage, control, prevent, cure, treat, and punish deviant and criminal behaviour have taken many forms.

Surgical and Chemical Treatments

- Frontal lobotomies have been used to control the outbursts of some psychiatric patients.

- Some male sex offenders have been castrated.

- Some alcoholics may be given the drug antabuse, which causes them to become violently ill if they drink alcohol.

- Some heroin addicts may be given the drug methadone as a less debilitating substitute.

Psychological Techniques

- Attempts have been made to identify youngsters who are at risk of becoming delinquent. Pre-emptive counselling or "scared straight" strategies have been used without much success.

- Comparative studies of various rehabilitative techniques invariably show group therapy to be much more effective in cutting down recidivism than other techniques, such as probation or incarceration. **Recidivism** is the probability that a released offender will repeat his or her crime. Group therapy, however, is expensive.

recidivism
the probability that a released offender will repeat his or her crime

- Behaviour modification processes can be very beneficial. The undesirable behaviour is targeted, the behaviours leading up to this point are itemized, and an attempt is made to alter an early, easy-to-change behaviour in the hope that it will prevent the person from reaching the undesirable behaviour. This kind of program depends on the willing participation of the subject.

Social Reform

Sometimes it is better to try to alter the social context within which the individual operates than to target the individual herself.

- Inner-city areas have been often targeted for community development programs. Activities, clubs, and sports are offered to focus the attention of the young on something constructive.

- Police deployment can be rearranged to give officers more immediate relationships with people in a community. A police officer in a car who appears only when there is a problem is intimidating; one who is an integrated part of the community is a helper. Community-based policing and officers on foot patrol and bicycles can help improve the police process. Police officers are the "gatekeepers" to the justice system, and they decide who is taken in to the system and who is kept out.

- Law reform could allow society to accommodate the widest diversity of behaviours. The decriminalization of such activities as communication for the purposes of prostitution, gambling, alcohol abuse, and marijuana possession would cut court cases (and expenses) by over 50 percent.

Environmental Design

It is fairly clear that certain physical environments seem to attract more crime than others (Newman, 1972). Densely populated, rundown, confined areas tend to have the highest crime rates. It becomes necessary, then, to build **defensible space —** areas that actively discourage criminal activity. There are four basic components to environmental design:

defensible space
areas that actively discourage criminal activity

- *Territoriality*   Areas and buildings should be designed and organized to make the residents feel that the space is their own. The design process could incorporate community organization techniques such as local committees.

- *Image*   A big part of making people feel attached to a place is the general appearance of it. Even low-rent housing can incorporate positive features such as landscaping. If you build a slum, you will produce slum behaviour.

- *Surveillance*   Buildings and parking areas should be easy to observe. Poorly lit, hidden recesses are natural environments for crime.

- *Activity level*   Communal areas and services should be organized so that there is a consistent flow of people.

CHAPTER SUMMARY

All of us have known people who are different by chance and some who are different by design. There are many behavioural patterns that may fall under either one of these categories or a combination of the two. Deviance is a relative concept along a number of dimensions, especially culture and time. Rates of deviance and crime vary from culture to culture and at different times in history. Some — perhaps most — of this variation is due to differences in the way we define and measure deviance; some is due to the under- or overattention paid to certain activities by authorities. Explanations of deviant behaviour abound; some concentrate on physiological factors, some on psychological factors, and others on sociocultural explanations of why people deviate. Most societies employ a series of sanctions and other measures to deal with, manage, control, punish, and sometimes cure deviant behaviour.

KEY TERMS

anomie	malsocialization
bourgeoisie	neutralization
conformity	non-participant observation
crime funnel	participant observation
decriminalization	prevalence
defensible space	primary deviation
deviant act	proletariat
deviant career	recidivism
differential association	sanctions
dissociation	secondary deviation
fantasy	social control
incidence	stigma
lumpenproletariat	vested interest

REFERENCES

Becker, H.S. (1963). *Outsiders: Studies in the sociology of deviance.* New York: The Free Press.

Criminal Code. (1985). RSC 1985, c. C-46, as amended.

Durkheim, É. (1951). *Suicide: A study in sociology* (J.A. Spaulding & G. Simpson, Trans., G. Simpson, Ed.). New York: The Free Press.

Government of Canada. (1982). *The criminal law in Canadian society.* Ottawa: Author.

Merton, R.K. (1957). *Social theory and social structure.* Glencoe, IL: The Free Press.

Newman, O. (1972). *Defensible space: Crime prevention through urban design.* New York: Macmillan.

Statistics Canada. (2002). The state: The legal system: Violent crime. In *Canada e-book.* Catalogue no. 11-404-XIE. http://142.206.72.67/04/046/04b_002a_e.htm.

Strauss, M.A., Gelles, R.J., & Steinmetz, S.K. (1981). *Behind closed doors.* Garden City, NY: Doubleday/Anchor.

Sutherland, H., & Cressey, D.R. (1960). *Principles of criminology* (ch. 4). Philadelphia: Lippincott.

Sykes, G., & Matza, D. (1957). Techniques of neutralization: A theory of delinquency. *American Sociological Review, 22,* 664-670.

CHAPTER 7

Family and Marriage

The family is the most fundamental institution in society. This chapter explores the structure and functioning of the family in modern Canadian society. It also examines the variables that surround the institution of marriage. Emphasis is placed on those factors that increasingly are causing families to become disorganized and reorganized. Finally, the chapter explores the changing nature of the family.

Chapter Objectives

After completing this chapter, you should be able to:

- Outline the major and minor functions that the family performs.

- Create a diagram of your own nuclear and extended families.

- Identify laws pertaining to marital partnerships, family obligations, and the rules of exogamy in Canada.

- Assess the strengths and weaknesses of differing marital systems.

- Relate case histories illustrating the different types of family disorganization and show any compensatory measures that were used to reorganize roles.

- Evaluate recent changes in the structure and functioning of the family as a social institution.

FAMILY

The definition of the family was tested in Canada when Helen Ann Dougherty, an American citizen, asked to live out her remaining years in peace with her two sisters in Toronto. She had been living for two years in Toronto after she left New York, where she no longer had friends or relatives. The bond of emotional dependency between the three survivors of Nazi concentration camps, who lost their parents and brother in World War II, did not sway the bureaucrats in Immigration Canada in approving her application for permanent status on humanitarian and compassionate grounds. The Immigration Department did not consider that she met the definition of a "de facto family member" or that she would suffer "disproportionate or undeserved hardship" in her return to New York, since her savings and social security pension provided her with the financial means to care for herself. In spite of the statement that the department's decision would not be reversed, Immigration Minister Denis Coderre changed the ruling after heavy public pressure. Mrs. Dougherty's lawyer argued that Immigration officials were "dead wrong" when they decided she was not a family member within the definition of family since a sister is a sibling. Section 12.4 of the Immigration Department's Internal Processing manual includes "sibling" in its definition of family (Malarek, 2003).

family
a group related by blood, marriage, or adoption

The **family** — traditionally a group related by blood, marriage, or adoption — is a universal social institution, which, as far as we know, has existed in all cultures throughout history. All attempts to rid a society of the family unit (for example, Soviet collectives, the Israeli kibbutz, North American hippie communes) have met with failure. The structure of the family unit has varied greatly from culture to culture and within our culture at different times. Currently, the nuclear family rather than the extended family is the most common family structure in Canada. Families are shrinking in size, and role relationships within the family are changing. It is no longer accurate to define the family solely as a husband and a wife and their children. Other combinations of people are also considered a family. The definition of family is being revised with changing social and political circumstances in Canadian society. Consequently, family could include a group of people who define themselves as family based on commitment, feelings of love, respect, and responsibility to and identification with one another (Schwartz & Scott, 1997). In this definition, feelings of belonging are integral to family life. The family has delegated some of its former functions to other agencies.

FAMILY FUNCTIONS

The functionalist theorist views the family as one institution among other social institutions (for example, education, health care) that has structures and functions that both connect it with society and make it distinct. The emphasis is on family strengths and contributions to society and how it helps maintain values across generations (Ward, 2002).

One reason the family is so enduring is that it is still the most efficient means of meeting some basic social needs. This is especially the case in the vital functions that the family performs.

1. *The family serves a reproductive function.* The family is a biological and/or nurturing group that has the purpose of continuing the species. The family is the accepted and legitimate means for replacing members of society.

2. *The family serves a maintenance function.* The human infant is dependent on adults for a longer period of time than any other animal. During the period when children are dependent, they need to be provided with food, shelter, warmth, etc., at least until they reach physical maturity. Today, government legislation ensures that these basic needs of families in general, and of children in particular, are met. The family also provides economic and emotional support for adults.

3. *The family serves a socialization function.* Socialization involves training the young to become fully functioning members of society. The family teaches children cultural norms, values, statuses, and roles through the use of discipline, example, association, and direct teaching. Children learn how they are expected to act and what they can expect of others. Children also receive status through the family. They are identified with their race, social class, ethnicity, and religious association through their **family of origin**, the family into which they are born. The **family of procreation** is the family that is created when people marry and have children. These concepts have become dated as a result of the changing family group.

4. *The family serves as a refuge*, a place of physical protection and emotional security. Generally, family members develop affectionate ties with one another that last after they are separated geographically. The family is the place where individuals practise interpersonal skills. These skills are crucial for developing meaningful relationships in society.

These are not the only functions of the family. However, some minor functions that the family performed in the past have largely been given up to other institutions in our society, and some notions of how the family should function have largely been abandoned:

- its role in caring for the aged;

- its role as a recreational unit;

- the notion that a family should be a political unit and display uniformity in its voting patterns; and

- the notion that the family should be a collective economic unit with shared resources, especially a common food supply.

Other institutions now give the family considerable aid in performing its functions. Some people see this distribution of responsibility as beneficial. Time and other resources may be freed up for other pursuits. Others see these changes as detrimental. The family that is protected from crisis and that delegates many of its responsibilities to other agencies, institutions, and government departments may face a greater risk of disintegrating. The importance of family teamwork is diminished.

FAMILY ROLES

According to the functionalist perspective, the family resembles all other complex institutions in society; it has a division of labour. Each family member performs a recognized and approved role, and this apportioning of roles maintains family structure. There is order and some degree of predictability, which lends stability to the family structure. One or more members provide the money for food, housing, and so on ("the breadwinner role"); one or more prepare meals, drive the children to activities, and so on ("the domestic role"). This system is dynamic, not static. Role changes are common, and in many families today the partners aim for more equal relations, with each committed to a career. The partners' roles are interchangeable; either or both partners can perform the breadwinner and domestic roles.

family of origin
the family into which an individual is born

family of procreation
the family that is created when people marry and have children

They share roles and are less hindered by gender-role stereotypes. Other types of families have members consisting of one parent, two same-sex parents, step-parents and couples without children, each member performing a distinct role.

A major contribution of the symbolic–interactionist perspective (referred by some today as the liberal theory) to the understanding of family relationships is an expansion of concepts about roles from the viewpoint of the individual rather than of society. Through interactions with others, especially significant people in our lives, we develop a sense of self and of the roles we are expected to fulfill. Role expectations come from past experiences. Symbolic interactionists contend that the best way to understand family relationships is to examine the meanings each member sees in others' actions and words. These meanings will affect behaviour directly. An interesting example is a conversation between spouses: "Why are you reading that book?" This could be interpreted by the other as "Why are you wasting your time?" or "Why didn't you choose another book?" The meaning read into the question will determine the response. Bernard concluded that men and women experience and perceive marriage and family life differently. In fact, women's and men's descriptions of family interactions are so different it seems as though they are talking about two different marriages (Bernard, 1972, 1982). Symbolic interactionists emphasize individual responsibility in shaping one's view of the world. They are criticized for ignoring social forces that influence us and bring about change to the family (Ward, 2002).

Explanations of other current theories such as the systems, feminist, and post-structuralist theories can be found in Baker's *Families: Changing Trends in Canada* (2001).

FAMILY STRUCTURE

In social sciences, the roles in a family can be depicted diagrammatically. A male is symbolized as a triangle, a female as a circle, and a marital or equivalent relationship as an equal sign. The older partner is shown to the left of the equal sign. Thus, a traditional Western marital relationship in which the husband is the older partner would be depicted as in figure 7.1.

Lineage, which depicts offspring, is shown as lines dropping from the equal sign. In figure 7.2, panel A shows a family with one male child. Panel B shows a family with one female child and one male child; the daughter is older than the son.

Family diagrams can also show disrupted structures (see figure 7.3). If a family member dies, then the symbol that represents the member is filled in. If the marriage or equivalent relationship ends, then the equal sign is crossed out. You can invent your own symbols to represent situations in which you find yourself professionally (for case notes) or personally (for journals and diaries).

nuclear family
a family composed of two generations, usually a married couple and their offspring

Traditionally, sociologists referred to the common family composition as a **nuclear family**, composed of two generations, usually a married couple and their offspring. Other variations of the family are common today. Single-parent families and families in which the adults are not legally married are examples. Each nuclear family goes through a life cycle. The particular cycle that a family goes through is peculiar to each family; however, there is an *ideal* cycle that most members of our society envision as the standard by which we can measure individual family cycles:

1. *A married couple (including unmarried cohabitants)* is called a **potential nuclear family**, regardless of whether or not they intend to have children.

2. *A family in which all the children are born and are still living at home* is called a **full nuclear family**. Possible disruptions in this state include the premature death of a spouse and the leaving home of an older child before succeeding children are born.

3. *A family in which all the children are grown and have left the family home* is called a **denuded nuclear family**. The *empty nest* is a more common name for this stage of family life. Again, this structure can be disrupted by the death of a spouse or a child who never leaves. The family has come full cycle. The couple is again on their own and the cycle is regenerated through their children, who are now part of potential nuclear families. (Figure 7.4 shows how the family structure at each stage of the cycle is represented.)

According to the steps to adulthood laid out above, the process appears to be sequential and irreversible. However, today these changes are not always one-time-only events that occur in this sequence. Young adults may no longer finish school, start a career, and then legally marry. They may stay in school and live with a partner, find a job, and subsequently, or simultaneously, return to school. They may continue to live with their parents, or move out and move back in, during their schooling, employment, and family-building years. They are delaying marriage (females average 27 and males 29). The growing tendency for young adults to live at home in their 20s and early 30s appears to be tied to periods of economic recession and slow recovery in which parents and children can benefit economically by sharing resources (Boyd & Norris, 1999). Most of us are members of two or more nuclear families in our lifetime. We play multiple social roles within this structure (son/daughter or stepson/stepdaughter, brother/sister or half/step-sibling, partner, father/mother or step-parent). Each role makes different demands on us, requires different skills, and emphasizes different aspects of our personality.

An **extended family** is defined as a family (any group that is related by blood, marriage, or adoption) that is (1) broader than the nuclear family and (2) recognized by the individual as being part of his or her family. There is, therefore, a psychological component to the extended family — the recognition of someone outside the nuclear family as a family member. Generally, the extended family comprises more than two generations.

For a variety of reasons, the nuclear family is now more common in Canada than the extended family. This prevalence is due in part to increased mobility in our society, which is a function both of the ability to move easily and of the necessity to move to where jobs are available.

The disappearance of the extended family is also due to our society's emphasis on the young leaving home to establish their independence. They tend to leave when their parents are middle-aged and spend the next 10 to 20 years setting up their own home and a totally separate existence. Typically, by the time the young have established themselves, they are approaching middle age and their parents have become dependent through retirement. This problem of dependency is dealt with in our society through governmental and social agency aid to senior citizens (for example, pensions and nursing homes). One unfortunate side effect of this process

potential nuclear family
a married couple (including unmarried cohabitants)

full nuclear family
a family in which all the children are born and are still living at home

denuded nuclear family
a family in which all the children are grown and have left the family home

extended family
a family that is broader than the nuclear family and recognized by the individual as being part of his or her family

FIGURE 7.1   Marriage or Equivalent Relationship

The triangle symbolizes a male, the circle symbolizes a female, and the equal sign symbolizes a marital or equivalent relationship. The older partner is shown to the left of the equal sign.

FIGURE 7.2   Offspring

(A)   (B)

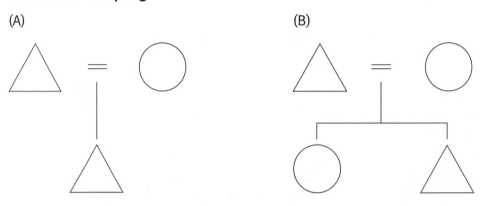

Lineage is shown as lines dropping from the equal sign. Panel A shows a family with one male child. Panel B shows a family with one female child and one male child; the daughter is older than the son.

FIGURE 7.3   Disrupted Structures

(A)   (B)

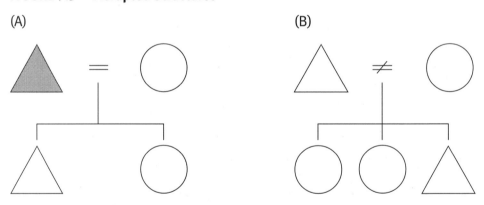

In panel A, a filled-in symbol indicates a family member who has died. In panel B, a crossed-out equal sign indicates a relationship that has ended (for example, through divorce).

is that the family is further fractured and the very young are often deprived of the company and wisdom of the very old. However, the function of the extended family is by no means over. Regular family gatherings are still held and baby-sitting help and temporary accommodation are still provided. In times of crisis, extended family members give emotional support or economic aid. An interesting idea developed in the fall of 2003 as a result of the double cohort entering universities and colleges in Ontario. With the shortage of student accommodation, a retirement home in

Toronto offered 43 spaces for students who would share the home with 100 seniors at a substantially less expensive rate than was available in student residences. How would this sharing of community affect the students and the elderly? How many students and retirement home residents would be interested in this arrangement?

An even broader concept than the extended family is **kin**, which is anybody to whom an individual is related, whether by birth or marriage, regardless of one's knowledge of their existence or one's recognition of them as family members. Kin was an important concept in Western culture for many centuries, and remains vital in some cultures today, but for the most part it has lost its currency in modern Canadian society.

kin
anybody to whom an individual is related, whether by birth or marriage

MARRIAGE

Until recently, marriage was defined as a socially recognized bond between members of the opposite sex. Social recognition is emphasized, rather than the legal tie, because some societies see common law marriage as being as permanent as legal marriage. The Ontario *Family Law Reform Act* of 1978 reinforced this emphasis. It put almost as many legal obligations on cohabitants as on legally married persons, especially where obligations to children are involved.

By 2003, there were an increasing number of homosexual marriage ceremonies, and the Canadian courts and government were in the process of redefining **marriage** as "the lawful union of two persons to the exclusion of all others."

marriage
the lawful union of two persons to the exclusion of all others

Most of us build our lives around the institution of marriage. We spend our early adult years selecting a partner. We adapt our personal goals to the personal goals of our marriage partners. We share possessions, time, and responsibility for children. In ideal marriages, we help each other through the problems of life. Less-than-ideal marriages may cause pain for one or both partners, and may end in divorce and the accompanying problems of readjustment and rebuilding.

Marriages differ across cultures and within our own society along a number of dimensions: the form a marriage takes, the process by which marriage partners are selected, the place of residence chosen by the partners, and the authority structure of the marriage.

Marital Structures

Our society practises **monogamy**, a marital system in which an individual is allowed only a single marriage partner. In recent years, however, the divorce rate has been climbing quite rapidly, and many divorced people marry new partners. The result is **serial monogamy**, the remarriage of divorced people to new partners. Some societies practise **polygamy**, a marital system in which an individual may have more than one spouse. There are three types of polygamy. In **polygyny**, a male is allowed more than one wife; the "possession" of extra wives is usually seen as marking the husband's socioeconomic and sexual status. In **polyandry** (less common), a female is allowed more than one husband; polyandry is usually based on demographic factors, especially a shortage of females in the population. Significantly, there is usually less family strife in polyandrous families than in polygynous ones, probably because in polygynous families wives are status objects (that is, something to be envied), whereas in polyandrous families, husbands have a simple

monogamy
a marital system in which an individual is allowed only a single marriage partner

serial monogamy
a marital system in which an individual takes two or more marriage partners in succession

polygamy
a marital system in which an individual may have more than one spouse

polygyny
a type of polygamy in which a male is allowed more than one wife

polyandry
a type of polygamy in which a female is allowed more than one husband

FIGURE 7.4   The Cycle of the Nuclear Family

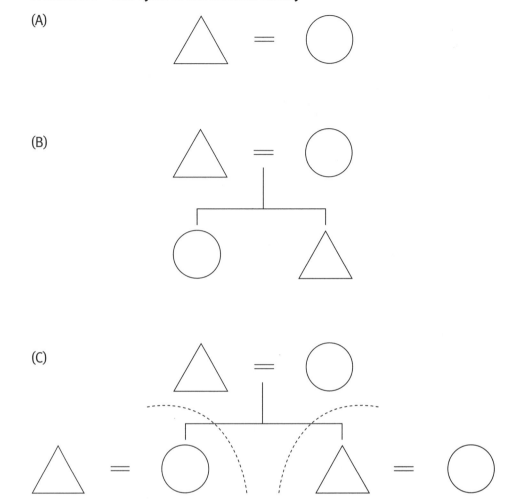

Panel A shows a potential nuclear family. Panel B shows a full nuclear family. Panel C shows a denuded nuclear family.

group marriage
a type of polygamy in which there is more than one husband and more than one wife but only one marriage tie and partners may be exchanged

choice — share a wife or go completely without. The third type of polygamy is **group marriage**, in which there is more than one husband and more than one wife but only one marriage tie and partners may be exchanged. Group marriage is not socially prescribed or accepted in any known society, but it has cropped up from time to time. Most polyandrous and polygynous societies are gradually becoming monogamous.

It is interesting to note that although polygamy is illegal in Canada, some religious groups practise it. In 1992, the attorney-general's office in British Columbia refused to charge a BC religious sect with polygamy; it believed it was unconstitutional in that it violated religious freedom guarantees and conflicted with the *Canadian Charter of Rights and Freedoms* (Robinson, 2003). Do you agree with this conclusion or do you believe monogamy should be upheld as the only type of marriage?

Marital Selection

Marriages differ in the process by which marriage partners are selected. There are two dimensions to this process: the basis for choice and the responsibility for choice.

BASIS FOR CHOICE

The basis for choice of a marital partner hinges on the concepts of exogamy and endogamy. **Exogamy** refers to social rules that require individuals to marry outside a specific social group. In our society, we are exogamous to age and to first cousins: we have to marry someone who is at least 18 (unless there is parental consent) and someone who is no closer related to us than a first cousin. **Endogamy** refers to social rules that require individuals to marry within a specific social group. Until recently, South Africa was endogamous to race (people were allowed to marry partners only of the same racial classification). Although Canada has no specific rules of endogamy, we do closely adhere to some very definite trends or patterns. The majority of Canadians marry people who are from the same social class, religious affiliation, racial and ethnic origin and who grew up close to their own family home. Although this tendency may be due in small part to prejudice against mixed marriages on any of the above dimensions, it is due in large part to frequency of contact and the fact that people who have similar backgrounds will develop similar interests and, therefore, increase their chances of sharing these interests. As immigration continues to change Canadian society and diversify family orientations, new sorts of endogamy are being created.

exogamy
social rules that require individuals to marry outside a specific social group

endogamy
social rules that require individuals to marry within a specific social group

RESPONSIBILITY FOR CHOICE

In Western society, responsibility for choosing a mate generally falls to the individual. In other societies and in some subcultures within our society, arranged marriages are common. There, responsibility for choosing a mate falls to parents, aunts, and uncles, who make a search for a suitable partner for the male (usually) when he reaches marriageable age. Very few arranged marriages are infant betrothals. When a female is found who approximates the desired qualifications, she is shown the qualities of her potential spouse. At this point, the two potential partners usually have the option of withdrawing from the deal. In arranged marriages, it is expected that the two partners will come to love each other as they share their achievements and tackle their problems together.

In Western cultures, we expect romantic love to be followed by marriage. It is only in the Western world of the 20th century that the notion of romantic love preceding marriage has become pervasive. For most of history, marriage has been a social, economic, and reproductive arrangement.

It is significant to note that arranged marriages have an extremely low breakup rate, whereas marriages based on romantic love have a much higher breakup rate. This difference in rates may be due in part to the societal values and assumptions underlying arranged marriages (for example, social stability is prized over individual fulfillment; marriage is a social, economic, and reproductive arrangement), and in part to our unreasonably high expectations, and correspondingly frequent and bitter disappointments, in marriage based on romantic love.

Marital Residence

Marriages differ in terms of where the newly married couple takes up residence after the marriage ceremony. There are three basic residence patterns that a new family can follow:

patrilocal marriage
a marriage in which the couple live with or near the husband's parents

matrilocal marriage
a marriage in which the couple live with or near the wife's parents

neolocal marriage
a marriage in which the couple live apart from both sets of parents

1. In **patrilocal marriages**, the newly married couple live with or near the husband's parents.

2. In **matrilocal marriages**, the newly married couple live with or near the wife's parents.

3. In **neolocal marriages**, the newly married couple live apart from both sets of parents.

In a society where most couples have to live away from parents because of the need to follow the jobs, the notion of choice of residence is somewhat outmoded. As a result, we emphasize not so much the place of residence of the couple as the set of parents who are called most frequently, most often visited, or turned to in time of crisis.

Authority Structure

Marriages also differ in their authority structures. There are three basic authority structures: patriarchal, matriarchal, and equalitarian. Variations in these structures occur between cultures, within cultures, and even within extended families.

patriarchal family
a marriage in which the husband/father is the formal authority figure

In a **patriarchal family**, the husband/father is the formal authority figure. He has the final say in important matters. This authority is based on his role, not extra skill, wisdom, or experience. In societies where patriarchal families are found, maleness confers authority and women have a limited or non-existent role in public life.

matriarchal family
a marriage in which the wife/mother is the formal authority figure

In a **matriarchal family**, the wife/mother is the formal authority figure. There is little evidence of an entire society with this dominant family structure (although some aboriginal societies appear to be matriarchies), but examples of this family can be found where a marital breakup has left the mother as the head of a single-parent family.

In our society, the family is continually approaching an equalitarian structure. In an **equalitarian family**, the couple jointly make important decisions concerning family matters. There is mutual respect for each one's opinions. Often, both partners are responsible for financial security as well. This equality often is difficult to achieve due to time constraints, jobs, and so on. This description underscores still existing power structures in the family.

equalitarian family
a marriage in which the couple jointly make important decisions concerning family matters

Marital Adjustment

An intimate relationship requires ongoing adjustment. The satisfaction that a couple draws from their relationship depends on a number of factors:

- the degree of commitment to the relationship;

- a willingness to work at the relationship; and

- external circumstances that are difficult to manage (for example, unanticipated illness, unemployment, and interference from relatives).

A good marriage requires effort as well as interpersonal skills, such as sensitivity, insight, and flexibility.

OTHER THEORIES OF THE FAMILY

Unlike functionalist theorists, who focus on the positive relationship between family and society and among family members, conflict theorists analyze negative influences, particularly power relationships within the family. Both functionalists and conflict theorists recognize that men and women tend to occupy different statuses and roles in society's institutions, with men tending to have higher incomes, more power, and status. None of these theorists see these conditions as involving relations of subordination and oppression. Conflict theorists focus on issues of class and fail to address the oppression of women, and functionalists don't relate inequality with oppression (Knuttila, 2002). Functionalists focus on social harmony and cannot adequately deal with or analyze change and conflict in the family.

Currently the most influential conflict-based theory is feminism. Feminist thinking is the driving force for much of the current research on the family. Feminist thinkers have different views on other issues, but generally agree that family relationships and society in general are based on the authority and power of men. They look at the political and social control enjoyed by men that contributes to subordination and oppression of women. As a result, women are limited in their opportunities and choices and are thwarted in reaching their full potential. Even when both partners work, there is an imbalance of household work, with women doing more of it (Ward, 1997). Feminist sociologists examine how women have been excluded from positions of power and leadership in society, the workplace, politics, academia, and the home.

Feminists' analyses have been at the forefront of studying family violence within the patriarchal structure of the family. They explain how family violence is part of a broader pattern of violence against women in society, reinforced by other social institutions (Knuttila, 2002). Feminist sociologists have effectively made violence against women a public issue. Their concern is supported by Statistics Canada's landmark 1993 Canadian Violence Against Women Survey. According to the survey, 29 percent of women who had been married or lived in a common law relationship revealed at least one incident of violence by their partner. Not only was the violence often repeated by many, it was all too often severe (Rodgers, 1994). Feminists who use conflict theory point out that as gender relations change and men lose power, some may use violence against women to reassert their power and status. Males are much more likely to be abusers and murderers than women, although both male and female children are victims of abuse.

Some feminist sociologists use the symbolic–interactionist approach, explaining how the association of strength and virility with violence is prevalent in so many areas of Canadian culture and how this produces violence. Feminists believe that the connection between masculinity and violence must be broken to effectively find a solution to this very serious social problem (Henslin, Glenday, Duffy, & Pupo, 2001).

Other topics of importance in family studies for feminist theorists are incest, sexual abuse, sex roles, and changing family forms.

FAMILY DISORGANIZATION

There are many factors in modern, urban, industrialized societies that serve to disrupt the normal functioning of family life. Often, circumstances will cause the roles performed by the various family members to be disrupted. There are four basic sources of family disorganization: structural strain, role failure, institutionalized evasions, and incest.

Structural Strain

In our society, we emphasize the nuclear family rather than the extended family. As a result, the family is much more structurally vulnerable to crises such as death or long-term disability. The nuclear family is not usually closely supported by the extended family. When a family member dies or is disabled, the roles he or she usually performs in the family have to be taken up by the surviving or able members. This burden is much greater on a small unit than on an extended unit, where there may be extra adults to take up the needed roles. Long-term disability may be an even greater burden on a nuclear family than the death of a member. There is a need not only to compensate for the roles left unfilled by the disabled member, but also to fill the new roles that are required for looking after the disabled member. Of course, grief and emotional stress are not felt any more deeply by one type of family structure than another, but the pressure to adjust is likely more acute in the nuclear family. Symbolic interactionists have contributed to the understanding of structural strain in their study of the concepts of role taking, role expectations, and role strain. As we interact with family members, we learn to put ourselves in their place. This is called role taking. As we interact with family, we anticipate their behaviour and shape our own behaviour to match. We develop role expectations. Problems may arise if our role expectations clash with others in our family. This clash could lead to **role strain**, a sense of discomfort or tension felt when we have difficulty meeting role expectations. For example, a stepfather who attempts to fill the role of a biological father may experience role strain (Porter, 1987).

role strain
a sense of discomfort or tension felt when we have difficulty meeting role expectations

Role Failure

A family can become disorganized if one of its members fails to perform adequately his or her designated roles. The breadwinner who cannot find employment cannot adequately provide for the maintenance of the family. An alcoholic parent cannot provide an adequate role model in the socialization of the children, and probably cannot be an adequate companion or sexual partner for his or her spouse. Role failure can induce structural strain through the non-performance of some roles and the need for other family members to cope with the member's role failure.

Institutionalized Evasions

Although we like to believe that marriages are forever, the social reality is far different from this ideal. To allow for marriage problems, we provide institutionalized evasions, such as divorce, annulment, and separation. These evasions are also potential causes of role reorganization in our society. As well as the economic, legal, and emotional strain that divorce may generate, newly single marriage partners face the added problem of being both mother and father to their children. They have to assume not only new roles but also roles that may be contradictory to their own role training. Adolescent children may also have to pick up roles for which they are not fully trained.

DIVORCE

One of the easier ways to recognize change in the Canadian family is by studying divorce. **Divorce** is defined as the dissolution of an existing marriage. Changes in divorce laws in the past few decades have made the divorce process much easier. The most recent *Divorce Act* was passed in June 1986, with a no-fault clause after one year of separation. That is, a divorce may be granted if, after a year of separation, the marriage partners assert marital breakdown without assigning blame or responsibility for the failure of the marriage. Most couples who seek a divorce use these grounds. However, families under stress may still opt for a more immediate solution by using the grounds of physical or mental cruelty. Figure 7.5 depicts the trends in marriage and divorce in Canada from 1967 to 1997. It illustrates how the new act affected the rates of marriage and divorce. The marriage rate increased slightly between 1986 and 1989, which may represent the backlog of people who were able to marry again after their divorces were finalized under the new act. As well, the divorce rate peaked following the new act since it became easier to obtain a divorce (Department of Justice Canada, 2000).

divorce
the dissolution of an existing marriage

More recent evidence confirms the impression that Canadians, having lived through nearly two decades of divorce laws, have learned that breaking up really can be hard to do. According to a Statistics Canada study (Statistics Canada, 2004; Galloway, 2004), the number of divorces dropped between 2000 and 2002. Reasons for this decline are likely tied to more people looking for stability in uncertain times, the realizations that people are often worse off after the divorce as a result of problems associated with single parenthood and other concers, few marriages, and more people living together without getting married. According to the study, the number of marriages that could be expected to end in divorce after 30 years hovers around 37 percent, with large regional variations.

There are a number of danger signals for divorce. Major signals are fundamental, early disagreements about matters such as money, savings, whether or not to have children, and how to bring up children. Other signals are one partner's sexual dissatisfaction in the marriage and a failure by the couple to accept each other's friendship relationships. Divorce is, however, often a solution to a problem rather than a problem in itself. A marriage is unsatisfactory when one partner would function better without the other, when one partner would always rather be alone than with the other, or when children would benefit from the absence of one parent.

It has been said that young children are hurt the most by divorce. In Canada, some 50 000 children encounter divorce annually. They find the transition difficult and are likely to suffer stress from thinking that they might have caused it, or wondering who will take care of them or where they will live. In the course of or after divorce, the daily family routine lacks regularity and consistency. Children want stability, assurance, and love. Nonetheless, research shows that children from a hostile two-parent home environment do better in a single-parent home after the initial year of separation has passed. Adolescents are more likely than young children to understand the separation, and at times are even relieved at such a resolution to family stress. Many children of divorced parents take responsibility and mature in interpersonal relations at an earlier age than their counterparts in intact families.

Societies can be classified by their acceptance of divorce. Some societies see the marital tie as being permanent and unbreakable. In such societies, no divorce is

FIGURE 7.5   Marriage and Divorce Rates in Canada, 1967–1997

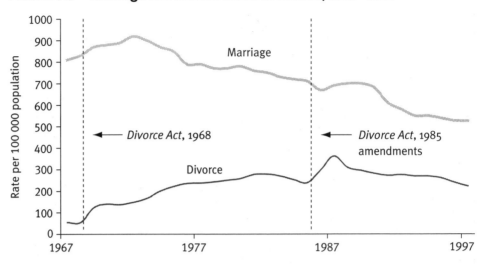

Source: Department of Justice Canada (2000).

possible. Other societies have a binding tie with some provision for divorce if the relationship can be shown to be clearly unworkable. Yet other societies have a loose marital tie in which divorce is easy to obtain. Is the most recent *Divorce Act* aimed at moving us from the second category to the third?

ANNULMENT

annulment
the dissolution of a marriage that was thought to exist but that in reality did not exist

Annulment is defined as the dissolution of a marriage that was thought to exist but that in reality did not exist. The situations that can give rise to annulment are many:

- If the person who officiated at the wedding ceremony was not qualified to perform the service, then the marriage is void.

- If one of the partners was under the age of consent, then their parents can declare the marriage null and void.

- If one of the partners was forced into the marriage, then it is not a legal marriage.

- If the marriage took place when one of the partners was "not of their right mind" (for example, mentally incompetent or incapacitated by drugs or alcohol), then the marriage contract is nullified.

- If the marriage is not consummated (if sexual intercourse does not occur), one partner can petition for annulment. Non-consummation is the most common basis for annulment. Only with consummation is a marriage fully recognized as being complete.

If annulment is granted, all record of that marriage is eliminated and it is as if it never took place.

The Roman Catholic Church has recently been criticized from within for its seemingly increasing tendency to grant annulments as a convenient way of getting around the Church's continued reluctance to recognize divorce.

SEPARATION

Separation is defined as the living apart of a still legally married couple. The term legal separation is often used these days, but it must be emphasized that it is the disbursement of possessions and children that is subject to legal contract, not the marital tie itself.

Incest

The family can also suffer disorganization if incest occurs within the group. **Incest** is a forbidden sexual relationship between members of the same family. In our society, incest has long been considered **taboo**, or so horrific that it is impolite even to mention it. In recent years, there has been a move to bring the problem of incest out of the closet. Society is just beginning to recognize the psychological devastation caused by incest. It has been estimated that over 90 percent of those with multiple personality disorder in Canada have suffered prolonged childhood abuse, which in many cases involved sexual abuse. These individuals dissociate and develop more than one personality as a survival strategy.

Not only is incest considered a deviant sexual practice, it is contrary to the *Criminal Code*. This has sometimes led the victims of incest to carry two burdens of guilt: (1) guilt for taking part in something that goes against society's norms; and (2) if the victim discloses the incest, guilt for being the instrument by which the family member is imprisoned. Consequently, many people believe that incest should be decriminalized and treated as a psychiatric disorder rather than a crime. Decriminalization may prompt those who have committed incest to seek help.

From a sociological perspective, the problem with incest is not the biological problems that may occur in a child of an incestuous liaison, but the role confusion that may ensue. For example, the offspring of an incestuous relationship between father and daughter is faced with the situation where his maternal grandfather is also his father; his father's wife is also his grandmother; and he and his mother share the same father. The result is role confusion or, more likely, role chaos.

It is not fully understood why primitive societies initiated rules against incest. Perhaps they noticed the emergence of genetic mutations over a number of generations; or perhaps they needed to marry off their children to other groups to maintain, begin, or enhance economic, political, and social ties between the groups. All societies have rules relating to incest, the form of which varies from one society to another. For example, the Azande of West Central Africa prescribed that a girl's first sexual intercourse should be with her father; this was purely an educational technique to ensure that one of the partners (they tended to be about 12 years old) knew what to do on their wedding night. Some societies forbid first-cousin marriages; others actively encourage it.

THE CHANGING FAMILY

According to Canada's 2001 census, the average Canadian family is shrinking. It consisted of 4 people in 1951 and had only 2.6 in 2001. An increasing number of couples are remaining childless, and more Canadians are living alone. It is obvious, though, that most Canadians choose to live in some form of a family. The 2001 census numbers reveal that 70 percent of all couples were married, down from 83 percent in 1981. Common law couples accounted for 14 percent of Canadian families, up from 6 percent in 1981. Only 44 percent of families were composed of dual parents who were married or living common law with children, and that number included same-sex couples raising children together. As of 2001, only one in four families were traditional nuclear families with two parents and their children.

Shifting Roles in the Family

There are many factors that have affected both spousal roles and parenting roles in present family life. The most obvious ones are (1) the increased prominence of common law unions, (2) the recognition and marriage of same-sex couples, (3) the frequency of divorce and remarriage resulting in single-parent families and blended families, (4) women in the workplace, and (5) reproductive technologies (Eichler, 1997, p. 66). This has led to complex consequences.

- The conception of spouses as husband (male) and wife (female) is blurred. With increasing numbers of same-sex unions and common law relationships, spousal roles have been redefined as partnerships between two people of the opposite or the same sex rather than as husband and wife roles.

- Parental roles have undergone tremendous changes as perceptions of the man as the breadwinner and woman as the caregiver are less evident. Sex roles are shifting more to androgyny in many families. More fathers are participating in day-to-day physical and emotional care of their children. The laws support fathers and mothers taking parental leave of 35 weeks in Canada with the arrival of a new baby. Approximately one in ten parental leaves are taken by men.

- Children increasingly are raised by a parent other than their biological one yet can maintain contact with the biological one with some kind of visitation and support arrangement.

- Parenting roles become even more confusing and complex with families created using reproductive technologies. Women may be biological mothers yet not give birth to the child. Surrogacy, egg and sperm donation, etc. have led to many ethical questions about parenthood.

Single-Parent Families

Single-parent families may arise as a result of death, separation, or divorce. Some individuals choose to have children but not to marry; and some single women become pregnant but marriage is not available to them. The proportion of single-parent families continues to grow. According to the 1996 census, almost one in every five children in this country lived with a lone parent. One reason for this growth is that individualism is valued in our society, often over social commitments. Divorce is accepted. Another significant social change is the slow increase of males among single parents. Lone-parent families headed by women continue to outnumber those headed by men by a factor of 4:1. The contention that mothers are better able to function as single parents is being challenged by those who argue that single fathers receive much more community support in parenting than single mothers do. Single-mother families are often socially and economically vulnerable. Mothers are expected to mother, while fathers get credit for stepping out of their traditional role to mother. Usually, fathers have better and more consistent financial resources to maintain their households than single mothers do. Good news for single parents emerged from the 2001 census, which found that although single-parent families were most closely linked to poverty in the past, their fortunes improved in the 1990s. This group made bigger gains over the decade than other families, with their median income jumping 19.4 percent. Most single mothers were finding jobs (Philp, 2003). The issue of teenage pregnancies is also of special concern because the core of Canada's poor are young, poorly educated women with children.

Blended Families

The traumatic experience of a divorce does not seem to discourage many people from remarrying. On average, there is a three- to four-year period between marriages. The family of a second marriage is likely to be different from the family of a first. Dependent children from a former marriage may be brought into the union. Blended families are made up of step-parents and siblings unrelated by blood. In step-relationships, children often have two fathers and two mothers, one being biological and the other a step-parent who may also be a social parent (the one more responsible for raising the child). For example, a very prevalent form of fatherhood is the non-exclusive (father role shared by another man — stepfather) and partial (the biological father does not have custody or live with the child but has visitation arrangements) father. If the stepfather adopts the child, the biological father is no longer the legal father.

A biological father to one child may become a social father in a new blended family with his own stepchildren and have less involvement with his own child. A father may be an exclusive parent (he alone has the father role to the child) to one of his children and a non-exclusive parent to another one. Mother relationships are very complex in blended families as well. After divorce, a biological and social mother is often no longer an exclusive mother, since her ex-husband usually enters into another relationship introducing a stepmother to the children. If her ex-husband gains custody, this will diminish her role as a social parent. In blended families, some children will be biological to one parent and not the other and some may be biological to both. The parent–child relationship will be different for each case (Eichler, 1997, pp. 72-80).

With the increase in complexity of family life, the socialization of children has become more complex, with conflict and role strain understandably being more common. The blended family involves transition for the children. Stress may arise over arrangements to meet the other biological parent. A child may not know how to relate to the step-parent. Discipline may become a thorny issue. Adjustments to step-siblings may be difficult, and complaints of favouritism may be a problem. On the positive side, some children welcome the blended family environment because it means more attention and more stable emotional and economic resources.

Common Law Families

According to Statistics Canada, the growth rates for all family structures were highest for common law families. Between 1991 and 1996, the rate of increase of common

common law couple
two people who are not
legally married to each
other but who live
together as sexual
partners

law families was about 16 times that for married couples. Traditionally, common law couples are two people of the opposite sex who are not legally married to each other but who live together as husband and wife in the same dwelling. However, the new social trends have led to a change in this definition. **Common law couples** are two people who are not legally married to each other but who live together as sexual partners. This type of family had increased by 28 percent from 1991. In 1991, one in nine couples were living common law; by 1996, the ratio was one in seven. Almost half of the common law families included children, whether born to the current union or brought to the family from previous unions. From 1991 to 1996, the number of children living in common law families grew by 52 percent.

Role designations can become unclear and complicated when considering who is the mother or father. A woman may have a child outside of marriage and have little contact with the biological father. She moves in with another man who becomes a social father, taking some parental and economic responsibility for this child. If the social father adopts the child, he becomes the legal father. If there is no adoption, who is liable for support payments if the couple separate, the biological or social father? Similar complications could arise if a mother abandons her child and the biological father is the primary caregiver who enters into a common law relationship.

With our largely urban and heterogeneous society and liberal sociocultural values and norms, there is a greater tolerance and acceptance of common law unions. Couples are increasingly choosing to live together without a formal marital ceremony, either as a prenuptial test of compatibility or as a permanent alternative. This social acceptance is facilitated by a growing number of married women who keep their own surname so that the couple is seen as two individuals rather than only as a couple (Eichler, 1997, pp. 49-50). Separated couples may not finalize costly divorce procedures before embarking on a new family arrangement. Property rights and child support obligations bind current common law arrangements.

Same-Sex Families

Recently, Canada has moved with changing social trends and radically altered its vision of the Canadian family. Canada's 2001 census included gay and lesbian households for the first time to reflect the growing recognition of homosexual relationships as family relationships that should be counted as part of the social fabric. Same-sex couples were already supported by the same economic and legal benefits and obligations given heterosexual common law couples. Nearly 3 percent of all common law couples declared themselves gay or lesbian; this was 0.5 percent of all couples, both married and common law. About 15 percent of the lesbian couples had children living with them, compared with 3 percent of male same-sex couples. Only two other countries at the time, the United States and New Zealand, included a same-sex option in their national census.

In May 2003, Ontario joined the Netherlands and Belgium as the only places in the world where same-sex couples could be legally married. The Ontario Court of Appeal as well as other provincial courts declared that refusing marriage to same-sex couples violated anti-discrimination measures in the *Canadian Charter of Rights and Freedoms*. The federal government did not appeal the ruling, which paved the way for civil marriages of same-sex couples in Canada. The federal law was in the process of being amended to define civil marriage as "the lawful union of two persons to the exclusion of all others." Traditions change to accommodate new realities. As the 2001 census verified, many same-sex couples have children — their own, adopted, or through reproductive technologies. Society has an interest in endorsing the desire of committed couples to give those children a stable home. The dramatic step of expanding the definition of marriage was an emotional issue that caused deep divisions in Canada. The new recognition did not affect a church's right to operate by its own religious rules and choose who to marry, but did divide marriage and religion even more than it already was.

Parenthood in these families is complex. With a lesbian couple, one mother may be biological and social and the co-mother is social. If adoption is the case, both are legal mothers. With gay co-fathers, one may be the biological parent to the child and the partner assumes a social father role. Other types of parenting relationships are also possible. Now, same-sex couples are allowed to adopt children in almost every province, and fertility clinics have opened the door to gay and lesbians conceiving children of their own genetic makeup. Many more gay men are embracing fatherhood, and this will likely increase with the legal right to marry. They can adopt a baby, hire a surrogate to carry a baby conceived with the sperm of one of them, or conceive a child with a lesbian couple and co-parent with them. It is important to note that surrogacy is an ethical issue in Canada and the government is debating a new federal law that would license fertility clinics and outlaw financial compensation to sperm and egg donors and to surrogates, aside from expenses. In Toronto, there are very popular parenting courses for same-sex couples who are considering parenthood (Philp, 2003).

Traditions of Immigrant Families

Many of Canada's new immigrants are coming from countries in Asia, the Caribbean, and Central and South America, bringing different traditions with them, including their own family traditions. Some of these immigrants rely heavily on their extended families for all aspects of their social life. A number of these traditions encourage arranged marriages. These immigrants are contributing to the variety of family types (Ward, 1997).

Aboriginal Families

Unlike non-aboriginal families, aboriginal families are attempting to return to practices and values that promote the traditional family life that was central to their nations prior to the arrival of European immigrants. With the Canadian government's failed attempts to assimilate them with policies such as separating children from their families and communities, the aboriginal peoples' interdependent and cooperative family unit that provided organization, stability, and spiritual well-being was severely disrupted. The statistics are compelling. As a result of parental abuse or neglect, 10 times more aboriginal children than non-aboriginal children are removed from their home. Seven times more aboriginal children than non-aboriginal children commit suicide. Wife abuse in these communities is seven times the national average (Timpson, 1995). Their traditional family life includes mutual responsibility, respect for women and children, and, above all, the general creed of caring and sharing (Royal Commission on Aboriginal Peoples, 1995).

CHAPTER SUMMARY

The family is a universal social institution. Its structure differs from society to society and over time, and its functions may grow or diminish or simply change, but the family itself endures because it meets some very basic human needs more efficiently and effectively than any alternative that has been tried. Common law, blended, and same-sex families, and sole parenting are adaptations of the family to current circumstances. The institution of marriage also is universal, occurring throughout the world and over time. There are variations in the number of spouses allowed, authority relationships, patterns of residence, and methods of selecting a partner. For all their endurance, though, families and marriages undergo disorganization for a variety of reasons and require reorganization of roles.

KEY TERMS

annulment

common law couple

denuded nuclear family

divorce

endogamy

equalitarian family

exogamy

extended family

family

family of origin

family of procreation

full nuclear family

group marriage

incest

kin

marriage

matriarchal family

matrilocal marriage

monogamy

neolocal marriage

nuclear family

patriarchal family

patrilocal marriage

polyandry

polygamy

polygyny

potential nuclear family

role strain

separation

serial monogamy

taboo

REFERENCES

Baker, M. (2001). *Families: Changing trends in Canada* (4th ed.). Toronto: McGraw-Hill Ryerson.

Bernard, J. (1972, 1982). *The future of marriage.* New York: Bantam.

Boyd, M., & Norris, D. (1999, Spring). The crowded nest: Young adults at home. *Canadian Social Trends*, Statistics Canada. Catalogue no. 11-008, pp. 2-5.

Department of Justice Canada. (2000). Marriage and divorce rates in Canada, 1967–1997. *Selected statistics on Canadian families and family law* (2nd ed.). Research Unit, Child Support Team, Department of Justice, p. 9. Reproduced with permission from the Department of Justice.

Divorce Act. (1986). SC 1986, c. 4.

Eichler, M. (1997). *Family shifts: Families, policies, and gender equality.* Toronto: Oxford University Press.

Family Law Reform Act (Ontario). (1978). RSO 1980, c. 152.

Galloway, G. (2004, May 5). Canadian divorce rate declining. *The Globe and Mail*, p. B13.

Henslin, J.M., Glenday, D., Duffy, A., & Pupo, N. (2001). *Sociology: A down-to-earth approach.* Toronto: Pearson Education Canada.

Knuttila, M. (2002). *Introducing sociology: A critical perspective.* Toronto: Oxford University Press.

Malarek, V. (2003, April 2). She is 75 and a Holocaust survivor: Why is Canada deporting Helen Ann Dougherty? *The Globe and Mail*, p. A1.

Malarek, V. (2003, April 4). Lawyer says case must be reviewed. *The Globe and Mail*, p. A12.

Philp, M. (2003, May 3). Gayby boom. *The Globe and Mail*, p. F4.

Philp, M. (2003, May 14). Single parents' fortunes improved in 1990s. *The Globe and Mail*, p. A4.

Porter, E. (1987). Conceptual frameworks for studying families. In *Family matters: Sociology and contemporary Canadian families* (pp. 41-61). Toronto: Methuen.

Robinson, B.A. (2003). Past hisory of polygyny in the Mormon church. http://www.religioustolerance.org/lds_poly.htm.

Rodgers, K. (1994, March). Wife assault: The findings of a national survey. *Juristat Service Bulletin, 14*, 1-21.

Royal Commission on Aboriginal Peoples. (1995). *Choosing life: Special report on suicide among aboriginal peoples.* Ottawa: Communications Group Publishing.

Schwartz, M.A., & Scott, B.M. (1997). *Marriages and families: Diversity and change.* Upper Saddle River, NJ: Prentice Hall.

Statistics Canada. (1997, October 14). *The daily* (pp. 1-5). Catalogue no. 11-001E.

Statistics Canada. (2004, May 4). *The daily.* http://www.statcan.ca/Daily/English/040504/d040504a.htm.

Timpson, J. (1995). Four decades of literature on native Canadian child welfare: Changing themes. *Child Welfare, 74,* 525.

Ward, M. (2002). *The family dynamic: A Canadian perspective* (2nd ed.). Toronto: ITP Nelson.

CHAPTER 8

Social Stratification

Social inequality is a fact of life. It includes all the measurements of superiority and inferiority between individuals, groups, and regions that arise in society. This chapter examines the different interpretations of the role and necessity of social stratification. It also considers mobility within the social structure, and the role that social inequality plays in such practical concerns as access to health care and educational opportunity.

Chapter Objectives

After completing this chapter, you should be able to:

- Enunciate your own ideas on the unequal distribution of wealth in society, and relate these ideas to one of the major theoretical perspectives.

- Evaluate factors that may enhance or decrease social mobility and life chances.

- Compare the Canadian stratification system and opportunities for social mobility with other social systems.

- Demonstrate how knowledge of socioeconomic status differences may be used in your chosen vocational field.

- Describe the relationship between socioeconomic status and the health care system, and between socioeconomic status and educational achievement.

  In the cultural mosaic of college students across the country are many im- migrant students who, with their families, have staked their hopes on a better life in Canada. They have many reasons for leaving their homeland. The list is long, with some reasons given as:

  - *a better future here*
  - *a better standard of living and lifestyle*
  - *better financial prospects*
  - *better health care and education opportunities*
  - *escape political persecution in homeland*
  - *more freedoms, feel safer here*
  - *find new adventures*
  - *want to learn English.*

It is not surprising that people all over the world dream of coming to Canada. The United Nations (2002) ranks Canada as one of the best places in the world to live in its Human Development Index. This sits well with most Canadians but can serve to mask some very real problems and encourage complacency in dealing with unresolved issues. There are an increasing number of homeless people in our cities, social problems continue to devastate aboriginal people on reservations, poverty is a reality for too many Canadian families, and many of our young are working on short-term contracts for minimum wage with no employment benefits.

BACKGROUND

social stratification
the process of ranking people in status levels according to some criteria of inferiority and superiority

social class
the social ranking of individuals on the basis of purely economic factors

socioeconomic status
the social ranking of individuals on a combination of social factors such as occupation, lifestyle, and family lineage and economic factors such as income, property ownership, and investments

Every known society ranks people in status levels according to some criteria of inferiority and superiority, in a process called **social stratification**. Stratification can take many forms. It can be based on such different criteria as race, religion, family background, property ownership, income, occupational prestige, age, gender, and ethnicity. If the social ranking of individuals is based on purely economic factors, the stratification is termed **social class**. More common, however, is a ranking on a combination of social factors such as occupation, lifestyle, and family lineage, and economic factors such as income, property ownership, and investments. This kind of stratification is termed **socioeconomic status**.

CONFLICT THEORY AND SOCIAL CLASS

The first person to systematically study the social significance of class differences was Karl Marx. In the mid-19th century, Marx outlined his view of the way society was structured in *The Manifesto of the Communist Party* and *Capital*. Marx was an economic determinist; he believed that all human relationships, laws, institutions, and so on, which he called the *superstructure* of society, revolve around economic arrangements. This superstructure was built on an economic base. What people believed, what they did, and how they felt about it ultimately depended on their economic role in society. This economic role depended on our relationship to the *means of production*, which Marx defined as things like factories, businesses, farms, equipment, and machinery. Marx suggested that individuals could have only two possible relationships to society as a whole: either to own the means of production, or to sell one's ability to work (one's labour) to the owners.

Thus, in Marx's view, society was made up of two large, hostile groups: the owners, whom he called the bourgeoisie, and the wage-workers, whom he called the proletariat. To Marx, this relationship was exploitive: the bourgeoisie were the exploiters and the proletariat were the exploited. The proletariat could survive in one of two ways:

1. The proletariat could sell their labour to the bourgeoisie. A man's ability to work had a deep, almost mystical significance to Karl Marx — a man was his work, and so to sell one's labour was to sell one's self.

2. The proletariat could become members of the lumpenproletariat, a group that existed outside the main society either through crime, deviance, begging, or some other means of subsistence. They were forced into this lifestyle by the exploitive bourgeoisie.

Marx believed that the gap between the bourgeoisie and the proletariat would widen forever. In Marx's terms "the rich will get richer and the poor will get babies," and hence have more mouths to feed and a smaller and smaller share of society's resources. Marx also described a middle class made up of small business owners and artisans (skilled workers). He predicted that this middle class, which he termed the **petite bourgeoisie**, would gradually disappear. He foresaw that skilled jobs would be replaced by machinery and that workers would become slaves to the machine, mere "machine-minders," while small companies would be swallowed up and forced into liquidation. As a result, the gap between the proletariat and the bourgeoisie would widen further still.

Although some of Marx's predictions have come true, he could not foresee some contrary trends. Machines have replaced many old skills, but machines have also been responsible for an increase in skilled jobs in many areas. Machines have to be designed, built, repaired, and maintained, and new jobs have evolved in order to deliver these skills. In the 1970s, small business ownership reached record highs. Even in the 1980s, when bankruptcies increased, many small industries and businesses mushroomed, especially those surrounding new technologies.

Eventually, Marx predicted, the gap between the bourgeoisie and the proletariat would become so great that the proletariat would become aware of the fact that they were being exploited and overthrow the bourgeoisie. The proletariat would then set up a communal state in which nobody would receive more than his fair share of societal rewards. This society would exclude the possibility of social class differences by eliminating differences in material wealth. For a number of reasons, however, this utopian ideal has not come to pass:

- It is difficult for modern workers with an automobile (or two) in the driveway, expensive electronic toys and gadgetry (for example, DVD players, computers, videogame systems, cell phones, satellite TV), union protection, 35-hour workweeks, and four weeks' holiday to see themselves as exploited.

- Those who could more easily see themselves as exploited (people on welfare, unemployment, or minimum wage) do not see the economic system itself as being at fault. Instead, they look for a more just application of the system. In fact, in the Western world of the 1980s and 1990s, the underclasses voted for conservative, right-wing politicians (for example, Margaret Thatcher, Ronald Reagan, and Brian Mulroney) rather than for candidates with leftist views.

- In the so-called communist world that was purportedly based on Marxist ideas (for example, Cuba, China, Romania), there seems to be significant evidence of differential access to society's rewards. These ongoing class differences may have been a factor in recent and growing dissatisfaction in "communist" societies.

petite bourgeoisie
a middle class made up of small business owners and artisans

SYMBOLIC INTERACTIONISM AND STATUS

Max Weber, a near contemporary of Marx, suggested that Marx's predictions would not come true because Marx overemphasized the role of economics and underemphasized the role of social factors in social stratification. Weber (1968), in contrast, emphasized *Stant* — in English, social standing or status. He maintained that even if people's access to society's material wealth were equalized, class or stratification differences would, before long, be re-established.

Weber was especially interested in the role that a person's lifestyle and life chances played in determining social standing. Weber argued that two people with equal economic positions could exhibit profoundly different **lifestyles**, or everyday ways in which lives are lived. Lifestyle includes recreation patterns, consumer patterns, socializing strategies, and ways of acquiring and maintaining material goods. For example, individual A might "spend it while he's got it," while individual B might invest or save his money in order to increase it; individual A might drink fine wine, while individual B might simply drink beer. Weber maintained that these different lifestyles, which are not entirely economically determined, differentiate among social strata.

Two individuals who occupy a similar socioeconomic status may also differ markedly in their chances of future advancement. That is, an individual's **life chances**, potential for future social mobility, are not determined solely by present social status. An individual who sees herself as potentially benefiting from the social system in the future is not going to do anything now to upset that social system. Thus, the promise of future reward for conformity becomes a fairly powerful social control that prevents the fulfillment of Marx's predictions.

lifestyle
the everyday way in which a life is lived

life chances
one's potential for future social mobility

FUNCTIONALIST THEORY

The idea that social classes are a necessary element of society has, surprisingly, been argued most strenuously by American sociologists (Davis & Moore, 1945). Functionalists believe that every social phenomenon has a function or purpose. Even deviant behaviour serves purposes such as providing social variety and, sometimes, simply providing society with ideas that are ahead of their time. Functionalists believe that if a social behaviour ceases to have a social function, it will disappear. If social stratification exists, it does so to perform some important social function. The functionalist theory runs as follows:

1. Society is based on the *division of labour*. That is, no one is an occupational island capable of meeting all of his or her needs. All members of society depend on the day-to-day performance of a number of interdependent skills by all other members of society to have their needs met.

2. Some of the tasks that need to be performed for society require a higher degree of skill than others do. Society is left with the problem of matching people with the appropriate skills and talents to the appropriate tasks.

3. The acquisition of a skill takes time; the higher the skill is, the longer it usually takes to acquire. This relationship creates some difficulty because, in most societies, the time taken to acquire a skill is usually a time of relative deprivation. Trainees tend to be paid much less than accomplished members of their chosen profession, and somewhat less than the general population.

4. Society needs to motivate the appropriate individuals from the limited pool of talent to aspire to the higher skills. Acquiring these skills will require individuals to deprive themselves while training, and to diligently apply

themselves in their positions once they have attained the skills. To offset this self-deprivation, society needs to provide some means of differentially rewarding these people for their efforts.

5. These rewards will tend to consist of status, material wealth, degrees of self-regulation, and leisure and recreation time.

The result of this skill-acquisition process is a system of socioeconomic status. That is, social inequality is a device by which society ensures that the most important positions are filled by the most qualified people.

There are some difficulties with this analysis of stratification, but most of the difficulties can be traced to ineffective application of the system rather than inherent faults. There is no guarantee, for example, that the most necessary jobs are the ones that receive the highest rewards. The functional importance of selling insurance may not be as that of some occupations, but in terms of prestige and income, insurance sellers are relatively highly rewarded. How can we compare the relative importance and difficulty of disparate skills such as those of a doctor and those of a mathematics professor? Whose absence would a society miss more, a professional athlete or a garbage collector?

THE SOCIAL LADDER

Having looked at theoretical explanations of why social strata occur, we turn now to descriptions of the current structure. The first major North American descriptive analysis of social class, *Yankee City* (1963), was undertaken in Newburyport, Massachusetts by W. Lloyd Warner in the 1940s and '50s. Warner and his associates identified six distinct social class structures:

1. At the top of the social ladder was the **upper-upper class**. This class consisted of individuals who were born into wealthy families — that is, families that had been wealthy for a long time and, thus, established at the top of the social ladder for a long period. The basis for membership in this group was inherited wealth and family background.

upper-upper class
a social class consisting of individuals who were born into wealthy families

2. The next-highest class was the **lower-upper class**, which consisted of individuals whose wealth, while equivalent to that of the upper-upper class, was newly gained, not inherited. The upper-upper class perceived these nouveau riche as being wealthy but lacking the breeding that they had acquired over time. For their part, the lower-upper class tended to view the upper-upper class as being the faded gentry whose status had not been achieved through work but simply ascribed at birth regardless of the personal worth of the individuals. One of Warner's most interesting findings was that class antagonism seemed to run stronger between these two upper-class groups than between any other two strata. They had separate clubs, they belonged to different voluntary and charitable organizations, and they did not intermarry.

lower-upper class
a social class consisting of individuals who have gained wealth and status through work

3. Warner also divided the middle classes into two distinct groups. The first, the **upper-middle class**, consisted of professional people, such as physicians, lawyers, and university professors, as well as a number of fairly successful small businessmen. This class seemed to have most in common

upper-middle class
a social class consisting of professionals

with the lower-upper class; they socialized, intermarried, belonged to the same organizations, and so on. They were probably bound together by a common feeling that they had achieved their status through their own blood, sweat, and tears.

lower-middle class
a social class consisting primarily of white-collar workers as well as skilled and semi-skilled blue-collar workers

4. The **lower-middle class**, the second of Warner's two middle classes, consisted of the bulk of white-collar workers, as well as skilled and semi-skilled blue-collar workers. Nowadays, we would probably place a middle-class group — the *middle-middle class* — between the upper-middle and the lower-middle classes. In this class would be skilled tradespeople and highly qualified white-collar workers.

5. At the base of the social ladder were the lower classes, again divided into upper and lower. The **upper-lower class** consisted of regularly employed but unskilled workers such as assembly-line workers, waitstaff, and janitorial workers.

upper-lower class
a social class consisting of regularly employed but unskilled workers

lower-lower class
a social class consisting of the working poor

6. The bottom-most class, the **lower-lower class**, consisted of the working poor — that is, those working for minimum wage or less, and those on welfare relief.

Warner calculated the position of every inhabitant of Newburyport on his social scale by constructing what he called an index of status characteristics. He measured people's occupation, the source of their income (for example, inherited wealth, investment earnings, fees for service, salary, wages, or public assistance), the style of house that they lived in, and the residential area in which that house was located. Of these four variables, Warner accorded the greatest weight to occupation. Warner's work is important because modern sociologists use social class systems and measure the socioeconomic status of an individual by methods that are essentially modifications of his pioneering work. In fact, much of the most prominent Canadian contribution to sociological knowledge (the works of Blishen and of Pineo and Goyder) seems to be derived from Warner's study.

The first adjustment that must be made to update Warner's work is to point out that the depiction of the social class system as a ladder is too simplistic. The social class system is certainly a vertical scale, and Canadians benefit greatly from the fact that our scale is somewhat easier to climb than the social scales of many of other countries. Nevertheless, the concept of a social ladder with rungs to be climbed belies the fact that some of the rungs are congested while others are quite sparsely populated and will probably remain so. Furthermore, the numbers of people in each class will change as the economy fluctuates and as whole groups become upwardly mobile (registered nurses) or downwardly mobile (store clerks), thus altering, if only incrementally, the shape of the class structure. The best pictorial depiction of Canada's social class system seems to be that of an inverted kite, with the vertical dimension showing position on the social scale and the horizontal dimension showing the relative number of people at various levels (see figure 8.1).

CANADA'S STRATIFICATION SYSTEM

In the 1960s, Bernard Blishen, a Canadian sociologist, produced a scale that could be used for ranking Canadians by the prestige of their occupations. Blishen's pioneering

FIGURE 8.1 Canada's Social Class System

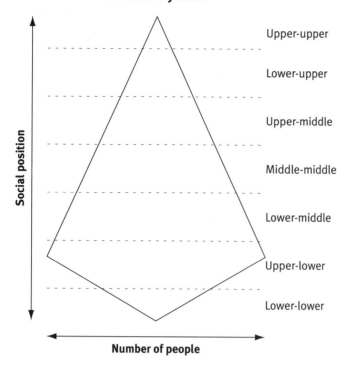

work has been replicated, modified, and improved not just in Canada but throughout the sociological world. Blishen wanted to combine the two most important variables extracted by Warner to distinguish social standing: income and occupation. Blishen sought, however, to refine the concept of occupation. He was more interested in the prestige of occupations. **Occupational prestige** is the social honour that other people accord you because of your occupation.

It should be pointed out that occupational prestige has no relationship to a person's ability to perform that role. The social honour accorded to somebody's role performance is called **esteem**, which is usually accorded not by the general public but by one's role set (for example, supervisor, colleagues, and clients). Thus, an individual can possess high occupational prestige and yet be held in low esteem because of his poor role performance, while another individual may be in a low-prestige occupation, but, through her diligence on the job, be accorded high esteem.

Using information from the 1951 Census of Canada, Blishen listed occupations that were found Canada-wide and worked out the average income for each occupation. He also constructed a survey wherein he listed these occupations and asked a random sample of Canadians to rank them according to prestige. The first result of note was the remarkable consistency with which Canadians from very different walks of life ranked occupations. By combining these prestige scores with average salaries, Blishen was able to list all the occupations in order. This scale has been rerun with every succeeding census, and the number of occupations listed has increased with each new version of the scale. The results are published under the title *A Socio-Economic Index for the Status of Occupations in Canada*, but it is more commonly referred to as the Blishen scale. The scale has shown practical value in predicting the distribution of some disorders in the population. It has also helped in ascertaining whether certain groups are at an educational disadvantage through a comparison of the educational achievement of one generation with the Blishen

occupational prestige
the social honour accorded to people on the basis of their occupation

esteem
the social honour accorded to people on the basis of their role performance

scores of the previous generation. Finally, the scale shows whether, over time, there is an upward flow of talent in the population.

John Porter, Canada's leading sociologist, provided us with the best theoretical description of the Canadian class system in his work *The Vertical Mosaic: An Analysis of Social Class and Power in Canada*. Porter acknowledged that the social class system was a vertical, gradually climbable ladder; in fact, he readily saw that the Blishen scale was an accurate model of the Canadian social class system. Porter, however, suggested that another very important Canadian social fact confused the whole picture of social standing in Canada — the fact that we are, by natural evolution and government decree, a multicultural society. The fact that many of us retain a strong identification with our ancestral homes changes the face of the social class system. There is a correlation between one's ethnic origin and the likely position one will achieve within the social class system. Certain occupations, and promotion within other occupations, seem to be more open or closed to various ethnic groups.

Thus, the Canadian class system is both vertical, in that it shows many of the elements of Warner's and Blishen's scales, and mosaic, in that the fragments of cultural groups from homelands have been reassembled on the Canadian landscape in such a way that an ethnic group can only penetrate so far up that scale.

GENDER STRATIFICATION

Despite considerable gains over the past 30 years, there are still major discrepancies in the socioeconomic status of men and women. In 1980, women made 52¢ for every dollar that men earned. By 2000, the gap had closed but was still considerable; women were earning 64¢ to the dollar (Statistics Canada, 2003).

Higher education is clearly the major facilitator of upward social mobility in Canada. In 1991, 27 percent of adults had a college or university education; by 2001, this had increased to 36 percent. In 2001, 34 percent of men had a university or college education, compared with 38 percent of women (Statistics Canada, 2003). In fact, women made tremendous inroads in average educational attainment throughout the 20th century. In 1920–21, the female percentage of total university full-time enrollment was 16.5 percent, and by 1997–98 it was 54.8 percent (Status of Women Canada, 2000). This increase in higher education for women leads to impressive gains in social status.

These figures are somewhat deceiving; the higher up the educational ladder you look, the lower the percentage of female students you find. Close to 60 percent of undergraduates are female; the male to female ratio at the master's level is almost equal, but at the PhD level, only about one-third of students are female. There may be a pyramid effect in place here. It was not until 1982 that the ratio of males to females at undergraduate level reached 50:50 for the first time. Now, this equity factor has advanced to the master's level. It may well be that a critical mass is needed at one level before the next sufficient numbers can advance to the next level.

In some professional degrees, women are making great gains. Almost half of all graduates in medical studies and research are women, and women are studying dentistry in increasing numbers. Women outnumber men by almost 2:1 in two formerly male-dominated professional fields: veterinary medicine and pharmacy (Statistics Canada, 2000).

Similar kinds of development can be found in occupational levels and income distribution. While women again have made significant inroads into the upper levels of the socioeconomic index, there are still major discrepancies. The proportion of women in senior management positions increased by 50 percent between 1987 and 2002 (16.9 percent to 25.1 percent of the total employed), but only one-quarter of senior management positions are occupied by women (Statistics Canada, 2003).

Women continue to remain underrepresented in the Canadian political system. At present, it remains an "old boys'" network. Canada is 37th in the world in terms of its collective female representation. Prime Minister Paul Martin wants to ensure that the Parliament of Canada is representative of the population. That means 52 percent of its members should be female (Galloway, 2003). This goal will be quite a challenge to attain. In traditional female occupations, females continue to be greatly overrepresented. Between 1987 and 2002, the percentage of women in nursing, therapy, and other health-related jobs remained the same at 87.3 percent. In clerical and administrative jobs, it rose from 74.4 percent to 75 percent (Statistics Canada, 2003).

At the other end of the occupational scale, the 10 lowest paid occupations account for only 1.1 percent of all male workers but 6 percent of female workers. There are roughly three times the number of men among the higher-paid occupations than men in lower-paid jobs, while for women there are five times as many women among lower-paid workers than there are women in higher-paid jobs. The upper levels could again succumb to the increasing critical mass of women in middle-income jobs and with higher education qualifications until upper-echelon jobs are equally split between males and females. The major lasting discrimination may, however, be at the bottom of the occupational ladder. It is difficult to see how the society can set about upgrading the skills of such vast numbers of undereducated, lowly paid female workers. This discrepancy may take a number of generations to even out.

SOCIAL MOBILITY

Most social class systems, to a greater or lesser extent, allow individuals to change their social standing. This process is called **social mobility**. We divide societies into two types based on the degree to which they allow social mobility:

1. An **open-class society** is a society that allows social mobility on the basis of individual achievement.

2. A **closed-class society** does not allow social mobility.

These two types of social class systems represent the ends of a continuum. Generally, societies fall somewhere between these extremes, toward one end or the other.

The Caste System

The most closed system that we know of was the old caste system of India, Pakistan, and Sri Lanka, remnants of which still exist. A **caste** (pronounced *kast*) is a totally closed social category. Members of the Indian caste system were born into a caste and died in that caste, and there was no possibility for social mobility in their lifetime. Marriage and all other social relationships had to take place between caste members.

social mobility
the ability of individuals to change their social standing

open-class society
a society that allows social mobility on the basis of individual achievement

closed-class society
a society that does not allow social mobility

caste
a totally closed social category

Contact with members of other castes was rigidly controlled. There was a prescribed ritual way in which a member of a lower caste approached a member of a higher caste. If the ritual was not carried out properly, the member of the higher caste was judged to be polluted and had to go through a ritual cleansing ceremony. The worst form of pollution came from contact with (which could be as oblique as walking in the shadow of) the group at the bottom of the social hierarchy, the untouchables.

One could not aspire to higher social status within the Indian caste system. The Hindu religion and its belief in reincarnation backed the system. Social mobility could occur only through reincarnation at a higher or lower social level. Caste members who ignored their caste obligations during their lifetime would come back at a lower level of existence, while those who met their caste obligations would come back at a higher level. Although this system seems harsh, it did confer some benefits on its members, and we can see some elements of the same process in our own society.

The caste system was built around an occupation and a geographical locality. For example, all the fishermen in a village would belong to one caste. The beneficial results of this system were that caste members could rely on a system of social, economic, and labour support in time of crisis. Everyone in a caste would pull together to help other caste members. Furthermore, adolescent identity crises were avoided, because members were born into occupational categories that they could not leave, and they could choose marital partners only from within their caste. However, the caste system tended to be stagnant, because there was no motivation to achieve, either individually or as a community.

Social control was very strict in the caste system; members who breached social etiquette were ostracized and became "outcaste" (outside the caste), lacking community support and income. When this consequence, or the threat of this consequence, was coupled with the fact that members ran the risk of coming back as a lower form of existence (as low as a flea in the intestine of a pig), there was considerable benefit to be derived from conformity to the system. Elements of this degree of social control can be seen in the close connection between the Judaeo–Christian ethic and the political system to which the majority of North Americans subscribe. Visions of hell, purgatory, and heaven, and scriptural writings about being content with one's lot and "having the poor always with us," have from time to time been invoked as ways of maintaining social order in times of deprivation in the Western world.

Open-Class Systems

The degree to which the class system of a society is open depends on a number of factors. These may include the relationship between life chances and ethnicity, the availability and distribution of educational opportunity, family size, the position of an individual in the birth order, the degree of industrialization of the area where an individual is born or resides, and the occupations of an individual's parents. All available indicators show that Canada is one of the most open societies in the world in terms of social mobility, second only to Israel. It is also interesting to note that a state's political structure — whether communist or capitalist — does not seem to affect the degree of social mobility.

vertical mobility
movement up or down
the social ladder

There are a number of ways of measuring mobility; the simplest is to look at **vertical mobility**, or the distance an individual moves up or down the social ladder in his or her lifetime. One important fact about an open-class society is that failure is as logical an outcome as success; individuals have an equal chance of climbing up and of sliding down the social ladder. Hence, vertical mobility can be divided into upward and downward mobility. A pool of social dropouts seems to be the necessary price to pay for the ability of others to achieve higher social standings.

In a second type of social mobility, **horizontal mobility**, an individual moves from one social position to another but remains at the same overall class level. For example, if a social service student transfers into the accounting program, her social role changes quite drastically but her social standing does not.

One of the most revealing measures of social mobility is **intergenerational mobility**, which is a comparison of an individual's adult social standing with that of his or her parents. The degree to which the current population's social standing differs from their parents is probably the best measure of the openness of our society that we possess.

Do Canadians believe that their class system is largely open to social mobility? An interesting study was carried out in 1996 by Jon Pammett, a Carleton University political scientist. He asked, "What are the most important requirements for getting ahead in Canada?" According to the results, Canadians ranked ambition, good education, hard work, and natural ability as the major keys to success. This appears to indicate "that individual characteristics are the most important determinants of any patterns of inequality that exist." It appears that Canadians believe we have an open class system (Pammett, 1996).

horizontal mobility
movement from one social position to another in the same class level

intergenerational mobility
movement in an individual adult's social standing in comparison with that of his or her parents

Embourgeoisement

One major trend that has recently been distinguished in social mobility is the increasing number of individuals who are living a middle-class lifestyle. This process of becoming middle class is called **embourgeoisement**, and it can refer either to an individual taking on a middle-class lifestyle or to the fact that an increasing percentage of the population is defined as being in the middle classes. About two-thirds of Canadians are currently defined as middle class. As a result of this high number of middle-class people, and the fact that another quarter of the population are lower class but think of themselves in middle-class terms, the value system and dominant ideology of Canadian society coincides with middle-class ideas and values. This is reflected in the operation of many Canadian institutions. It could work to the disadvantage of those who have not had early socialization into middle-class values and who also lack the economic resources to be independent of government-sponsored public institutions — that is, the lower social classes.

embourgeoisement
the process of becoming middle class

HEALTH AND SOCIAL CLASS

Patterns of health, illness, and access to health care are strongly related to social class. Although the universality of medicare in Canada means that we are not deprived of access to health care as some people are in the United States, some groups in Canada do receive better care than others. There is much "extra" care that can be bought, over and above the basic necessities provided by such programs as OHIP.

The vast majority of known diseases attack all social groups, but they do not attack them equally. Lung and chest disorders are much higher among the lower classes, and are probably related to the type of jobs they do, area of residence (often in poorer urban areas downwind of factories), and the high incidence of cigarette smoking. The middle class have higher rates of stress-related diseases such as hypertension, ulcers, and heart irregularities. The upper classes have higher levels of disorders related to excess, such as gout and alcoholism. Life expectancy also varies among the social classes; it is as much as eight years greater for those in the middle and upper classes than for those in the lower classes.

Many of Canada's wealthier citizens have access to subsidized drug plans, dental plans, and optical plans. It is fair to say that the lower one's income is, the less likely one will receive any form of help with these health care options.

Economics of Health Care

The governments of societies with predominantly socialist or mixed economies provide a wide range of social welfare benefits, including medical care. These societies usually agree on the principle that health care is a fundamental right of all citizens and that governments should provide care in more or less equal fashion. Most health care facilities are owned and operated by various levels of government. Health care professionals are, in effect, civil servants paid by the government. In Canada, legislation provides all citizens with government-funded access to hospitalization and physician services.

Medicine in Canada is not socialized; physicians operate privately and bill the government of the province where they practise. Fee schedules are regulated between provincial governments and bodies representing physicians. Some services, such as dental work and plastic surgery, are considered cosmetic or non-essential, and individuals have to pay for these services themselves; the status of other services, such as fertilization, sex changes, and in-vitro conceptions, is being debated. All other Western capitalist societies, except the United States, provide government assistance in health care, and many (for example, the United Kingdom, Japan, Sweden, and Australia) have systems as comprehensive as Canada's. The maintenance of a basic level of health is seen in these countries as a necessary and important benefit for society. However, because of government involvement in the health care system, administrative costs are often quite high; a large and steady flow of paper is needed to justify the activities of institutions to the government.

The United States is unique among industrialized countries in that its government has no program that ensures that Americans have access to health care. Medicine is predominantly a private, for-profit industry in which more money buys better care. Poor Americans have minimal access to health care. As a result, the richest country in the world has a population that is less healthy, on the whole, than the populations of other industrialized countries. In some social groups in the United States, the death rate for infants in the first year of life is about the same as that in poor African and Asian nations. The death rate for middle-aged men in the United States is twice as high as that in Canada or Western Europe.

The for-profit, direct-fee system of health care is very profitable for physicians and groups that own hospitals. These physicians and groups make up a powerful special interest group that devotes considerable time, money, and energy to opposing proposals for a national health care program. The financial rewards offered by this system to those who work within it have lured many money-oriented Canadian physicians south of the border, thus depriving the Canadian health care system of their services.

SOCIAL CLASS AND EDUCATIONAL OPPORTUNITY

The best way to ensure equality of opportunity for improving life chances appears to be a free universal system of education with compulsory attendance, in which the only discriminator is learning ability and hard work. This is far more difficult to achieve than it first seems. There are several reasons for inequalities of opportunity.

Education in Canada

Under the Canadian constitution, education is a provincial rather than a federal responsibility, except for the education of aboriginal people and military personnel. This provincial control has produced a great deal of diversity among the education systems of the various provinces. There appear to be regional disparities in the education of the population in different provinces. For example, more Ontarians have degrees, certificates, or diplomas and spend more years in school than do Newfoundlanders (taking into account the difference in population). Provincial wealth, availability of employment, and rural residence are among the reasons for the differences. There are even variations in education within provinces. Most decisions concerning elementary and secondary education are made at the local community level by elected school boards. Therefore, in most cases, the community in which you live will determine what education system is available.

Inequality of access exists for students whose situation (for example, remote habitation, small numbers of students, physical handicaps, or severe allergies to the environment) would make the traditional classroom environment impractical or impossible. This circumstance may be alleviated through distance education. At one time, students received educational materials through the mail. Today, technological advances in information systems can help meet the growing demand for distance education, while allowing a greater sophistication in methods and subjects covered. Courses can be and are offered at elementary, secondary, and postsecondary levels.

Regardless of the available methods of education, the most important inhibitor of educational progress is the fact that a child spends four or five years of life processing information before he or she gets to the school system. Many skills are acquired, developed, or, more significantly, limited during these years, and so some children may already be further ahead than others by the time they get to school. These skills include problem-solving strategies, language facility, methods of coping with frustration and stress, and attention span. Some inhibitors of educational progress may depend on the social class standing of the parents, and other class-related factors can come into play later.

Role of Finances in Education

Finances play a role in the education system, even though it is free to students. The textbooks and materials available to students are limited by the government's funding of the education system, and supplementary materials are more likely to be available in middle- and upper-class homes. In our current educational and technological climate, students with access to late-model computers will have an educational advantage over those who do not. Evidence suggests that the educational grants and loans available to students at the postsecondary level are more commonly used by the middle classes than by the lower classes for which they were intended.

Living in a low-income family may also place subtle (or not-so-subtle) pressure on adolescent students to abandon schooling for work at a relatively young age in order to contribute to the family income. Getting a job can also be a way of making up for the relative deprivation that adolescents may feel when they see a friend who has left school acquiring consumer goods that are not available to them because they are still in school. Although middle-class incomes are higher overall than lower-class ones, lower-class jobs usually pay more initially than middle-class jobs. (Maximum income is realized very early in lower-class jobs and careers.) These material motivations and rewards can be attractive enough to lure someone away from school. Unfortunately, early success is often followed by financial struggle as individuals marry, raise children, and pay off the mortgage.

Differences in income between lower- and middle-class families are likely to be evident in different resources available in the home. Middle-class homes tend to be more spacious and better equipped with facilities and tools for private, uninterrupted study or just general reading, such as a separate room, a computer, a desk, and appropriate lighting, than lower-class homes. A child with access to a word-processing program with a spell-checking function may get better marks on writing assignments, although be no better at spelling, than a child without access to such resources.

The pressure to conform is a further income-related difficulty for lower-class students. Peers, especially middle-class peers, will be wearing shoes and clothing as marketed by cultural icons. Because students often judge each other by outward appearances, this pressure accentuates class differences. If lower-class children do not conform by dressing in the prevailing style, then teachers and administrators may judge them negatively, perhaps perceiving their "grunginess" as a political statement more than a necessity. The gap between the haves and the have-nots is widening in Canada, especially in Ontario. Downward mobility as a result of downsizing and marital breakups is swelling the ranks of the lower social classes. In an effort to curtail fashion wars, some public schools have adopted school uniforms, but even uniforms can reveal disparities in social standing, because different grades and cuts of cloth are readily discernible.

Social Class and Language

Lower-class families tend to be larger than middle-class families. This fact, coupled with the fact that lower-class houses tend to be smaller and less well equipped than middle-class homes, strains resources even further and increases the probability that study facilities will be inadequate. Large family size may also have an effect on children's language skills. Because children tend to learn language from adult models, the more interaction a child has with adult models, the more opportunity the child has for acquiring adequate language skills. If there are two parents and two children in a family, each child can, in theory, have continuous, one-to-one interaction with a parent. This can never be the case if there are two parents and four children or, increasingly, one parent and two or three children.

Basil Bernstein, a British conflict theorist, has demonstrated (1971) how the poverty of language spoken in the home can adversely affect a child's chances for intellectual development. He has outlined two patterns of speech. One is an **elaborate language code**, which emphasizes verbalization and conceptualization and involves complex sentences and extensive use of adjectives, adverbs, and conjunctions. This pattern of speech is a suitable vehicle for abstract thought and is, importantly, the language system used by all teachers. Elaborate language codes are more likely to be found in middle-class homes than in lower-class homes, and middle-class children will sooner recognize the patterns of speech employed by teachers than will lower-class children.

The other speech pattern, a **restricted language code**, is typical of lower-class homes. It consists of short, clipped sentences, with few adverbs and adjectives, used repetitiously, and lacks conjunctions and subordinate clauses. This speech pattern emphasizes concrete, tangible, here-and-now things and is inadequate to express complex information or arguments. Lower-class children enter school with their restricted language code and are presented with an elaborate language code as the mode of instruction — virtually a foreign language. School is structured to encourage children who have command of an elaborate language code; students are selected and streamed unequally on the basis of their different backgrounds.

elaborate language code
a speech pattern that emphasizes verbalization and conceptualization and involves complex sentences and extensive use of adjectives, adverbs, and conjunctions

restricted language code
a speech pattern that consists of short, clipped sentences, with few adverbs and adjectives, used repetitiously, and lacks conjunctions and subordinate clauses

Class and Value Orientations

There seems to be a considerable difference between the values of middle-class and lower-class people. Middle-class values typically emphasize ambition, achievement, manipulation of the environment to one's advantage, possessiveness, and especially deferred gratification. **Deferred gratification** is the willingness to put off rewards until a later time in the belief that they will increase. The dominant value system for lower-class families, in contrast, is that of **immediate gratification**, in which all of one's resources are used for present pleasures. The fable of the industrious ant and the carefree grasshopper teaches the distinction between deferred and immediate gratification.

Most of these middle-class values are inherent in our education system and are accepted without question by teachers and the majority of citizens. In fact, when we also consider the importance of individual rights and the desirability of property ownership in Canadian society, it is evident that our laws, our education system, our political system, and our religious institutions are at one in holding these values. This "coincidence" of value systems works well for the vast majority of us because we feel comfortable with the values that are ingrained in us and expressed in the institutions around us.

Imagine, however, being brought up in a different value system and being confronted with this uniform and somewhat strange environment. Lower-class values are different. They tend to be fatalistic in the belief that achievement is not possible and that immediate gratification is the order of the day. If you lack possessions, you either develop an exaggerated need for possessions or, more likely, do not hold them in great value. If you do not know what tomorrow will bring, you live for today. All of these values are at odds with the predominant values and the raison d'être of the education system. Thus, lower-class children run the risk of feeling alienated from the very institution that is designed to give them the opportunity to break the cycle of poverty.

deferred gratification
the willingness to put off rewards until a later time in the belief that they will increase

immediate gratification
the use of all of one's resources for present pleasures

Parental Education

Perhaps the single biggest factor in the probability that a child will do well at school is the educational level of the parent. A well-educated parent gives the child an advantage in a number of ways:

- The parent will tend to put more value on and show greater interest in education. The child will grow up with the belief that education is an important and beneficial process, not a punishment.

- The parent can give the child more assistance with homework and can construct extra work.

- The parent knows the system. When dealing with this large formal organization, he or she is on familiar ground.

- The parent is more likely to be able to solve and explain problems, which encourages the child to look for and understand the reasons for things. In disciplining the child, for example, the parent is more likely to explain why a behaviour is wrong and what behaviour should be substituted; there may be punishment, but not only punishment.

CHAPTER SUMMARY

All societies have ways of unequally ranking people and, as a result, unequally distributing wealth. In Western industrialized societies, the most prevalent measure and means of ranking is socioeconomic status. One's status is assessed primarily on the basis of economic wealth and occupational prestige. The major schools of thought in sociology differ in their views of social stratification. Conflict theorists perceive it as a way of maintaining the status quo and exploiting working people. Functionalists perceive status differences as an enticement to achieve. Symbolic interactionists see it as a personal expression of one's lifestyle and concomitant life chances. Societies differ in the amount of social mobility that they allow their citizens. Some societies greatly restrict mobility, essentially requiring people to follow in the footsteps of their parents; others claim to use only individual merit as a basis for assigning status. Social standing has practical implications for such things as health status, access to health care, disease distribution, and educational advancement.

KEY TERMS

caste

closed-class society

deferred gratification

elaborate language code

embourgeoisement

esteem

horizontal mobility

immediate gratification

intergenerational mobility

life chances

lifestyle

lower-lower class

lower-middle class

lower-upper class

occupational prestige

open-class society

petite bourgeoisie

restricted language code

social class

social mobility

social stratification

socioeconomic status

upper-lower class

upper-middle class

upper-upper class

vertical mobility

REFERENCES

Bernstein, B. (1971). *Class, codes, and control: Vol. I. Theoretical studies towards a sociology of language.* London: Routledge & Kegan Paul.

Blishen, B.R. (1967). A socio-economic index for the status of occupations in Canada. *Canadian Review of Sociology and Anthropology, 4,* 41-57.

Davis, K., & Moore, W.E. (1945, April). Some principles of stratification. *American Sociological Review, 10,* 242-249.

Galloway, G. (2003, November 14). Martin calls for 52 per cent women MPs. *The Globe and Mail,* p. 45.

Goyder, J., & Pineo, P. (1979). Social class self-identification. In J.F. Curtis & W.G. Scott (Eds.), *Social stratification in Canada* (pp. 431-437). Scarborough, ON: Prentice-Hall Canada.

Marx, K. (1933). *Capital* (E. Paul & C. Paul, Trans.). London: J.M. Dent & Sons.

Marx, K., & Engels, F. (1965). *Manifesto of the Communist Party.* Moscow: Progress Publishers.

Pammett, J. (1996). Getting ahead around the world. In A. Frizzell & J.H. Pammett (Eds.), *Social inequality in Canada* (pp. 67-86). Ottawa: Carleton University Press.

Porter, J. (1965). *The vertical mosaic: An analysis of social class and power in Canada.* Toronto: University of Toronto Press.

Statistics Canada. (2003, March 11). *The daily.* http://www.statcan.ca/Daily/English/030311/d030311a.htm.

Statistics Canada. (2000). *Education in Canada: A statistical review*. Table 41, p. 153, Catalogue no. 81-229.

Statistics Canada. (2003). *Women in Canada: Work chapter updates*. Labour Force Survey. Table 11. Distribution of employment, by occupation, 1987, 1994 and 2002. Catalogue no. 89F0133XIE.

Status of Women Canada. (2000). Women's history month 2000 — Table 4. http://www.swc-cfc.gc.ca/dates/whm/2000/stats_e.html.

United Nations. (2002). *Human development report 2002*. http://hdr.undp.org/reports/global/2002/en/pdf/HDR%20PR_HD1.pdf.

Warner, W.L., Low, J.O., Lunt, P.S., & Sole, L. (1963). *Yankee city* (abridged ed.). New Haven, CT: Yale University Press.

Weber, M. (1968). *Economy and society* (G. Roth & C. Wittich, Eds.). New York: Bedminster Press.

CHAPTER 9

Changes in Society

Social change is a fact of life. It is evident in all aspects of our social relationships. This chapter examines the underlying problems, issues, and dissatisfactions that are the genesis of social change. It also looks at the individuals and groups that facilitate changes in the social structure. Finally, this chapter considers general social trends and some more specific social changes.

Chapter Objectives

After completing this chapter, you should be able to:

- Describe a recent social change that was clearly a benefit to one sector of society and equally clearly a detriment to another sector.

- Describe and give examples of the three social psychological states that often stem from societal problems.

- Describe and give examples of the three types of social movement, and identify the major change agents within them.

- Describe and give examples of the general trends of formalization, urbanization, urbanism, technologization, and globalization.

- Describe and give examples of changes in beliefs, values, skill levels, and institutions that have affected Canadians in the last decade.

- Show how the social readjustment rating scale demonstrates the complexity of the relationship between sociological, psychological, and physiological variables.

Lloyd Axworthy, an internationally respected Canadian statesman, argued in his book Navigating a New World *(2003) that "human security" — putting the interest of people ahead of the nation state and multinationals — must be the top priority for the 21st century. David Boyd, senior associate at the University of Victoria's Eco-Research Chair in Environmental Law and Policy, provides us with hope as he describes seven signs of progress that symbolize the extraordinary potential and ingenuity of human beings. He is not suggesting the world's problems are solved. However, he focuses on "7 modern-day wonders of the world" instead of the global problems of terrorism, war, disease, poverty, and environmental degradation.*

This good news comes from facts given by the United Nations, the Food and Agriculture Organization of the United Nations, and the World Meteorological Organization, all reliable sources:

- Democracy   *Since 1990, more than 100 nations cast aside military dictatorships or one-party rule and chose elected governments.*

- Population   *As a result of efforts to empower women and encourage family planning, the rate of population growth is now declining.*

- Food   *Despite the addition of 3 billion humans to the world's population since 1960, fewer people in total are malnourished today than in 1970. Global food production has grown at a faster rate than the population.*

- Literacy   *Literacy is a cornerstone of a healthy, prosperous society because it is a tool to improve our standard of living. The literacy rate in the developing world has jumped from 47 percent to 73 percent since 1970.*

- Environment   *The global production of ozone-depleting chemicals has dropped more than 80 percent, and Canadian production of such chemicals is down 95 percent. Several ground-breaking international agreements have been reached to protect the environment.*

- Health   *In developing countries, a child born today will live an average of 8 years longer than a child born 30 years ago.*

- Poverty   *The world's poor are not getting poorer. Between 1975 and 1998, average per capita income doubled in developing countries (adjusted for inflation); in other words, people in the world's have-not nations have twice the buying power they had 25 years ago. (Boyd, 2002)*

BACKGROUND

North America is often said to be the fastest changing society of all time — more things have been invented, produced, altered, and destroyed in the last 60 years than in the rest of history combined. At the same time, however, many critics would maintain that a large percentage of the changes are superficial, that the basic structure of the society has remained remarkably unchanged, and that other changes have had a detrimental effect.

There is a subtle but important difference between the concepts of social change and progress. **Social change** is simply any way in which society is now different from the way it was previously; that is, it is an objective measure with no implication of good or bad change. In contrast, **progress** is an idea of change for the good. It is important to point out that one person's idea of progress may be another person's idea of regress or change for the bad. A social change that benefits one individual or one group may simultaneously harm another. For example, rigid control on industrial pollution would significantly improve our environment and probably our health, yet it may also lead to economic difficulties for industries and businesses, which could result in shutdowns, layoffs, and bankruptcies.

social change
any way in which society is now different from the way it was previously

progress
social change for the good

We may ask whether people welcome change in their social environment or whether they fear it. Habits, customs, fundamental social institutions (for example, the family and religion), and socialization into society's various roles (for example, sex roles) are powerful forces that help to maintain stability and continuity in our society. When we look at these forces closely, however, we can discern changes in our beliefs, perceptions, and behaviour involving every aspect of society. Some of these changes are the result of crisis. For example, the recognition of the incidence of violence in the home is changing family structure. Battered spouses are increasingly given support by community services to help them when leaving their marriages.

Other changes occur over a long time, such as the shift away from a patriarchal society. Only a few powerful women have been recorded in history. Most of these women had an ascribed status (for example, queens of England). In almost all societies, women were at one time a powerless group and were often considered the property of men. In some patriarchal societies, such as Saudi Arabia, this is still the case. In Canadian society, women's lives have gradually changed as a result of greater attention to individual rights and through sustained effort to eliminate sexism and sexual harassment. It is widely recognized that women are having a positive influence in the workplace. Many people believe that the traditional female traits of sensitivity and emotionality can play a major role in creating more humane and, hence, more effective organizations.

THE PROCESS OF SOCIAL CHANGE

Social Change and Social Problems

Social change is usually precipitated by the existence of a particular **social problem**, a social phenomenon that is perceived as detrimental to society by a large proportion of the population and, therefore, in need of correction. A social problem implies the possibility of a solution. There may, however, be disagreement about what the most appropriate solution is. If the crime rate is increasing, is the answer to increase the police force, create more jobs, reform the school system, or some combination of all three?

social problem
a social phenomenon that is perceived as detrimental to society by a large proportion of the population and, therefore, in need of correction

Social change may also be precipitated by a **social issue**, a controversial subject in a society on which there is no general agreement — for example, the setting up and funding of abortion clinics, or the laws surrounding possession of small quantities of marijuana. A social change that accepts the reality underlying an issue may occur, but the issue is likely to remain contentious, no matter how it is resolved.

social issue
a controversial subject in a society on which there is no general agreement

In general, social problems and social issues do not exist and are not contested on a purely abstract level; they have an impact on the lives of individuals. It is the impact of general trends on individual lives that contributes to the next stage in our model of social change. In abstract theory, a restrictive monetary policy may have "benefits" for the economy. In the real world, however, such a policy destroys the lives of small businesspeople who go bankrupt, executives whose firms fold, skilled workers who are laid off, and labourers whose work is done for a pittance in less-developed countries. We have increasing rates of separation and divorce, but this general trend does not tell us about the disruption in the lives of millions of men, women, and children.

The process of change that is precipitated by social problems and issues is modelled in figure 9.1.

FIGURE 9.1 **Model of Social Change**

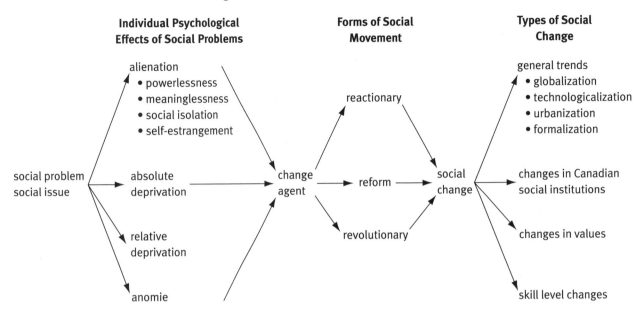

Individual Effects of Social Problems

There are three major social psychological states from which an individual suffers as a result of general social problems: alienation, anomie, and relative deprivation.

ALIENATION

alienation
a sense of lacking control over one's life

Alienation is a sense of lacking control over one's life. From time to time, we all feel that we are at the mercy of "the slings and arrows of outrageous fortune," but an alienated person feels this on a chronic, ongoing basis. Encompassed within a general feeling of alienation is:

- *A sense of powerlessness*   One feels that all meaningful decisions about life, work, and future are being made elsewhere by bosses, unions, government departments, etc., and one seems to have little input into those decisions.

- *A sense of meaninglessness*   One feels that one's life lacks purpose or direction. In modern society, the very thing that gives most of us a sense of meaning in life — our work — has been eroded either by the growing numbers of unemployed or by the fact that many employed people are performing monotonous, mind-numbing tasks.

- *A sense of social isolation*   Many people complain that their neighbourhood, community, or family group is not as close as it used to be, and that primary relationships are harder to initiate and maintain.

- *A sense of self-estrangement*   One feels that the world is passing one by, and that one spends too much time wishing one were doing something else.

ANOMIE

Anomie is a sense of confusion about society's norms and goals. In modern industrial society, we have so many conflicting goals, values, and norms available to us that it often becomes very difficult to choose a direction. A person is said to be in an anomic state when he or she is chronically unable to make such choices and, consequently, ends up in a state of inertia, depression, escapism, or deviance. In extreme anomic states, the only choice that seems available may be suicide. (For discussion of Durkheim's study of anomic suicide, see chapter 1.)

RELATIVE DEPRIVATION

Relative deprivation is a sense that one is not getting a fair share of society's rewards. Straightforward deprivation (not possessing something) is much easier to accept, because most of us are in the same boat. In a state of relative (and psychologically damaging) deprivation, in contrast, others who are in otherwise similar situations have things that you do not or you are now deprived of something you previously possessed, for example, a job.

relative deprivation
a sense that one is not getting a fair share of society's rewards

PRECIPITATORS OF CHANGE

The initial stages of these sociopsychological states are not disruptive. Thousands of citizens suffer degrees of alienation, anomie, and relative deprivation. It is not until they realize that there are a substantial number of other individuals in the same circumstances that any major move is made to alleviate the situation. Such was the case with Canada's hepatitis C victims who sought compensation for contracting the disease from contaminated blood supplies. **Change agents** are people capable of being the first to speak up and motivate others to band together and act. As this activity gains momentum, it becomes what is known as a **social movement**, a secondary group whose aim is to promote or prevent social change.

In any social movement, sustained effort and commitment requires effective leadership. This leadership must skillfully articulate the goals and beliefs of the movement in its attempt to coordinate collective action. Many resources (money, time, coordination of effort, leadership, persistence, etc.) are needed to mobilize collective action. For example, the environmental movement relies on large donations to sustain the leadership and marketing necessary to increase awareness of the cause and educate the public concerning its role in bringing about change.

change agents
people capable of motivating others to band together and act

social movement
a secondary group whose aim is to promote or prevent social change

SOURCES OF DISCONTENT

Absolute Deprivation

Absolute deprivation consists of the structural disadvantages that are rooted either in unequal opportunities or in deteriorating life conditions. According to this view of discontent, the greater the disadvantage a group faces, the more likely a social movement will arise. Absolute deprivations are not personal perceptions of deprivation, as are relative deprivations; rather, they are concrete situations that are deeply rooted in the social structure of society. Structured inequalities among people often lead to grievances.

Ideologies are used to define and explain these grievances. **Ideologies** are beliefs or values that are used to justify and legitimate alternatives to existing social inequalities. They identify the "good guys" and the "bad guys" and help define

absolute deprivation
structural disadvantages that are rooted either in unequal opportunities or in deteriorating life conditions

ideology
beliefs or values that are used to justify and legitimate alternatives to existing social inequalities

collective goals and strategies for achieving these goals. Ideologies also provide moral justification for the existence of social movements and help promote commitment to the cause.

Economic and occupational inequalities are two of the most common sources of discontent. For example, the social movement to improve the status of women has concentrated on the barriers to income equality based on structurally restricted opportunities for women in the workforce. Discontent based on inequality is also the source of many ethnic and racial movements.

The First Nations peoples of Canada have longstanding grievances generated by the social structure of Canadian society. Their discontent is based on real incidents of discrimination rooted in structurally based inequalities. An example of this type of inequality may be found in our justice system, which led to the wrongful conviction of Donald Marshall Jr., a Mi'kmaq in Nova Scotia. It is a fact of history that these Canadians have been treated unfairly and have lost control of their existence, whether through restricted land use, lack of autonomy over their lives, or an unfair justice system run by other Canadians. This unfair treatment has led to deteriorating living conditions and has often diminished aboriginal self-respect.

Relative Deprivation

Some sociologists argue that the reality of being disadvantaged is not sufficient to stir discontent strong enough to incite social movements. What is necessary is the subjective feeling inherent in relative deprivation; it is the *perception* of being unfairly or unjustly treated that precipitates change. This perception is formed in beliefs and experiences in which one feels deprived relative to one's expectation of fair and just treatment. Rebellion occurs if individuals become frustrated with unfulfilled expectations and when they believe they are not getting the rewards to which they are entitled. This deprivation creates the force to do something to change the antagonizing situation. If relative deprivation is taken as the cause of discontent of First Nations Canadians, one could argue that aboriginals' expectations of equality with whites have developed much more quickly than actual improvements in their conditions; this highlighted the disparity and precipitated the will to force change, and led to incidents like the standoff at Oka in the summer of 1990.

TYPES OF SOCIAL MOVEMENTS

Social movements do not occur in static societies; they occur in societies that are already undergoing a considerable amount of social change. In such a society, some people are afraid that there is too much change, while others may wish to accelerate the rate of change. There are three basic types of social movements: reactionary, reform, and revolutionary.

Reactionary Social Movements

reactionary social movement
a social movement that wants either to keep things as they are and prevent further changes or to restore some previously existing situation that is perceived as being better than the current situation

Reactionary social movements are movements that want either to keep things as they are and prevent further changes or to restore some previously existing situation that is perceived as being better than the current situation. Examples of reactionary social movements are the pro-life movement, which wants to return our abortion laws to the way they read before 1967; the temperance movement, which sought severe restrictions on alcohol consumption; the movement to reinstate capital punishment; the movement away from feminist ideals; and the movement to reverse the extension of basic rights to homosexuals.

Reform Social Movements

Reform social movements are movements that generally agree with society's current goals but that seek some modification or improvement in the way that society is trying to achieve its goals. Most of our political parties seem to be committed to almost identical ends, but they criticize the way that others are implementing policies. They often state that while there is nothing wrong with the goals, their opponents' methods will never achieve those goals. These movements often seek to introduce specific legal reforms by lobbying and influencing power groups through manipulation and threats. Pro-choice and pro-life activists both seek to change legislation concerning abortion, but to different ends. Pro-choicers want to make access to abortion easier, whereas pro-lifers want to bring back earlier and tougher anti-abortion legislation.

reform social movement
a social movement that generally agrees with society's current goals but that seeks some modification or improvement in the way that society is trying to achieve its goals

Revolutionary Social Movements

Revolutionary social movements seek to drastically redefine society's goals or the very nature and structure of society. Their aim is to replace the established order. The Parti québécois seeks to partition Canada and to subvert the official goal of establishing a fully bilingual country. Revolutionary social movements often use violent means in their attempt to dislodge the established authorities from their positions of power, but a revolution does not necessarily imply violence. A revolution is defined by the goal of fundamental change, not the means by which this goal is achieved.

revolutionary social movement
a social movement that seeks to drastically redefine society's goals or the very nature and structure of society

If the social movement is successful, it will accomplish a change in the way that society operates. For example, the feminist movement started out as a strident minority group about 30 years ago and was generally rejected. The movement has since accomplished significant changes in the law and especially in people's attitudes to issues such as equal pay for work of equal value, daycare provision, and sexual assault laws. Although a social movement may achieve fairly significant social change, the new social situation is often a compromise. For example, even members of the feminist movement still refer to the issues above as "women's" issues, not as issues that are vital to society as a whole.

TYPES OF SOCIAL CHANGE

General Social Trends

URBANIZATION

Some changes are almost universal, or at least typical of industrialized countries. One worldwide trend is **urbanization**, which is the growth and development of cities, often at the expense of rural areas. It is estimated that about three-quarters of Canadians live in urban areas. Cities grow both physically and in terms of population. Physically, cities grow both vertically and horizontally. Most vertical growth in cities takes the form of large, impersonal buildings that fail to foster communication between

urbanization
the growth and development of cities, often at the expense of rural areas

people, and the number of structures that are located totally underground is increasing. At present, nearly all of these underground structures are commercial ventures, but there is no logical reason why they cannot also include residential areas. The sociological consequences of subterranean residential areas are unclear.

suburbanization
the appropriation and use of productive farmland to build roads and residential and commercial areas

The horizontal or outward growth of cities is known as **suburbanization**. In this process, productive farmland is appropriated and used to build roads and residential and commercial areas. Across North America, the population is growing faster in suburbs than it is in city cores. Millions of acres of previously arable land is now occupied by family dwellings. The motivating factor in the growth of suburbs has been the need to provide housing for the burgeoning population. Governments have assisted this growth by providing better transportation systems and various programs that make it easier for prospective homeowners to obtain and carry mortgages. Improvements in agricultural technology have lessened the impact of the loss of farm land.

The suburban explosion has generated its own social difficulties. Suburban living requires a lot of energy. More fuel is required to heat and cool large, detached homes than a similar number of dwellings within a complex. And commuting from the suburbs to the city for work, leisure, and shopping purposes also consumes energy. Some social critics maintain that the uniformity of the suburban layout is sterile, lacking both the sense of community of rural villages and the exciting variety of cities. Modern suburbs can, however, be quite varied both in terms of architecture and, in an age of increasing multiculturalism, population composition. Economic restrictions tend to produce suburbs that are homogeneous in terms of the occupational prestige and socioeconomic status of the residents. Perhaps, then, we are simply faced with the task of defining community in a way that is more appropriate to modern values and technology.

exurbanites
people who have moved well beyond a city's limits but still retain an attachment to the city

A growing phenomenon is exurbanism. **Exurbanites** are people who have moved well beyond a city's limits but still retain an attachment to the city. Exurbanites often "invade" an existing rural village, bringing with them their urban values and lifestyles. This influx can be the source of tension between the original residents and the newcomers. The original residents see the newcomers as significantly undermining their lifestyle, while the newcomers may see the originals as cold and inhospitable.

Canadian cities have lost population from their core areas to the suburbs. In large cities such as Toronto, however, the core areas typically contain some of the most desirable and expensive housing (for example, Rosedale). Cities also grow in terms of population. Much of this increase is due to immigration, whether from within Canada or without. Rural areas, especially, lose many of their young and talented to the cities. As the city population grows denser, criminal and deviant behaviours tend to increase. As we can see by these examples, the very social changes that occur in the name of progress can themselves become the social problems of the future.

URBANISM

urbanism
the cluster of norms, values, and material possessions that originate from the requirements of city living

Does life in cities differ significantly from life in rural areas? Is there a lifestyle typical of city dwelling? If there is a lifestyle that has been generated by the evolution of large urban structures, one may well expect that modern electronic communication and transportation systems have now made it possible to live an urbanized lifestyle while physically residing outside the city. **Urbanism** is the cluster of norms, values, and material possessions that originate from the requirements of city living. Louis Wirth (1938), an American sociologist, said that city life has three defining traits:

1. a large number of residents,

2. a high population density, and

3. a heterogeneous population.

It is impossible to get to know everybody in a city; there are too many people, and it is likely that among the large number of people there will be different types of people that an individual has no desire to know. In this great human diversity, people perform specialized tasks to satisfy certain markets. Thus, people tend to meet each other only in specific, temporary situations. One result of this is the seeming "coldness" of city life. People's tendency to keep to themselves is called **privatization**. Because of the proximity of large numbers of people in the city, it is impossible for individuals to maintain much in the way of their own private, physical space. To compensate for this lack of physical space, urbanites set up their own social distance. By not interacting closely with their immediate neighbours, people can achieve in social terms what population density deprives them of in physical terms.

Sociological writings on the privatization that exists (and that may be growing) in cities often make a value judgment — namely, that the rural lifestyle is in some way superior to the urban. One of the first scholars to write about the differences between rural and urban lifestyles was the 19th century German social scientist Ferdinand Tonnies. Tonnies suggested that large cities produced their own cultural features. In his analysis of rural and urban lifestyles, he used the German terms *gemeinschaft* and *gesellschaft*. The closest translation of *gemeinschaft* is "community," but to Tonnies, **gemeinschaft** meant a living organism, involving an underlying consensus or mutual understanding, based on kinship, common locality of residence, and friendship. One can sense the bias toward this lifestyle from the positive phrasing of the characteristics.

Our current conception of the term **community** as a *small, closely knit, homogeneous society* would easily substitute for *gemeinschaft*. The concept of *gesellschaft* is a little more difficult to define. Basically, **gesellschaft** refers to the large-scale, formal, heterogeneous lifestyle typical of modern urban/industrial complexes. Tonnies suggested that the world was on an irresistible path that was drifting away from *gemeinschaft* and toward *gesellschaft*. Most of Tonnies's writings were tinged with regret at the passing of *gemeinschaft*-like society. The phrase "the eclipse of community" was coined by later sociologists to describe and, again, regret this trend. It is easy to see that in much sociological writing, as well as in much news reporting and politicking, there exists to this day an anti-urban bias.

There are different ways of looking at human interactions within a large city. It is possible, for example, for relatively close-knit "communities" to grow within small sectors of the city. There are many examples of what are called urban villages within Canadian cities. An **urban village** is a network of social relationships among some residents of a city. If this network is bound to a certain locality, it is called a **neighbourhood**. The Locke Street area of Hamilton, Ontario, for example, is very homogeneous in social and artistic interests and in the socioeconomic status of its inhabitants, and as a result it is a close-knit community. Most of the people know each other, see each other on a regular basis, and feel a sense of belonging.

privatization
people's tendency to keep to themselves

gemeinschaft
according to Tonnies, a living organism, involving an underlying consensus or mutual understanding, based on kinship, common locality of residence, and friendship

community
a small, closely knit, homogeneous society

gesellschaft
the large-scale, formal, heterogeneous lifestyle typical of modern urban/industrial complexes

urban village
a network of social relationships among some residents of a city

neighbourhood
a network of social relationships that is bound to a certain locality

Even if the social network is not tied to locality, people who live in various parts of a city can maintain close relationships with each other. They can share festivities, triumphs, and tragedies; meet on a regular basis; give each other social, economic, and physical support when needed; and generally be emotionally attached to each other. Just because a group is not attached by place does not mean that it has any less sense of community.

The continuing increase in population of the city comes largely at the expense of rural areas. Very often it is the younger people from rural areas who migrate into the cities, thus leaving an age imbalance in the countryside. City living is distinctly different from rural living in that the urban environment produces a constant bombardment of unnatural stimuli. There is traffic noise from motor vehicles and even aircraft, telephones constantly ringing, a barrage of advertisements in various media, and noise from numerous machines. People in cities learn to ignore irrelevant information as they go about their daily lives. City residents can sleep with streetcars rumbling by their homes or planes taking off and landing over their heads.

HUMAN ECOLOGY Urban sociologists assume that the physical surroundings of one's area of residence will shape one's behaviour and interactions. Most surveys of urban dwellers suggest that more than three-quarters of them would prefer to live in the suburbs or the country, yet an increasing number of people are gravitating toward the city. This anomaly can be accounted for on economic grounds. People move to places that are perceived to offer greater job opportunities and economic rewards, and put aside any preference they might have for a particular living pattern. The shift in Canadian residential patterns has been dramatic. One hundred years ago, Canada's population lived predominantly in rural areas and few lived in cities; this situation is now completely reversed.

An urban sociologist would ask such questions as:

- How would the building of a new physical structure affect human relationships in a community?

- Why does the incidence of crime and deviance increase as the population in an area grows more dense?

- What are the attractions of large shopping malls for groups of youths?

- If low-income housing is to be built, what are the relative merits of concentrating it in one area or dispersing it in smaller units among more expensive housing?

Thus, urban sociology can be very useful in community planning, policing, community development, and public health planning.

urban planning
the improvement of community living by the deliberate creation or changing of physical environments

URBAN PLANNING **Urban planning** is the improvement of community living by deliberately creating or changing physical environments. Urban planners are professionals who are employed by municipal governments, or sometimes privately contracted, to create comprehensive, long-range plans to ensure that city growth and development is controlled and organized. Over the past 25 years, there has been a growing concern that citizen participation should play a role in the planning process. Many municipal governments now employ urban sociologists to help construct impact studies and to devise questionnaires that will assess the needs and interests of those affected by urban development. Planners, architects, developers, and politicians may be able to understand proposed projects from an aesthetic, technical, or economic perspective, but they are not usually affected personally by their projects and do not necessarily share the value systems and lifestyles of those who are affected. They have to recognize that physical changes to the cityscape alter social relationships. Even something as seemingly beneficent as the clearing of a slum and the relocation of the residents to more modern housing can have a devastating impact on the social support systems that people who live in the slum have developed. Urban sociologists can help planners, developers, and politicians understand that the physical structure of a house does not itself give rise to the complex network of social relationships, duties, rights, and obligations of which a home is made.

The difficulty faced by urban planners is that their recommendations will almost always mean economic, social, and political benefits to some and economic, social, and political costs to others. They make recommendations, they do not make decisions. A great deal of input can come from citizen participation, sociological research, and planners themselves, without this input ever being taken into consideration. Two good examples of this fact are the implementation of a two-tiered regional government in Ontario and the failure to integrate municipal housing appropriately into new surveys.

By the 1970s, the vast majority of sociologists had long since come to the conclusion that Ontario's city hall–style governments were out of date and costly. In any given region of the province, there were a number of city and town governments duplicating facilities at great cost. Urban sociologists suggested that regional government would remove a great deal of this duplicated expense. They suggested that cities and their **hinterlands**, regions that service and identify with a particular city, be amalgamated into regional governments.

Although the suggestion to change to one-tier regions made economic sense, it was not politically popular. Small communities feared that they would lose their autonomy in the face of the massive voting power of city areas. The provincial government had two feasible solutions: force regional government through or leave things as they were. In an attempt to pacify everybody, the Ontario government invented two-tier regional government. All the old municipal governments continued to exist, still duplicating many services, and on top of this there was added another level of government with representatives from all the municipalities. This model of government caused more duplication of services and an extra bureaucracy for taxpayers to fund.

Another well-researched sociological phenomenon was the plan to build large-scale municipal and Ontario housing surveys. People feared that these government housing projects would become instant ghettos and that social disintegration would inevitably follow, with the legions of disadvantaged feeding off each other's alienation. A large grouping of disadvantaged people is known to create a culture of poverty — a tendency to rely on welfare, a lack of job motivation, a lack of interest in educational achievement, and so on — that is handed down from generation to generation. The proposed solution was to build small units of subsidized housing into every survey that was erected, thus avoiding the conditions for creating a culture of poverty and, at the same time, surrounding disadvantaged children with other, achievement-oriented role models. The window of opportunity was wide open in the early 1970s, at the height of the housing boom; early integration would have gone unquestioned. There were also attempts to "integrate" such units into existing neighbourhoods,

hinterland
the region that services and identifies with a particular city

although, not surprisingly, established residents resisted integration efforts. Where developers tried to integrate subsidized housing into new surveys, their pursuit of economies of scale often led them to incorporate many more units than the suggested numbers. Fewer and more dispersed units would have ensured more interaction between advantaged and disadvantaged residents.

INDUSTRIALIZATION

industrialization
the substitution of technology for manual labour as the basis of production

automation
the replacement of people by machines

A further major trend has been the technologization or **industrialization** of our society. Technology is increasingly being substituted for manual labour as the basis of production. We depend more and more on machines to perform tasks that would previously be done by humans. Technology, in the form of VCRs, DVD players, personal computers, and video games, dominates even our leisure-time activities. In the workplace, **automation** (the replacement of people by machines) and computer control of job functions has caused many old skills to become redundant, and more and more people are losing jobs as a result. Workers are becoming deskilled as the modern technologies are taking the skills out of jobs. People once did the calculating, manipulating, and designing that is now done by computers. At the same time, new skills have been introduced, and society is faced with the problem of not having sufficient numbers of people with these new skills. In the changing job market, many of the jobs now available to high school graduates will disappear in the near future and will be replaced by jobs that do not yet exist.

Another consequence of the rapid expansion of technology is computer sophistication. The proliferation of computer-related technologies has ushered in the Information Age. Information has become a highly valued commodity. The more information one possesses, the greater advantage one has over the competition. A major concern of these technologies is the difficulty in controlling who obtains information about us.

In a *gemeinschaft* society where a small, harmonious group of people share work, leisure, and home life, there is little thought of privacy. However, most Canadians have never experienced this closeness with neighbours. Most live in a *gesellschaft* society where work, leisure, and home are compartmentalized and where the right to privacy is taken for granted. However, with the increasing sophistication of computer technology and the great decrease in the cost of gathering information, this privacy is in jeopardy. The information about you no longer belongs to you alone. It is gleaned from a variety of data sources and stored in databases. Credit bureaus may know more about you than you do yourself. Most of us are unaware of the regulations designed to protect our right to privacy. Therefore, it may very well be that these rights are being violated.

Cyberspace raises a major privacy concern. Legislation is needed to protect those who use the Internet. Internet surfers are able to obtain information, services, and products from around the world. Electronic transactions leave a data trail of personal information that can be sold, reused, or combined with other databases without our knowledge.

globalization
the increasing tendency for practices and values to cross national boundaries and for worldwide practices to shape everyday activities

GLOBALIZATION

Another trend is **globalization**, the increasing tendency for practices and values to cross national boundaries and for worldwide practices to shape everyday activities.

Throughout most of the world, you can buy a McDonald's hamburger and the latest designer jeans, you can phone home across continents with a calling card, and you can watch American soap operas and other TV programs beamed in via satellite. E-mail makes communication virtually instantaneous. Many companies are multinational in scope, and their employees travel to and converse with branches in other countries daily.

The process of globalization suggests that we must question our previous notions of what constitutes a society. Especially questionable is the extent to which we can continue to think of societies as having physical boundaries. As large groups migrate, travel becomes easier, and cultures diffuse, the idea of territory in the physical sense may become outdated. This process will inevitably cause instability for a portion of the population. Many will cling more firmly to roots than ever before, defining society in terms of private ownership of "their" land. Distance is no longer an inhibitor to social relationships. We can be anywhere in the world in a day, we can hear voices from the other side of the world moments after pressing a few buttons, and we can instantaneously communicate documents, letters, and pictures. So many of the limitations that made us define the world in narrow temporal and spatial ways have been removed. It is inevitable that other temporal and spatial restrictions will have to be redefined, including what we define as a society.

Many countries have followed Canada's lead in instituting a policy of multiculturalism — a policy that simply acknowledges an existing social fact. Combining this approved maintenance of cultural heritage with ease of communication with and travel to "homelands" makes the assimilation of cultural groups less and less likely. Globalization may not, therefore, lead to greater homogeneity of cultures; it may well foster differences. Ethnicity will become increasingly more significant than nationality. Worldwide social networks that preserve and enhance cultural distinctions have already arisen. Globalization allows people to choose traits from a worldwide menu and adapt them to fit their own distinctive ways.

Many of these social changes were made possible initially by economic and political changes. In the last few hundred years, there seems to have been, for better or worse, an inexorable movement toward Western liberal democracy and capitalism. The most recent symbol of this trend is the tearing down of the Berlin Wall. These and other events have led many people to fear rampant American cultural and economic imperialism. At the same time, globalized groups have emerged to fight worldwide battles against poverty, to establish civil rights, and to protect the global ecology. Wariness of cultural domination is still understandable. The language of globalization and of the international elite is English, as is the majority of material on the Internet. In Europe alone, globalization is changing the cultural landscape as native languages are giving way to English (Rifkin, 2001). Popular music is dominated by acts from the United States, Britain, Canada, and Australia. Most internationally distributed movies come out of Hollywood. American television, chain restaurants and hotels, and computer software are available everywhere in the world. CNN disseminates America's perspective and viewpoint worldwide.

Economic globalization appears to be evolving independent of government controls. The free trade movement that stimulated the formation of the North American free trade agreement (NAFTA) and the European Union may have been facilitated by politicians, but the economic well-being of nation states now appears to be beyond the control of any particular national government. An increasing number of activities cannot be dealt with by civil or criminal law within a single country, or by alliances of a small group of companies. Local business law has great difficulty governing the activity of multinational companies, and local communication controls and obscenity laws are inadequate to deal with the growth and content of the Internet. In their interactions with multinational corporations, governments become caught in a paradox: they need foreign investment, exports, and imports, yet each transaction can further erode their own sovereignty.

formalization
the increasing dependence on bureaucratic and legalistic definitions of human relationships

Another aspect of globalization is **formalization** — the increasing dependence on bureaucratic and legalistic definitions of human relationships. Trust, faith, the personal touch, and a sense of community are being replaced with contracts, legalistic attitudes, protocol, and privatization. Can globalization produce a "global village," or will it be an extreme form of *gesellschaft*? Even such areas as the games people play show elements of this trend. The sports pages of newspapers are apparently more concerned with union–management negotiations, franchise shifting, stadium deals, player strikes, and the role of player agents than they are with athletic excellence.

The world is made up of close to 190 nations. Although national sovereignty is still acknowledged, these nations have become a global village with their fortunes and futures intertwined. The global society has multiplied into thousands of nongovernmental organizations that address worldwide and regional issues of concern. However, there is a dark side to globalization. The modern tools of global management, organization, and finance can be used by the global elite to forget, ignore, and even exploit the dispossessed people of the world (refugees, child victims of war, AIDS victims, unemployed youth, etc.) (Axworthy, 2003).

Advocates of globalization argue that free and open trade and an expansion of commercial relationships and activities of all kinds are the keys to a brighter future for everyone. The assumption that commerce spurs culture is misguided. In fact, the opposite is more often the case. New cultural activists argue that culture leads to the creation of commerce and government, not the other way around. People first establish a common language, agreed-upon codes of behaviour, and a shared sense of purpose. Only when cultures are well developed is there enough trust to support commercial and governmental institutions (Rifkin, 2001).

A cultural backlash to globalization has been evident at protests during G8 conferences, etc. This collectivity points to global corporations, such as Monsanto, AOL-Time Warner, McDonald's, and Merck, which are undermining cultural diversity and destroying the viability of local communities. Local cultures are reawakening worldwide. In India, consumers trashed McDonald's for violating Hindu dietary laws. In France, angry farmers uprooted Monsanto's genetically engineered crops, claiming they are a threat to French cultural sovereignty over food productions. In Canada, some local communities have fought to keep out Wal-Mart. They feared it would replace small-town culture with suburban superstores (Rifkin, 2001).

For Canadians who believe that globalization is a positive process, they would have been encouraged after reading the headline in *The Globe and Mail* on January 10, 2002, "Canada Jumps in Ranking on Globalization" (McKenna, 2002).

It appears that Canada has great potential in the capacity to manoeuvre and manage in a global context. It ranked seventh overall, ahead of the United States and France, as a society that is adapting best to globalization. The criteria included the degree of economic integration, the level and frequency of political engagement, personal contact with other people, and the use of technology, especially the Internet (Axworthy, 2003).

Changes in Social Institutions

The social institutions of the family, religion, education, health care, and welfare have undergone significant changes since the end of World War II. Among the many changes to the Canadian family have been the following:

- family size has decreased;

- the number of single-parent families has increased;

- common law marriage has become more common;

- same-sex relationships have been recognized;

- although the extended family is less important, an increasing number of grandparents are taking an active role in caring for their grandchildren. This care ranges from babysitting on a regular basis to raising them. This change can be attributed to increasing family pressures in which parents need support and to the increase in immigrant families in which a multigenerational household is more common;

- the family home is relocated quite frequently; and

- authority relationships have changed.

The Canadian divorce rate has fluctuated dramatically. Rates rose sharply in 1987 after changes to the federal law were introduced in 1986. By the late 1990s, though, rates were dropping. It may be that more people are choosing common law relationships, so the dissolution of their relationships does not show up in divorce statistics. It also may be that more people are separating without going through the formal step of divorce. The average age of first marriage has been rising since the early 1970s. In 1970, the average age of marriage in Canada was 25.1 for men and 22.7 for women (Vanier Institute of the Family, 1994). According to Statistics Canada (Mitchell, 1998), the average age of first marriage for men in 1996 was 29.3 years and for women, 27.3 years. The delay in marriage is delaying the starting of families.

Changes in People's Skill Levels

The demand for skilled workers in the population has grown tremendously in the last 20 years. As a result, more young people are staying in school and going to postsecondary institutions. Canada has also placed strict qualification restrictions on immigrants, requiring that they show they possess a skill that is in short supply in the country.

Changes in Beliefs and Values

A recent and growing trend has been a shift to economic conservatism, with an emphasis on cutting back expenditures rather than maintaining or increasing spending. In turn, society has adopted a more conservative attitude toward social programs; people are questioning the need for some programs and restricting the allocation of funds to many others. People also seem to be turning, or returning, to religious organizations in search of guidance in a society that offers less and less direction and purpose to daily living.

These social changes do not happen in abstraction; they have real physical, psychological, and emotional effects on individuals. Thomas Holmes (1967), a Seattle physician, theorized that the number of social changes an individual undergoes in a short period of time is directly related to the probability that the individual will contract a disease or suffer an injury. Holmes produced a social readjustment rating scale that assigns a score to every social change that an individual could undergo (see figure 9.2). For example, the most radical change is the death of a spouse, which is scored at 100; divorce is scored at 73; and even Christmas, during which some people change their habits, is scored at 12. It should be noted that Holmes was not concerned with whether a change in an individual's life was positive or negative; the general idea is that a sociological event (a change in living condition) has psychological and physiological effects (for example, stress, fatigue, strain, and overextension of bodily defence mechanisms). These effects hinder a person's ability to concentrate and hence increase the likelihood of an accident. They could also make the person so rundown that he or she would be more susceptible to disease. Perhaps the major value of Holmes's study is that it demonstrates that, although we may teach sociology, psychology, and physiology as independent disciplines, in the real world any phenomenon usually is an interaction of all three processes.

CHAPTER SUMMARY

Change is a constant, especially in societies that are already changing. Social changes and problems unnerve and dissatisfy people in various ways, and cause some of them to seek solutions to these problems. By banding together, they can often bring about change, but the result is rarely exactly what was intended, and so the whole cycle starts over again. Change is not an abstraction; it affects all of us socially, mentally, and even sometimes physically.

FIGURE 9.2   Scoring for the Holmes-Rahe Social Readjustment Scale

Less than 150 life change units = 30% chance of illness
150-299 life change units   = 50% chance of illness
300 or more life change units   = 80% chance of illness

Life events	Score
Death of spouse	100
Divorce	73
Marital separation from mate	65
Detention in jail, other institution	63
Death of a close family member	63
Major personal injury or illness	53
Marriage	50
Fired from work	47
Marital reconciliation	45
Retirement	45
Major change in health or behaviour of a family member	44
Pregnancy	40
Sexual difficulties	39
Gaining a new family member (e.g., through birth, adoption, oldster moving)	39
Major business re-adjustment (e.g., merger, bankruptcy)	39
Major change in financial status	38
Death of close friend	37
Change to different line of work	36
Major change in the number of arguments with spouse	35
Taking out a mortgage or loan for a major purchase	31
Foreclosure on a mortgage or loan	30
Major change in responsibilities at work	29
Son or daughter leaving home (e.g., marriage, college)	29
Trouble with in-laws	29
Outstanding personal achievement	28
Spouse beginning or ceasing to work outside the home	26
Beginning or ceasing formal schooling	26
Major change in living conditions	25
Revision of personal habits (dress, manners, friends)	24
Trouble with boss	23
Major change in working hours or conditions	20
Change in residence	20
Change to a new school	20
Major change in usual type and/or amount of recreation	19
Major change in church activities (a lot more or less)	19
Major change in social activities (clubs, movies, visits)	18
Taking out a mortgage or loan for a lesser purchase (e.g., car, TV, freezer)	17
Major change in sleeping habits	16
Major change in the number of family get-togethers	15
Major change in eating habits	15
Vacation	13
Christmas season	12
Minor violations of the law (e.g., traffic tickets)	11

Total _____

KEY TERMS

absolute deprivation	progress
alienation	reactionary social movement
automation	reform social movement
change agents	relative deprivation
community	revolutionary social movement
exurbanites	social change
formalization	social issue
gemeinschaft	social movement
gesellschaft	social problem
globalization	suburbanization
hinterland	urban planning
ideology	urban village
industrialization	urbanism
neighbourhood	urbanization
privatization	

REFERENCES

Axworthy, L. (2003). *Navigating a new world: Canada's global future*. Toronto: Alfred A. Knopf Canada.

Boyd, D. (2002, December). Seven modern-day wonders of the world. http://www.galtglobalreview.com/world/seven_wonders.html.

Holmes, T.H., & Rahe, R.H. (1967). The social readjustment rating scale. *Journal of Psychosomatic Research, 11*, 213-218.

McKenna, B. (2002, January 10). Canada jumps in ranking on globalization. *The Globe and Mail*, p. B8.

Mitchell, A. (1998, January 30). Divorce rate dives with cuts in legal aid. *The Globe and Mail*, pp. A1, A10.

Rifkin, J. (2001, July 2). World culture resists bowing to commerce. *Los Angeles Times*. Available at http://www.globalpolicy.org/ngos/role/globdem/globprot/2001/0702rifk.htm.

Tonnies, F. (1957). *Community and society*. East Lansing, MI: Michigan State University Press.

Vanier Institute of the Family. (1994, January). *Profiling Canada's families*. Ottawa: Author.

Wirth, L. (1938). Urbanism as a way of life. *American Journal of Sociology, 44*, 1-24.

Research Methods

All social sciences attempt to increase knowledge through the use of scientific techniques of inquiry. Sociology attempts to produce objective information about human interaction through the use of techniques that, at best, try to be scientific. This chapter discusses the nature of science, its applicability to sociology, the strategies and ethics of research, the techniques of social research, and the difficulties associated with doing research on and about humans.

THE IDEA OF A SOCIAL SCIENCE

In chapter 1, we showed how Durkheim had suggested that the rules of the scientific method could be applied to the study of social facts. If sociology can be called a science, it is a young science, and it is also what is known as a soft science. A soft science has no universally applicable laws; instead, it relies mostly on generalizations that seem to hold up most of the time and under most conditions. Durkheim's pioneering study of suicide, undertaken over 100 years ago, was very recent in comparison with the founding works in such disciplines as mathematics, astronomy, physics, medicine, and biology.

Few sociological research findings have been formulated, even approximately, into laws of human interaction. For the most part, we have to be satisfied with generalizations (such as 70 percent of abusive parents were abused as children), sequences (for example, given a family history of poor supervision, lack of affection and attention, harsh and inconsistent discipline, and lack of family integration, there is a 95 percent probability that a child will get in trouble with the law during adolescence), or correlation (such as automobile accidents increase in proportion to the amount of alcohol consumed).

Sociology may be relatively lacking in **hard data** (information gathered under the most rigorous of scientific procedures), but this does not mean that sociology is unscientific. Science is not a mystical entity; it is merely a way of doing things. Science is the pursuit of objective knowledge accumulated from observation. It is a method of systematically acquiring, ordering, interpreting, evaluating, and explaining information.

hard data
information gathered under the most rigorous of scientific procedures

STEPS IN THE SCIENTIFIC METHOD

1. Formulate the question to be answered or the problem to be solved.

2. Develop a **hypothesis** about the problem — that is, a statement that can be empirically tested.

hypothesis
a statement that can be empirically tested

3. Collect data that will test whether the hypothesis is supported or not supported.

4. Analyze and organize the data into generalizations, sequences, and correlations, and explain the significance of each.

5. Formulate a theory that explains all of the conclusions derived from an analysis of the data.

empiricism
the systematic gathering of evidence through observations and procedures that can be repeated and verified by others

Scientific knowledge is gained through the empirical approach. **Empiricism** is the systematic gathering of evidence through observations and procedures that can be repeated and verified by others. We can gain important ideas through discussion, argument, assertions, and opinions, but these ideas are not scientific without solid evidence gained by testing them. The scientific attitude, therefore, is skeptical; scientists need observable evidence to make objective assumptions. Evidence is gathered by testing these assumptions. To be tested appropriately, the assumptions must be precise. The test must also be reliable — that is, the observations must recur repeatedly under prescribed circumstances. To get useful information, then, the demands of testability, precision, and reliability must be met.

RECURRING RESEARCH ISSUES

Pure and Applied Sciences

pure science
the pursuit of new knowledge for the sake of increasing science's total store of knowledge

The pursuit of new knowledge for the sake of increasing science's total store of knowledge is called **pure science**. This basic research has no direct, practical benefit. Pure science seeks only to discover laws and generalizations. A study to see whether there is any social, psychological, or physical distinctiveness about a group of violence-prone people that is not found in the rest of society is an example of pure science. In contrast, applied science is the use of science to solve problems of immediate, practical importance. If we were able to identify a chemical imbalance in the study group that makes them prone to violence, then applied scientists could set about looking for ways to correct the chemical imbalance.

Should sociology be conducted as an applied or a pure science? Should sociologists simply generate new knowledge about human interaction and leave its applications to administrators, social workers, medical personnel, peace officers, policy makers, community planners, and advertising executives, or should sociologists play a direct role in the use of the knowledge? The answers to these questions are not easy, and are often a topic of debate.

Some argue that scientists are completely free of any responsibility for the uses to which the knowledge they generate is put; sociologists, as scientists, should stay ethically neutral. To be unaffected by the biases and preferences of interested parties and by any potential consequences of the use of scientific findings is to be **value-free**.

value-free
to be unaffected by the biases and preferences of interested parties and by any potential consequences of the use of scientific findings

Other scientists argue that no matter how hard you try, you simply cannot be value-free. You value the subject you are studying; otherwise, you would not have chosen it. In sorting needed from unneeded data, you pass a judgment, and usually you have to report to a supervising or financing body with its own interests. If it is not possible to remain value-free, then you should try to exercise some control over the uses to which your findings are put. Action involvement is the deliberate attempt by the scientist to exercise some control over the way in which his or her findings are used.

Laboratory or Field Settings

A **laboratory** is any situation or facility that is devoted solely to research. The researcher is able to maintain strict control over the situation. By its very nature, however, the situation is an artificial one. A question thus arises about the extent to which it is possible to generalize from this laboratory research to real-life situations. For example, will research subjects act naturally if they are aware that they are being observed? A **field setting** is an environment or situation that occurs naturally; the researcher visits this situation and observes behaviour in its "natural" environment.

In most human research, the participants know that they are being observed, and this awareness itself may produce changes in behaviour. Such change in behaviour was first noticed in a series of studies carried out at the Western Electric Plant at Hawthorne, Illinois. The studies were intended to examine factors that affected worker productivity. A group of workers were subjected to changes in temperature, lighting, work hours, and so on, and the subsequent effect on productivity was observed. The researchers noticed that no matter what they tried, even dimming the lights, an increase in productivity resulted. Something else, then, was affecting them. It soon became clear that awareness of being specially treated and being under scrutiny was having a greater effect than the environmental changes. Since the time of that series of studies, behaviour that results from the researcher's intervention rather than natural behaviour has been called the **Hawthorne effect**. We will later discuss ways in which researchers can avoid this outcome as much as possible.

The Truthfulness of Self-Reporting

Researchers who use self-reporting by subjects often assume that the responses are truthful. There remains the possibility, however, that the responses are not truthful; these are called response sets. There are three basic types of response sets:

1. A tendency to agree with the statements of an authority regardless of their content is called **response acquiescence** (or "yea saying").

2. A tendency to answer items in an uncommon direction, often in terms of what the respondent considers funny, is called **response deviation**.

3. A tendency to answer questions in a direction that the respondent considers is most socially acceptable, regardless of whether the answer is right or correct, is called **social desirability response**.

SOME BASIC CONCEPTS

Before we discuss the techniques and strategies used in social research, let us explain some basic concepts that will recur throughout this appendix.

One important distinction is that between the reliability and the validity of a research instrument. The questions surrounding both are important, whether the instrument is a mechanical or electronic device or a questionnaire. **Reliability** is the consistency with which an instrument measures a response or an effect when the

---

laboratory
any situation or facility that is devoted solely to research

field setting
an environment or situation that occurs naturally; the researcher visits this situation and observes behaviour in its "natural" environment

Hawthorne effect
behaviour that results from the researcher's intervention rather than natural behaviour

response acquiescence
a tendency to agree with the statements of an authority regardless of their content

response deviation
a tendency to answer items in an uncommon direction

social desirability response
a tendency to answer questions in a direction that the respondent considers most socially acceptable

reliability
the consistency with which an instrument measures a response or an effect when the instrument is used by the researcher again or by another researcher under the same conditions

validity
the degree to which a test actually measures what it says it measures

variable
a characteristic that can change or differ

independent variable
a variable that is thought to be a factor contributing to the cause of the outcome being studied

dependent variable
a variable that is thought to be the outcome or effect of the interaction of variables

intervening variable
a variable that distorts the hypothesized relationship between the independent and dependent variables

operational definition
a measurement that is meaningful for the purposes of an experiment

correlation
the measurement of interdependence among variables

positive correlation
a correlation between variables in which the variables either increase together or decrease together

inverse correlation
a correlation between variables in which one variable increases as the other decreases

spurious correlation
an apparent relationship between two variables that makes no sense

instrument is used by the researcher again or by another researcher under the same conditions. For example, if we wanted to test a person's reaction times, we could set up an experiment to see how quickly an individual can move his finger from one electronic button to another on a given signal. For this test to be considered reliable, we would have to ensure that the conditions are the same for all respondents and that we always fairly administer the test. The **validity** of a test is the degree to which a test actually measures what it says it measures. In our example, we would have to ascertain whether the movement of a finger from one electronic button to another is an accurate measure of reaction time.

Any given research study measures the interaction of variables. A **variable** is a characteristic that can change or differ. Variables can be almost anything about which you want to learn something: age, sex, race, social class, homicide rates, incidence of disease, divorce rates, market share, ethnicity, family violence, or consumer patterns. In any research study, the scientist must distinguish three types of variables: independent, dependent, and intervening. An **independent variable** is a variable that is thought to be a factor contributing to the cause of the outcome being studied. In our sample study of reaction times, we may hypothesize that age is an independent variable that causes reaction time to change. A **dependent variable** is a variable that is thought to be the outcome or effect of the interaction of variables. In our example, reaction time is the dependent variable. Sometimes, something seems to get in the way of a clear relationship between the independent and dependent variables and obscures the outcome. An **intervening variable** is a variable that distorts the hypothesized relationship between the independent and dependent variables. In our example, intervening variables could be fatigue, illness, or stress.

In the course of our research, we may find it useful to compare categories of independent variables against categories of dependent variables. For example, we may hypothesize that different age categories have slower or faster response rates. The difficulty we face in comparing one set of theoretical categories (young, middle-aged, and old respondents) with another (quick, medium, and slow reaction times) is making theoretical categories *measurable categories*. To do this, we produce what is called an **operational definition** — a measurement that is meaningful for the purposes of an experiment. Some such measurements are fairly standardized. For example, most psychologists and sociologists use 18–40 to define young adulthood, 40–65 to define middle age, and 65+ to constitute old age. Other measurements have to be adapted solely for the purpose of an ongoing experiment — for example, what constitutes a quick reaction time.

In a research study, the scientist often hopes to find a consistent relationship between independent and dependent variables. A **correlation** is the measurement of interdependence among variables. A **positive correlation** between variables is observed when the variables either increase together or decrease together. In our sample study of reaction times, there may be a positive correlation between fitness level and reaction time — that is, as fitness levels improve, reaction time quickens. An **inverse correlation** between variables is observed when one variable increases as the other decreases. In our example, as age increases, reaction time may slow. The fact that two variables are highly correlated does not necessarily mean that one causes another. A **spurious correlation** between variables is an apparent relationship between two variables that makes no sense. In our example, we could find that people wearing dark shirts have faster reaction times than people wearing light shirts. We would not want to conclude on the basis of this observation that the colour of one's shirt in any way is a reliable predictor of reaction time.

RESEARCH DESIGNS

Research designs can be divided into four basic types, although elements of more than one of these types can be found in some studies. Some designs produce harder data than others — that is, some collect data using more rigorous procedures than others. In the following discussion, we will look at designs in the order of the rigour of their procedures, and in the order of the data produced, from hardest to softest. The nature of the subject under study and such extraneous factors as time and money determine the research design to be used. As we shall see, it is often the case that the nature of sociological study makes the most rigorous research procedures, which produce the hardest data, unavailable to sociologists. The fourth type of research design, the descriptive survey, produces the softest data but is the most frequently used design in social research.

Planned Experiments

The planned experiment uses the most rigorous procedures of all research designs and produces the hardest data. However, it is rarely found in its pure form in social science research. For a study to be a true experiment, a number of conditions have to be met:

- The experimenter must be able to randomly assign research subjects to experimental procedures; some will be subjected to the procedure being tested, while others will be set aside as a comparison. In many social science studies, the subject matter being investigated is controversial, socially undesirable, or even sociopathological. It is clearly unethical to randomly assign subjects to such states as dysfunctional families, alcoholism, abusive behaviour, or sexual deviation just to study outcomes.

- The experimenter has to be aware of all the variables that may affect the outcome of the study. Because sociologists study human beings and human states, it is probably impossible to know everything that is currently affecting the performance and behaviour of research subjects. For example, your ability to understand this section of the chapter may depend on your prior educational experience, your attitude toward sociology in general, whether you studied last night, whether you have the flu, or any number of other possible conditions.

- The experimenter has to be able to control and manipulate all of the independent variables and to observe the effect of this manipulation on the dependent variable. In studies of human beings and human states, it is not possible to know all such variables, so sociologists cannot manipulate experimental variables as other scientists can. Even if sociologists did know all such variables, it would be very difficult to control such things as feelings of grief, levels of stress, and attention spans. And even if sociologists could overcome these obstacles, there would remain the major ethical problem of not having the right to exercise such a degree of behavioural control over fellow humans.

Because of the conditions that have to be met, experimental designs are often not available to sociologists. Some designs that purport to be experiments do not meet these conditions. Consequently, sociologists often have to use another type of research design — most frequently, a longitudinal study.

Longitudinal Designs

cohort
a group of people of similar social standing, usually the same age group

Longitudinal studies, sometimes also called prospective studies, typically follow one or more **cohorts** (a group of people of similar social standing, usually the same age group) over a period of time. The study measures changes in the group and attempts to explain what has caused or influenced the change. This change factor could be a natural consequence of the passage of time — for example, an illness — or something introduced by the researcher — for example, a new educational technique. The starting point of the study is usually referred to as T1 and the end point as T2. The group is tested at T1 in its **initial state** and tested again at T2 in its **subsequent state**. The period of time used in the study varies depending on the nature of the study. Studying the effects of a headache tablet may only take 15 minutes, whereas studying the effects of a college program on a student's behaviour and attitudes may take a number of years.

initial state
the condition of a group at the prescribed starting point (T1) of a study

subsequent state
the condition of a group at the prescribed end point (T2) of a study

In a longitudinal or prospective study, subjects can be allocated to groups. For example, in a study of recidivism rates, one group of subjects can be those in jail for a year and another can be those on probation. At the end of the study period, the groups can be tested to see which group has the lower recidivism rate.

There are several drawbacks to longitudinal research design:

- It is complicated to execute.

- It can take a long time.

- It can be expensive.

- Subjects may drop out of the study as time goes on: they can relocate, become ill, die, or simply decide that it is not something that they want to do anymore.

- If the subjects who remain in the study group differ significantly from those who leave, there is a risk that the sample will be biased or skewed.

- The longer the study runs, the more likely it is that the research staff will change, impairing continuity.

Retrospective Designs (Ex Post Facto Studies)

Sometimes, it is not possible to study an event until after it has taken place — for example, the spread of disease, incidents of juvenile crime, or dropping out of school. In a retrospective or *ex post facto* (after the fact) study, the researcher starts at T2 (the end point in a longitudinal study) and searches back through records, people's memories, case histories, etc., to discover the event or condition (T1) that has led to certain effects on one group and not on another.

Retrospective studies are open to mistakes and distortions because researchers must rely on records and memories. Memories are fallible; people forget things that happened even a short time ago, let alone years ago. People also have selective memories — that is, they reinterpret the past on the basis of current information. Records can have omissions, contain inaccurate transcriptions, or simply be lost. Even with these shortcomings, retrospective studies are sometimes the only type of design available if the event being studied has already occurred.

Descriptive Surveys (Cross-Sectional Studies)

Most sociological studies take the form of a survey that indicates what a segment of society is like at the point in time of its study. Cross-sectional studies require less time and are less expensive than longitudinal studies and are therefore more common. They do not demand continuity or long-term cooperation among subjects or researchers and are therefore easier to execute. However, cross-sectional studies lack a temporal perspective; they produce, in effect, a snapshot of a segment of society at one point in time. This data slice fails to show how and why a segment of society changes over time.

In a cross-sectional study, the researcher asks a list of questions of an appropriate group of people to ascertain what is going on. There are some severe limitations to this design:

- It describes only the segment of society being studied and can only approximately suggest whether the findings are relevant to the whole society.

- It is accurate only for the point in time of study. Attitudes, behaviours, and values change, so even the group being studied may not produce the same responses at another point in time.

- From the data collected only recurring correlations, not causes, can be observed.

In a later section of this chapter, we examine in greater depth three types of descriptive surveys: interviews, questionnaires, and observational studies.

Combining Designs

To get around some of the weaknesses of the different types of research designs, researchers often combine elements of more than one type of design. Two examples of combined designs are time-lag designs and sequential designs.

TIME-LAG DESIGN

The time-lag design is used when a researcher wants to compare people of the same age, but at different times. It addresses problems of the influences on behaviour of cultural and historic factors as people of different cohorts are examined. For example, a study might compare the morals of 20-year-old college students in 1968 and the morals of today's 20-year-old students. Age is held constant and historic eras are compared. This is a retrospective study with a cross-sectional design.

SEQUENTIAL DESIGN

The sequential design begins with a cross-sectional study using several groups of people of different ages. Months or years after the original test, the same groups of people are retested as in a longitudinal study. Simultaneously, a new group of people are tested at each age level in order to control for changes that may have occurred in the original group because of dropping out, the effects of retesting, or of experiences peculiar to a cohort. This research method combines elements of cross-sectional and longitudinal designs.

INITIATING RESEARCH

A good starting point for any piece of research is to write out a proposal. A proposal is mandatory if you are applying for a grant, but it is still a good idea even if you are doing it for your own enlightenment. The proposal will lend structure and direction to your research. There are five major steps in putting together a research proposal:

1. *State your objective and research question clearly and precisely*   Once you have ideas to pursue, questions to answer, or hypotheses to test, write down these thoughts in detail. As you look through this detailed description, formulate, as clearly as you can, what you wish to gain by doing this study. Write out this objective as precisely as possible. List some questions you want to answer in your study. If you list 10 or more questions, your study either is too vague or is in reality more than one study. Check with others to see whether they think your objective is clear, your project is feasible, and your questions are appropriate.

2. *Do a thorough background literature search*   Background research will tell you if the kind of study that you want to do has already been done. Background research will also help you to shape your study questions more precisely as you see them in the light of other research. When you have reviewed the background literature, do a brief writeup, concentrating on those elements that are most directly related to your own research. If you are not breaking new ground, show how your research throws new light on old problems or how your new approach will be more beneficial to clients or others.

   Background reading should include all relevant materials. You should search out any laws that surround the issue that you are studying, previous research reported in professional journals, social commentary in magazines or on TV, experiences of people who have worked in the field. You can even use anecdotal evidence such as novels, autobiographies, and diaries. Remember that different types of information have different levels of validity. *Primary sources* — the findings of properly constructed research — provide the strongest data. *Secondary sources* include reports from institutions specifically set up to deal with a social phenomenon. *Tertiary sources* provide the weakest information, usually in the form of anecdotes. Many useful insights can be derived from tertiary sources, but they must not be thought of as scientific fact.

   There is much useful information around on just about every aspect of society, and it is often already in statistical form. All agencies that are specifically set up to deal with one aspect of society publish official statistics in the form of monthly, quarterly, and/or annual reports. Among these agencies are police, hospitals, social service agencies, the registrar general, the census bureau, the city directory, governments (municipal, provincial, and federal), and the United Nations. Newspapers, magazines, TV programs, periodicals, popular journals, and historical novels all contain information on social phenomena of varying degrees of reliability and validity. All should be researched.

3. *Always have a general strategy in mind*   Your objective and research questions will usually shape your strategy. Decide whether your research will take the form of a survey, an observational study, a longitudinal study, or another kind of study. If there is more than one strategy that is possible, which is most practical in terms of time, cost, level of difficulty, labour, etc.?

4. *Outline in advance what you will consider the successful conclusion of your study*   Put these criteria into exact numbers, and be prepared to defend your criteria for success — they cannot be arbitrary. For example, if a minimum of 70 percent of respondents report having experienced a phenomenon at least twice in the last 12 months, then this will have been shown to be a significant happening.

5. *Keep the proposal part of the research as concise and as precise as possible*   Unnecessarily long research proposals tend to indicate a lack of effective communication and clarity of thought on the part of the researcher. As part of the process of writing your research proposal, keep appendices and supporting documents to a minimum.

THE STRUCTURE OF SOCIAL RESEARCH

1. Topic Selection and Hypothesis Formulation

The first stage of any research is the selection of a topic. The best topics come out of your own interests. A good topic will strike you as provocative and full of possibilities, and it will give you a chance to deepen your knowledge about something that already interests you or that you feel you should know more about. Having selected your topic, you will then have to develop your thesis about the topic, and from this generate a testable hypothesis. A *thesis* is a brief statement of your main beliefs about your topic. A *hypothesis* is a statement of what you expect to find from your research, stated in such a way that it directs your research by suggesting a relationship between two variables that can be tested. For example, your hypothesis could be, "College students who participate in varsity sports have a lower dropout rate than those who don't." You can now start deciding what kind of information you will need to either support or to reject your hypothesis.

2. Population Definition

Once you have decided on your hypothesis, you then ask yourself, "Who are the people whom I need to study to get the desired results"? The total number of people who could be included in the study is called the **population**. The population is usually defined by the hypothesis. In our example of varsity sports and dropout rates, the population is full-time college students, because only full-time students are allowed to play varsity sports. In most studies, it is impossible to study the total

population
the total number of people who could be included in a study

population because of limits on time, effort, and money. For example, there might be about 5000 full-time students at just one college, and well over 100 000 full-time students at all Ontario colleges. However, there are occasions when you will want to take what is called a *total sample* — that is, study the whole population.

3. Sample Generation

sample
a small group taken from the population in such a way as to represent that population

More often than not, we study a sample of the population. A **sample** is a small group taken from the population in such a way as to represent that population. The idea is that anything that we find out about the sample should also hold true for the population. The sample has to be taken from the population. In our example of varsity and dropout rates, all sample members must be full-time college students. The problematic part of taking a sample is ensuring that it is representative of the population. To do this, one of three different types of samples can be drawn:

random sample
a sample drawn purely by chance, in which every member of the population has an exactly equal chance of being selected

1. A **random sample** is a sample drawn purely by chance so that every member of the population has an exactly equal chance of being selected. To take a random sample, you have to know exactly who is in the population so that they can be given their equal chance of selection. In our example, it is possible to get a complete list of all full-time students at a particular college. We could take a total sample, but since there are, say, only 100 varsity athletes, we could simply compare them with 100 other students. Therefore, we would sample 100 out of 5000 students. That is, we would take a 100/5000, or 1/50, sample. There are a number of ways of doing this. For example, we could list all 5000 names on 5000 slips of paper and pull 100 out of a hat, or we could assign each name a number from 0001 to 5000 and ask a computer to randomly generate 100 numbers from 1 to 5000, and then pick those names whose numbers correspond to the computer-generated set of numbers. A random sample is the most scientifically valid kind of sample because there is no possibility of the researcher interfering in any way in who is and is not selected. However, some difficulties can arise with random sampling. If we are randomly selecting 100 from 5000, then it logically follows that any given 100 people have an exactly equal chance of being selected as any other 100 people. How useful is our sample, for comparison purposes, if we draw 100 male technology students yet we know that 50 percent of varsity athletes are female and only 25 percent of varsity athletes come from technology courses? Such a bias in a random sample suggests that we sometimes do need some control over who becomes part of a study.

stratified random sample
a random sample that includes categories of people who are most important to a study; these categories are represented proportionately within the whole sample, yet within each category subjects are randomly sampled

2. A **stratified random sample** is a random sample that includes categories of people who are most important to a study; these categories are represented proportionately within the whole sample, yet within each category subjects are randomly sampled. For example, if we know that there are 500 male business students among our 5000 students — that is, that they make up 10 percent of the population — then we want to ensure that 10 percent of our sample (of 100) are male business students. We would put the names of the 500 business students into a hat and draw 10 of them out at random. We would repeat this process for female business students,

male and female applied arts students, male and female health sciences students, and so on. Hence, each group is proportionately represented (the stratified part) but within categories the participants have been randomly selected.

3. Sometimes we have no way of knowing the individual names of everyone who could be included in the study, or it is just too inconvenient in terms of time, effort, and money to keep tabs on the randomization process. In this case, we could resort to a **quota sample** — a sampling technique in which the first given number of people encountered who fit the research criteria are included in the sample. We can get a little more sophisticated than just telling interviewers to get a certain number of respondents. We can, for example, tell one interviewer to get responses from the first 10 male business students that he or she encounters, another to study the first 7 female health sciences students that he or she encounters, and so on.

There are a number of advantages to quota sampling. You always get a 100 percent response; if someone refuses to be included in your study, you just move on to the next person who fits your criteria, and you keep going until you have filled your quota. Quota sampling is cheap — it requires no expensive computer generation of random numbers; it is quick — time is not wasted fine-tuning who is and who is not eligible for random selection to complete your population list; and it is easy — just hit the streets, the mall, the cafeteria, and so on and do it.

There are also a number of serious disadvantages to quota sampling. There is no way of knowing whether a sample is representative of the population. Certain types of people congregate at certain places at specific times of day, so samples taken at those times may overrepresent certain groups. Because quota sampling requires that people be approached personally rather than chosen randomly (by computer, for example), it inevitably involves **selection bias** — the unconscious tendency of any individual to prefer some people to others. Hence, certain types of people are more likely than others to be included in a quota sample.

4. Comparison Group Allocation

Once a sample has been generated, the next task is often to allocate them into two separate groups for the purpose of the study. Only one of these groups will be subjected to the process being studied; the other group will be encouraged to carry on behaving in some traditional pattern to serve as a comparison group. The new procedure that is being tested is called the **manoeuvre**. The **experimental group** is the group that undergoes the manoeuvre. The **control group** is a comparison group as similar to the experimental group as possible except that it does not undergo the manoeuvre. Dividing the sample into experimental and control groups is called **allocation**.

This allocation process can be achieved by one of a number of means. We could randomly allocate by drawing the names out of a hat and alternately placing names in the control group and in the experimental group. We could use a system called **matched pairs** in which one of two subjects who are as alike as possible is allocated to the experimental group and one to the control group. Identical twins are

quota sample
a sampling technique in which the first given number of people encountered who fit the research criteria are included in the sample

selection bias
the unconscious tendency of any individual to prefer some people to others

manoeuvre
a procedure being tested

experimental group
the group of subjects in a study who undergo a manoeuvre

control group
a comparison group of subjects in a study who do not undergo a manoeuvre

allocation
the process of dividing a sample into experimental and control groups

matched pairs
a type of allocation in which one of two subjects who are as alike as possible is allocated to the experimental group and one to the control group

natural selection
a type of allocation in which individuals are allocated to the experimental group or the control group on the basis of whether they are subjected to a phenomenon or not

the perfect example of matched pairs. Finally, we could let **natural selection** occur. That is, we could wait to see which individuals are subjected to a phenomenon and which are not; the first are the experimental group and the remainder are the control group. In our example of varsity sports and dropout rates, those who participate in varsity sports are the experimental group and those who do not participate are the control group, because varsity sports participation is the manoeuvre under study.

5. Testing and Comparative Measurement

Once the comparison groups have been selected, their status on entering the study has to be established. Thus, the two groups are tested at the time of entry (T1) into the study to establish their initial state. In our example of varsity sports and dropout rates, we would probably want to know more than just whether they want to participate in varsity sports or not. We would also measure other factors that might contribute to college dropout rates, such as whether they have part-time jobs, what their high school grades were, their reasons for enrolling in a particular course of study, and so on.

Once the comparison groups have been subjected to the manoeuvre (for example, one school year), their subsequent state at the designated conclusion of the study (T2) is measured. The subsequent state of each group is compared with its initial state to see which group has changed more. Even a control group that has been subjected to a placebo (a course of action that is not supposed to produce any change) may change its status somewhat. The important point is to see which group has changed more.

6. Conclusions and Recommendations

Once these comparative measures have been obtained, it is now possible to start writing conclusions about the observed data. These conclusions should, initially, be confined to statements of what the facts demonstrate; they should not attempt to evaluate the procedure. Once the facts of the case have been stated, you can then infer how much of the result is due to real differences and how much may be due to outside interference, such as the design of the study. Having stated your conclusions and discussed their acceptability, you now can make recommendations on practical courses of action that may follow from your conclusions.

In our example of varsity sports and dropout rates, if we find that varsity athletes have significantly lower dropout rates than other students, we would want to investigate whether the conclusion was a result of the way we drew our sample of non-varsity athletes, or whether varsity athletes were "taken care of" to ensure their continued eligibility. If we found we could dismiss these latter speculations as non-factors in the research, we would have to consider the practical use of this information. Because it is logically, economically, and physically impossible to make all students into varsity athletes, we would have to determine what it is about varsity athletics that keeps people in school. Maybe it is not the nature of sports, but the extra meaning they give to attendance at school. If this is true, then we can start to investigate what other kinds of activities might fulfill the same role for other students, and then set up programs to get them involved. Thus, we see another facet of research — the completion of one study often leads to new questions to investigate and new studies to pursue. In fact, this is the nature of science itself.

METHODS OF DATA COLLECTION

There are many ways in which sociologists collect data to test hypotheses. In the following section, we look at some of the more common techniques. We start by considering the informal or "soft" methods, whose primary function is to point the researcher in the right direction and to initiate ideas about the appropriate questions to ask in a subsequent, more formal study. There are times, however, when informal, less reliable techniques are the only ones available to the researcher. After considering some informal methods, we examine some more formal methods that yield "harder" data.

Informal Methods

KEY INFORMANTS

A **key informant** is an individual who has been enmeshed in a social situation for a long period of time and who makes it his or her business to be aware of all the activities of the group. The social situation in question could be a workplace, a community, a neighbourhood, a family, a church, or a sports team. A key informant can, in a colloquial fashion, provide the researcher with important information to set up the study. For example, if you want to examine family ties in a small rural community, supposing them to be very close-knit, you might casually interview an elder of the village. In the course of your conversation, he informs you that "Those young'uns that don't move to the city spend all their time visiting it, and when they move there they don't visit home as much as they should." From this statement you formulate a series of hypotheses about the migration patterns and changing value systems of young rural dwellers, the impact of urbanism on family relationships and the probability that rural communities will have an increasingly "old" population. Needless to say, you have to verify this information with more solid evidence, because your key informant may simply be a gossip voicing the old lament that things aren't what they used to be; or maybe his opinion about young people of the village reflects his family situation but not everybody's. However, you still have managed to frame some questions that are worth investigating.

key informant
an individual who has been enmeshed in a social situation for a long period of time and who makes it his or her business to be aware of all the activities of the group

LETTERS AND DIARIES

A researcher who is interested in studying something in the fairly distant past may have to rely on the informal written communications of that time. For example, you could be researching the adaptation of a group to a new country of residence and want to trace some of the changes over time. By examining the changing tone of letters and diaries of the group, you may be able to trace a path of increasing acculturation as you come across fewer references to what they miss and more references to the things they have and do in their new environment.

There are limitations in the use of letters and diaries as a research tool. Only a limited portion of the population write letters and even fewer keep diaries. You have to question whether the letter writers are representative of the whole population. Perhaps the people who wrote were unusually prone to melancholy and nostalgia, while those who did not write adapted more quickly and had no time to write. Another important facet of letter writing to keep in mind when using letters as a research tool is that people often state things in a way that they think their recipient wants to hear. For example, they may play up their homesickness in order to emphasize to the people they left behind that they are missed.

The method used for the analysis of documentary evidence is called content analysis. **Content analysis** is the search for recurring themes in documents. The researcher decides on the "units" to be measured — for example, references to homesickness — and then examines documents for the frequency of references and their intensity, counting the ones that are clear and unambiguous.

content analysis
the search for recurring
themes in documents

CASE NOTES AND RECORDS

One way to carry out *ex post facto* studies is to analyze data such as social workers' case notes, medical records, judicial dispositions, probation officers' files, and student records. Most of these documents contain a large amount of quantifiable data or can be subjected to content analysis. Some of them, especially case notes, tend to be highly subjective and unsystematic. No two recorders take their notes in the same way, and some miss data or record inaccurately. Many of the idiosyncrasies that make case notes and records somewhat problematic as research tools are being minimized by the increasing use of computers in record keeping. The demands of computerization ensure that record keeping is systematic and rigorous.

CASE STUDIES

case study
a detailed description,
including a longitudinal
investigation, of an
individual rather than
a cohort

The **case study** is a detailed description, including a longitudinal investigation, of an individual rather than a cohort. The main drawback of case studies is that the information they provide about individuals may not pertain to the population, and thus generalized conclusions may not be drawn from the results. However, case studies may provide some evidence of a phenomenon that warrants further study.

Observational Studies

If the subjects to be studied form a group that tends to gather together in a specific place for an extended period of time, the best way of studying them may be to directly observe their behaviour. Many groups can and have been studied in this way. Small villages, neighbourhoods, work groups, children in play groups, school classes, inmates of institutions, primitive tribes, hospital patients, street gangs, and sports teams are just a few of the groups that have been studied. In conducting an observational study, the researcher can either become an active member of the group or observe the group from its perimeter.

open observation
an observational method
in which the researcher
informs the group that
they are being studied

closed observation
an observational method
in which the researcher
studies the group without
their knowledge

The researcher must also decide whether to conduct **open observation** — that is, inform the group that they are being studied — or **closed observation** — study the group without their knowledge. With open observation, you run the risk that your presence and the subjects' knowledge that they are being studied will alter the very behaviour that you hope to study in its natural environment; you also run the risk that the group will be hostile to your endeavours. If you present yourself appropriately, the group is likely to accept you. You should delay recording your observations until your presence is taken for granted. People cannot act outside of their normative pattern for long. You can then pursue your study in greater ethical comfort, because you will not be spying. With closed observation, unless you are screened completely from the subjects, you are likely to be somewhat visible, perhaps simply as a stranger. Because strangers unwittingly alter the behaviour of a settled group, not as much as knowledge that they are being studied does, but still enough, it is advisable to delay recording your observations for a time. If, in the course of a closed study, some of the subjects gain knowledge that they are being studied, the disruption may irreparably skew the study results, and may well imperil the researcher. Many social scientists object to closed studies on the ground that they are a form of spying.

PARTICIPANT OBSERVATION

When the researcher plays an active role in the group being studied, the technique is called participant observation. By taking an active role in the group, the researcher usually achieves a much deeper insight into what drives the group's behaviour. Participant observation entails a number of risks and difficulties. By becoming emotionally attached to the group being studied, the researcher may lose his or her objectivity. If the researcher sees that the group is taking a course of action that will have serious negative consequences and so, as a "friend," intercedes on their behalf, the researcher has failed in her or his goal as a researcher — to observe the natural history of the group. If, however, the researcher stands by and objectively observes while the group self-destructs, then the researcher is faced with her or his own conscience and the awareness that some action could have rescued the group.

NON-PARTICIPANT OBSERVATION

In some cases, it is not possible for the social scientist to become an active member of the group being studied. Children's play groups, for example, would be very difficult for a full-grown adult to penetrate. Such studies have to be undertaken as non-participant observation — that is, a research method in which the researcher observes the activities of the group being studied as an outsider. It is much easier to maintain impartiality as an outside observer than as an active participant, but losing the ability to feel things as the group feels them and see things as they see them takes away from the depth of the study.

DATA RECORDING IN OBSERVATIONAL STUDIES

Recording data in both participant and non-participant observational studies presents some difficulties. It is sometimes difficult, especially in closed studies, to record data at the exact time that the behaviour of interest actually occurs. This does not mean that data collecting is unsystematic. Before the study begins, devices for recording data are set up and decisions about the recording procedure are made. It is important to note here that in all study designs, of all sciences, these methodological decisions have to be made before the onset of the study.

SOCIO-METRIC DIAGRAMS   If the group being studied meets at a certain spot all the time, the researcher could start with a drawing of the location. A school classroom, a daycare centre, a hospital ward, and so on can be diagrammed very easily. The researcher makes multiple copies of the diagram and, at periodic intervals, draws figures representing specific people to show who is interacting with whom and in what location. It is difficult to represent phenomena like the intensity of the interaction, but a resourceful researcher can invent symbols to represent such things. Over time, these diagrams indicate trends in the relationships between individuals in the group.

TIME-SAMPLE CHARTS Time-sample charting involves splitting the day into appropriate time periods (for example, 30-minute intervals) and then randomly selecting from each time period a shorter period (for example, a 5-minute spell). The activities and interrelationships of the subject group in that shorter spell are charted, and every longer period is sampled in this fashion for the length of the study. The chart may look like table 10.1. Other techniques available include notebook jottings, diaries, and tape recordings.

Survey Research

Often it is not possible to directly observe the behaviour of the sample group, especially if they are a more widespread cross-section of the society. To get around this difficulty, the researcher has to rely on the actors' reports of their own actions, which usually take the form of answers to a set of diagnostic questions. Survey research may also be preferred in studies of private behaviour that it would be inappropriate to observe, or when direct observation could be used but a survey would be significantly cheaper and quicker. Surveys usually take the form of questionnaires or interviews. The distinctions between questionnaires and interviews are discussed further below. Both techniques essentially involve putting a series of questions to a sample of the population for their response.

PRINCIPLES OF SURVEY RESEARCH

informed consent
a research requirement that ensures that subjects know the nature of the research and are willing participants in it

1. Respondents are allowed **informed consent** — a research requirement that ensures that subjects know the nature of the research and are willing participants in it. The obtaining of consent usually takes the form of a written or spoken preamble to the survey that outlines in general terms what the survey is about, why it is being done, for whom it is being done, who is being questioned, and to what use the results will be put. During this preamble, it is usual to emphasize to respondents that participation in the study is purely voluntary and that, while their involvement would be greatly appreciated, they retain the right to say no.

guaranteed anonymity
a research requirement that assures subjects that their responses will be kept confidential

2. Respondents must also be **guaranteed anonymity** — that is, they must be assured that their responses will be kept confidential. Nobody should be able to isolate and identify the response of an individual. All data will be presented in categories of responses, not individual ones.

3. Questions should be sequenced appropriately. Two principles apply here. First, the independent variables of the study should be listed before the dependent ones. Second, easy-to-answer questions should be listed first, followed by the more difficult, abstract, and personal questions. Because independent variables tend to consist of data such as age, sex, and occupation (and are therefore easily stated), and dependent variables tend to be based on opinions, behaviours, and attitudes (and are therefore more difficult to elicit), the two elements of survey design almost always coincide.

TABLE 10.1   Time-Sample Chart

Time	Individual	Interactions	Interaction type
0835	Jack Frost	Santa & elves	Winter sports
0915	Rin Tin Tin	Snoopy & Lassie	Fire hydrant assessment

QUESTIONNAIRES

A **questionnaire** is an organized, systematic printed list of questions. The questionnaire is distributed to a sample of respondents either by hand or by mail. Respondents fill in answers to the questions in private, and then hand or mail the document back.

The questionnaire approach has a number of advantages. Large numbers of people may be surveyed fairly easily at minimal expense. The data from questionnaires are standardized and easy to summarize. Respondents mark their own answers and are given written instructions, which minimizes the recruitment, training, and travel of research assistants. The questionnaire is an excellent assurance of anonymity: respondents answer in private and their completed documents are handed in with a multitude of others. This confidentiality encourages honest completion.

The questionnaire approach also has a number of disadvantages. Questions can be misunderstood, and with no researcher present to explain further, the question may go unanswered or be "incorrectly" answered. The omission of a significant question from the questionnaire may not come to light until the study is close to completion.

A serious and growing problem with questionnaires is **non-response** — the unwillingness of subjects to participate in a survey. Statistical estimates suggest that an absolute minimum of 75 percent return is needed for the results of a questionnaire to be considered valid. Increasingly, the initial return rate is below 40 percent. The researcher has to follow up by phoning all members of the sample, asking them if they have returned their questionnaire; if they have, the researcher crosses them off the list of non-respondents; if they have not, the researcher must ask them to complete and return their questionnaire. A number of successive bouts of phoning around, gradually whittling down the list of non-respondents, is often necessary to obtain a decent return rate. The time and cost needed to do such followups must be planned for in the original research design. Even if 80 percent of the questionnaires are returned, the researcher is left with the nagging doubt that the remaining 20 percent may be a very important response group that would have dramatically changed the overall results. Maybe the fact that they did not respond is a significant statement about the issue being studied.

INTERVIEWS

In an interview, the printed list of questions that would make up a questionnaire is called an interview schedule. The **interview** itself is the face-to-face encounter in which the researcher asks a question, the subject verbally responds, and the researcher records the response. The response rate for interviews tends to be initially much higher than that for questionnaires. A living person may be harder to resist than a sheet of paper that can be placed in a drawer and lost forever. An interview can be structured in such a way as to allow the researcher to explain misunderstood questions or to provide supplementary questions if something new and unprovided for comes up. Thus, the interview provides the researcher with greater flexibility in questioning respondents.

questionnaire
an organized, systematic printed list of questions

non-response
the unwillingness of subjects to participate in a survey

interview
a face-to-face research encounter in which a researcher asks a question, the subject verbally responds, and the researcher records the response

The researcher conducting interviews has to be conscious of a variety of personal biases. Respondents in an interview situation know that the results are not completely anonymous — that is, the interviewer knows how they have answered. As a result, respondents may provide misinformation or omit data deliberately to avoid social embarrassment. Respondents may also respond personally to the interviewer on the basis of favourable or unfavourable impressions of the researcher's appearance, clothing style, or demeanour. Respondents may also provide distorted answers if they respond to questions as they imagine the interviewer wants them to. Face-to-face respondents are more likely to opt for socially acceptable answers to questions, especially if their true feelings are not in line with general public opinion.

A further difficulty associated with the interview process is that information can be lost or misconstrued in a variety of ways: through the interviewer's understanding of the questions, his or her ability to communicate them, the respondents' understanding of the questions, their ability to enunciate an answer, the interviewer's understanding of the respondents' answers, and his or her ability to record the answer accurately. To guard against miscommunication, interviewers have to be adequately trained to ensure that they understand the questions to be asked; that they do not inadvertently communicate (by facial expression, body posture, or tone of voice) to respondents their own feelings about the issue; and that their communication of the question is clear and understandable. These measures cannot, however, ensure that respondents hear and understand the question correctly. When respondents communicate their response, it is important that the interviewer understand the response clearly and record it accurately.

Personal interviews that follow a systematic sampling plan will provide solid data if a number of checks are carried out:

- To ensure that quality information is obtained, interviewers should be provided with detailed training.

- Practice sessions in which interviewers can be evaluated should be conducted.

- Interviewers should be given precise instructions concerning how to recruit respondents and conduct the interview.

- All interviews must be conducted in a consistent manner.

- The senior researchers can re-interview a subsample of the subjects.

Although the interview approach is more expensive than questionnaires, it is more flexible and has the potential to yield more accurate data. Interviewers can explain the purpose of the investigation to respondents, establish rapport, discuss the interview, and respond to questions at any time. These factors will aid in cooperation. Interviewers can listen to responses and simultaneously observe respondents. Facial expression, tone of voice, and body language can be assessed to supplement the information, especially with regard to the veracity of the responses.

DIFFICULTIES IN DRAWING UP QUESTIONNAIRES AND INTERVIEW SCHEDULES

TYPE OF QUESTIONS   You must choose between structured, *forced-choice* questions and unstructured, *open-ended* questions. Forced-choice questions provide a question and a series of alternative answers from which respondents must select one (unless the nature of the study allows more than one alternative answer). The advantage of forced-choice questioning is that the answers are easily categorized and quantified: it is simply a matter of adding up the way certain types of people answered and comparing their answers with the answers given by other types of people. The disadvantage of forced-choice questioning is that the only answers elicited are those that you have set; there is no flexibility, even though some respondents may want to answer a question in an unanticipated way. Open-ended questions allow this flexibility; you write them in such a way that respondents can answer at length if they want to, not just by checking off a box. Open-ended questioning may elicit useful information that you have not even thought about. However, this approach requires extensive content analysis to quantify the data, which is a time-consuming and difficult process.

LOADED WORDS   You must avoid phrasing questions using words that may produce overly emotional reactions from respondents. Many words carry significance, sometimes positive, sometimes negative, even if you intend to use them in a denotative, non-threatening way. Such words include "drugs," "gay," "strike," "boss," and "bureaucracy." Titles and professions may also conjure up emotional responses that are strongly positive or negative depending on the respondent. Professions such as lawyer, politician, psychiatrist, and doctor often produce this kind of reaction.

INAPPROPRIATE RESPONSE CATEGORIES   A number of things can go wrong when you set up response categories in a forced-choice questionnaire or interview. There are two reasons to avoid using loaded words as response categories: (1) some respondents might automatically shun categories that use loaded words; and (2) some respondents might see such categories as safe havens that give them an easy and secure option. Often, terms like "average" and "adequate" will attract respondents when they are set in the centre of a continuum of possible answers. If possible, avoid providing safe, middle-ground answer categories. Also be sure to set up clearly visible, accurately aligned answer categories; if the questions are open-ended, leave sufficient space to communicate to respondents that you are expecting more than a one-word answer.

LEADING QUESTIONS   Avoid phrasing questions in such a way as to suggest that respondents should answer in a socially accepted way or to indicate an expected behaviour pattern. If you ask a group of parents, "How much time do you devote to helping your children with homework?" it becomes virtually impossible to say "None." Instead, ask two questions: "Is it appropriate for parents to involve themselves in a child's homework?" and "If yes, how much is an appropriate time for a parent to be involved?" Similarly, only a grouch would say "No" to a question such as, "Are you in favour of extending services available to senior citizens?" Such a question is known as a *motherhood statement*. If you specify that these extended services involve a full-scale recreation centre that will be opened on the respondent's block, at municipal taxpayers' sole expense, and will replace the preschool and ball diamonds that were originally planned for the neighbourhood, the response may be somewhat different.

Keep your questions as simple, short, and straightforward as possible. If a question seems long and complex to you, it will almost certainly be too long and too complex for respondents; if possible, break it down into a couple of questions. Also avoid questions that may annoy, embarrass, or antagonize respondents. For example, questions about income or use of intoxicants may be problematic for many people.

VAGUE WORDING   Peruse your questions to ensure that the wording is clear and concise. Many words can be ambiguous; as simple a word as "you" can be either single or plural. For example, a seemingly straightforward question like, "How often have you used the library in the last two months?" is actually vague and ambiguous. First, "you" may be singular or plural. Second, the verb "used," to some respondents, could mean "walked in to check the football scores," whereas you meant "sat down and studied for a certain period of time." Third, "library" is not specified; you may mean "college library," but respondents may think "public library." Finally, "last two months" is not a specific time period but a relative one; it depends on when the respondent is answering the questionnaire. Let's rephrase the question: "How often did you personally study (for more than 30 minutes) in the college library in September and October of 2004?" This version is much more specific, and likely to generate better data, than the original.

A good way to iron out many of these potential wrinkles in your survey is to do a **pilot study** — that is, try out a draft copy of the questionnaire or interview schedule on a convenient group of respondents. You can ask this group not only to answer the questionnaire but also to comment on the questions. The group does not have to be a scientifically drawn sample because the results will not be counted in the final study.

pilot study
a method of evaluating a proposed study in which a convenient group of respondents answers and comments on a draft questionnaire or interview schedule

RESEARCH ETHICS

Numerous difficulties confront researchers who study human behaviour. Ethical concerns regarding human rights and dignity do not permit some research, even though the information gathered could be useful. Researchers must take care never to endanger the physical, mental, and emotional well-being of their subjects. Most institutions involved in research (for example, universities, hospitals, and education boards) have review boards that scrutinize proposed research to ensure that subjects are not endangered.

Researchers must respect the individual's freedom to decline to participate in research or to discontinue participation at any time. Potential subjects must be informed of all features of the study that could affect their willingness to participate.

Observing people in their daily routine or obtaining information about them is an invasion of privacy; appropriate permission, informed consent, and a guarantee of anonymity should ensure that the rights of the individual are upheld. Subjects should not be deceived about the purpose of the study, but it is not necessary to tell them what hypothesis is being studied. For example, if your hypothesis is that young women are more responsible drivers than young men, you would simply inform your subjects that you are doing a comparative analysis of the driving habits of males and females.

KEY TERMS

allocation	matched pairs
case study	natural selection
closed observation	non-response
cohort	open observation
content analysis	operational definition
control group	pilot study
correlation	population
dependent variable	positive correlation
empiricism	pure science
experimental group	questionnaire
field setting	quota sample
guaranteed anonymity	random sample
hard data	reliability
Hawthorne effect	response acquiescence
hypothesis	response deviation
independent variable	sample
informed consent	selection bias
initial state	social desirability response
intervening variable	spurious correlation
interview	stratified random sample
inverse correlation	subsequent state
key informant	validity
laboratory	value-free
manoeuvre	variable

Glossary of Terms

A

absolute deprivation
structural disadvantages that are rooted either in unequal opportunities or in deteriorating life conditions

acculturation
the process of adjusting to the ways of a new society

achieved status
a social position that an individual has gained through his or her efforts and abilities

action involvement
the deliberate attempt by scientists to exercise some control over the way in which their findings are used

age-specific birth rate
the number of live births per 1000 people of a given age group in the population per annum

ageism
discrimination based on age

agents of socialization
large-scale settings or institutions that help to shape our norms and values

alienation
a sense of lacking control over one's life

allocation
the process of dividing a sample into experimental and control groups

androgyny
the presence of both traditional feminine and masculine traits within individuals of both sexes

annulment
the dissolution of a marriage that was thought to exist but that in reality did not exist

anomie
a state in which the individual is chronically unable to make choices; a state of confusion that arises when an individual is faced with a conflict of choices in a society that provides no clear guidelines

apartheid
South Africa's government-enforced policy of segregation from 1948 to 1990

applied science
the application of the knowledge gained in pure science to everyday, practical use

argot
a unique language of a subculture with specialized vocabulary and idioms

artifacts
material possessions that are specific to a culture

ascribed status
a social position that society gives to an individual regardless of his or her merit or desire

assimilation
a process of cultural accommodation in which one group is completely absorbed by another

authority
the established right to make decisions about and to order the actions of others

automation
the replacement of people by machines

B

baby boom
an unusually large cohort of infants born in a relatively short period of time

beliefs
ideas that tell people what should exist or happen in a particular situation

birth control
any technique that prevents the birth of a child

birth rate
the number of live births per 1000 population per annum

Blishen scale
a measure of the relative social prestige of occupations

bourgeoisie
owners of the means of production

brain drain
the migration of skilled people from places that need their talents in search of material rewards in places that already have a skilled population

bureaucracy
a highly structured secondary group that is governed by a detailed set of rules and that has a marked division of labour

case study
a detailed description, including a longitudinal investigation, of an individual rather than a cohort

caste
a totally closed social category

censorship
the withholding of information released to the public that might influence public opinion

change agents
people capable of motivating others to band together and act

civil rights
the rights of individuals to not be treated as second-class citizens, especially the right of freedom from servitude

cloning
the technique of producing a genetically identical duplicate of an organism

closed observation
an observational method in which the researcher studies the group without their knowledge

closed-class society
a society that does not allow social mobility

cohort
a group of people of similar social standing, usually the same age group

collective behaviour
a relatively unorganized pattern of mass social interaction

collective panic
a sudden, overwhelming terror experienced by a group of people who desperately attempt to flee when they believe there are not enough escape routes in a perilous situation

common law couple
two people who are not legally married to each other but who live together as sexual partners

community
a small, closely knit, homogeneous society

compartmentalization
the separation of the parts of one's life that are inconsistent or in conflict so that one does not have to deal with the two things simultaneously

conflict theory
a theoretical perspective that stresses conflict, power differences, and social change as permanent characteristics of society

conformity
the tendency of people to behave within society's norms

content analysis
the search for recurring themes in documents

contraception
any device that prevents conception from taking place

control group
a comparison group of subjects in a study who do not undergo a manoeuvre

correlation
the measurement of interdependence among variables

craze
an excessive and unreasonable enthusiasm to rush toward something desired

crime funnel
a depiction of how an increasing amount of crime goes unresolved the further one progresses through the justice system

crowd
a temporary collection of people in close physical proximity

crude death rate
the number of deaths per 1000 population per annum

cultural diffusion
the process by which cultural elements spread from group to group within a society, or from one society to another

cultural lag
a process in which some areas of society do not change as quickly as the rest of society

cultural pluralism
a process of cultural accommodation in which one group is added to another and retains much of its cultural heritage and practices

cultural relativity
the idea that every cultural trait can only be fully understood and evaluated by the standards of right and wrong of the society in which it originated

cultural trait
the smallest unit of culture that can be identified

culture
everything people think, everything people do, and everything people possess because they belong to a particular society

culture-bound
meaningful within a cultural context and less meaningful when removed from that context

culture shock
a feeling of being bombarded by so many new stimuli (ideas, activities, lifestyles, etc.) that adjustment seems impossible

D

decriminalization
removing an act from coverage by the *Criminal Code*

defensible space
areas that actively discourage criminal activity

deferred gratification
the willingness to put off rewards until a later time in the belief that they will increase

deinstitutionalization
the attempt to return as many institutionalized people to the community as possible, replacing total institutionalized care with outreach programs, community-based services, out-patient clinics, and other programs

demographic transition theory
a model of how societies progress from a state of balanced populations as a result of high birth rates and high death rates, through periods of rapid population growth, to a state of balanced population with low birth and death rates

demography
the study of populations

denuded nuclear family
a family in which all the children are grown and have left the family home

dependent variable
a variable that is thought to be the outcome or effect of the interaction of variables

deviant act
a single behaviour that is contrary to society's norms

deviant behaviour
behaviour that is outside socially accepted boundaries

deviant career
a lifestyle based on involvement in a deviant activity

differential association
a theory that any person can be trained to adopt and follow a pattern of deviant or criminal behaviour

discrimination
any action that is taken on the basis of a prejudice

disease
an objective pathology of the body

dissociation
a feeling of inner numbness

division of labour
the tendency for general tasks and roles to become increasingly specialized

divorce
the dissolution of an existing marriage

E

education
the deliberate and organized transmission of values, knowledge, and skills

elaborate language code
a speech pattern that emphasizes verbalization and conceptualization and involves complex sentences and extensive use of adjectives, adverbs, and conjunctions

embourgeoisement
the process of becoming middle class

emigration
movement out of a geographical area

empathy
the ability to imaginatively place oneself in the situation of another individual

empiricism
the systematic gathering of evidence through observations and procedures that can be repeated and verified by others

endogamy
social rules that require individuals to marry within a specific social group

equalitarian family
a marriage in which the husband and the wife jointly make important decisions concerning family matters

esteem
the social honour accorded to people on the basis of their role performance

ethnicity
a shared cultural heritage and a sense of peoplehood

ethnocentrism
the evaluation of other cultures in terms of one's own cultural values and standards

exogamy
social rules that require individuals to marry outside a specific social group

experimental group
the group of subjects in a study who undergo a manoeuvre

extended family
a family that is broader than the nuclear family and recognized by the individual as being part of his or her family

exurbanites
people who have moved well beyond a city's limits but still retain an attachment to the city

F

fad
an unusual piece of popular culture that is quickly and enthusiastically adopted by a small part of the population

family
a group related by blood, marriage, or adoption

family of origin
the family into which an individual is born

family of procreation
the family that is created when people marry and have children

family planning
the conscious decisions a couple has to make about reproduction

fantasy
imagination unrestrained by reality

fashion
the current, short-lived custom in dress, manners, speech, etc., that is adopted by large groups of people

fear
the anticipation or actual experience of pain or severe distress

fecundity
the maximum biological capacity for reproduction that a population can achieve

feminist
an advocate of the movement for women to have political, economic, and social rights equal to those of men

fertility
the actual reproductive performance of a population

field setting
an environment or situation that occurs naturally; the researcher visits this situation and observes behaviour in its "natural" environment

formal organization
a secondary group in which roles, resources, and technology are coordinated to achieve a goal by means of a process that is formalized through written rules and procedures

formalization
the increasing dependence on bureaucratic and legalistic definitions of human relationships

full nuclear family
a family in which all the children are born and are still living at home

functionalism
a theoretical perspective that stresses the way in which each part of society functions to meet the needs of the society as a whole

future shock
a feeling that society is changing so rapidly in technological terms, and new stimuli arise so quickly, that it is difficult or impossible to adapt to the changes

G

gemeinschaft
according to Tonnies, a living organism, involving an underlying consensus or mutual understanding, based on kinship, common locality of residence, and friendship

gender
recognition of maleness or femaleness as designated by society

gender identity
one's sense of being male or female

gender roles
culturally defined positions and activities that are considered sex-appropriate within a society

gender socialization
a complex learning process in which people learn to be masculine and feminine according to society's expectations

generalized other
the concept of ourselves that we think exists in the community

gerontology
the study of the aging process

gesellschaft
the large-scale, formal, heterogeneous lifestyle typical of modern urban/industrial complexes

globalization
the increasing tendency for practices and values to cross national boundaries and for worldwide practices to shape everyday activities

group
a collectivity of individuals sharing a common interest or bond

group marriage
a type of polygamy in which there is more than one husband and more than one wife but only one marriage tie and partners may be exchanged

guaranteed anonymity
a research requirement that assures subjects that their responses will be kept confidential

H

hard data
information gathered under the most rigorous of scientific procedures

Hawthorne effect
behaviour that results from the researcher's intervention rather than natural behaviour

health care
deliberate activity directed toward improving health

hinterland
the region that services and identifies with a particular city

holistic medicine
an approach to health care that directs attention to the whole person as well as to the importance of the social and physical environment

horizontal mobility
movement from one social position to another in the same class level

hospices
institutions with a homelike atmosphere specifically for the dying and their friends and family

hypothesis
a suggestion or assumption that two social facts are related in a previously unsuspected way; a statement that can be empirically tested

I

ideology
a manner of thinking characteristic of a whole society or culture; beliefs or values that are used to justify and legitimate alternatives to existing social inequalities

illness
the subjective sense that one is not well

immediate gratification
the use of all of one's resources for present pleasures

immigration
movement into a geographical area

in-grouping
the process by which an individual receives a sense of acceptance by and belonging to a group

incest
a forbidden sexual relationship between members of the same family

incidence
the number of new cases of a disorder that arise in a given year

independent variable
a variable that is thought to be a factor contributing to the cause of the outcome being studied

industrialization
the substitution of technology for manual labour as the basis of production

infant mortality rate
the number of deaths per 1000 children less than one year of age per annum

influence
the ability to affect the actions and decisions of others beyond one's authority to do so; an indirect way of getting individuals to cooperate or conform to expectations

informed consent
a research requirement that ensures that subjects know the nature of the research and are willing participants in it

initial state
the condition of a group at the prescribed starting point (T1) of a study

institution
an established way of dealing with a social need

interaction
the two-way process of communication between people and their assessment of the nature of that communication

intergenerational mobility
movement in an individual adult's social standing in comparison with that of his or her parents

internalization
a norm learned so well, it is thought of, not as culturally taught, but as part of human nature; learning that is so efficient that social responses are automatic and the individual is not aware that they are learned or patterned

intervening variable
a variable that distorts the hypothesized relationship between the independent and dependent variables

interview
a face-to-face research encounter in which a researcher asks a question, the subject verbally responds, and the researcher records the response

inverse correlation
a correlation between variables in which one variable increases as the other decreases

J

Jensenism
the prejudicial belief that one race is collectively more intelligent than another

K

key informant
an individual who has been enmeshed in a social situation for a long period of time and who makes it his or her business to be aware of all the activities of the group

kin
anybody to whom an individual is related, whether by birth or marriage

L

laboratory
any situation or facility that is devoted solely to research

latent function
the underlying or hidden purposes that evolve in a social institution

life chances
one's potential for future social mobility

life expectancy
the average age of death in the population in a given year

life span
the upper limit of survival of a human body

lifestyle
the everyday way in which a life is lived

looking-glass self
the picture that we get of ourselves from the reactions of other people to us

lower-lower class
a social class consisting of the working poor

lower-middle class
a social class consisting primarily of white-collar workers as well as skilled and semi-skilled blue-collar workers

lower-upper class
a social class consisting of individuals who have gained wealth and status through work

lumpenproletariat
people who live outside the economic system imposed by the bourgeoisie

lynch mob
a vigilante crowd intent on punishing others with its own version of law and order

M

macrosociology
the study of large groups and social processes that affect the whole society

malsocialization
poor integration of a culture's norms and values

manifest destiny
the belief that white people were given dominion over North America as a result of divine intervention, and were thus justified in removing the aboriginal nations

manifest function
the designed and evident purpose of a social institution

manoeuvre
a procedure being tested

marginal persons
individuals who find themselves on the fringes of many groups but not fully immersed in any one group

marriage
the lawful union of two persons to the exclusion of all others

mass
a group of people who share an idea or an objective or react in the same way to the same event, but who are not in close proximity to one another

mass hysteria
a frightening misunderstanding that is shared by a large number of people who become very anxious

matched pairs
a type of allocation in which one of two subjects who are as alike as possible is allocated to the experimental group and one to the control group

matriarchal family
a marriage in which the wife/mother is the formal authority figure

matrilocal marriage
a marriage in which the couple live with or near the wife's parents

mechanical solidarity
solidarity in which individuals resemble each other in all aspects of their lives

melting pot
a process of cultural accommodation in which one group is almost completely absorbed by another but contributes something distinctive to the whole

microsociology
the study of individuals and small groups

migration
any movement of a population between two geographical areas

minority group
a collection of people who share common traits and hold significantly less power than society's dominant groups

mob
an emotionally aroused crowd bent on violent and hostile action

monogamy
a marital system in which an individual is allowed only a single marriage partner

morbidity
the rate of illness in a population

mortality
the number of deaths in a population

multiculturalism
government-assisted cultural pluralism

multiple roles
behavioural patterns associated with the different statuses that an individual holds in his or her many primary and secondary group affiliations

N

natural selection
a type of allocation in which individuals are allocated to the experimental group or the control group on the basis of whether they are subjected to a phenomenon or not

neighbourhood
a network of social relationships that is bound to a certain locality

neolocal marriage
a marriage in which the couple live apart from both sets of parents

neutralization
the process of excusing deviant behaviour on the grounds of mitigating circumstances

non-participant observation
a research method in which the researcher observes the activities of the group being studied as an outsider

non-response
the unwillingness of subjects to participate in a survey

norm
an established pattern of behaviour or an appropriate response to a social situation; standards of conduct and rules for behaviour that tell us how we should and should not behave

normative behaviour
behaviour that is within socially accepted boundaries

nuclear family
a family composed of two generations, usually a married couple and their offspring

O

objectivity
seeing things as they are, not as they ought to be

occupational prestige
the social honour accorded to people on the basis of their occupation

occupational socialization
the preparation of students for entering the job market

open observation
an observational method in which the researcher informs the group that they are being studied

open-class society
a society that allows social mobility on the basis of individual achievement

operational definition
a measurement that is meaningful for the purposes of an experiment

organic solidarity
solidarity in which the parts of society perform different functions and are interdependent

out-grouping
the process by which an individual receives a sense of rejection by and exclusion from a group

P

participant observation
a research method in which the researcher plays an active role in the group being studied

patriarchal family
a marriage in which the husband/father is the formal authority figure

patrilocal marriage
a marriage in which the couple live with or near the husband's parents

peers
other people of approximately the same age and social status

personal fable
a belief that the individual is immune to life's crises

petite bourgeoisie
a middle class made up of small business owners and artisans

pilot study
a method of evaluating a proposed study in which a convenient group of respondents answers and comments on a draft questionnaire or interview schedule

polyandry
a type of polygamy in which a female is allowed more than one husband

polygamy
a marital system in which an individual may have more than one spouse

polygyny
a type of polygamy in which a male is allowed more than one wife

population
the total number of people who could be included in a study

positive correlation
a correlation between variables in which the variables either increase together or decrease together

potential nuclear family
a married couple (including unmarried cohabitants)

power
the ability to control the actions of others regardless of their wishes

prejudice
a preconceived idea that the behaviours and personality traits of an individual can be predicted on the basis of the human categories to which the individual belongs

prescriptions
the rules and directions of behaviour that are set down and recommended

prevalence
the total number of cases of a disorder that exist

primary deviation
deviant behaviour that occurs prior to the society's knowledge of the individual's behaviour

primary group
a collection of individuals who gather together simply for the sake of being together

privatization
people's tendency to keep to themselves

progress
social change for the good

projection
the rationalizing of a problem by claiming that someone else is really responsible

proletariat
workers for the bourgeoisie

propaganda
the manipulation of ideas or opinions through the presentation of limited, selective, or false information to induce the public to accept a particular view

proscriptions
the banning or condemnation of certain behaviour

public
a large number of people who share a common attitude on an issue

public opinion
the attitude about a particular issue that is held by the members of a public

pure science
the search for laws and generalizations; the pursuit of new knowledge for the sake of increasing science's total store of knowledge

Q

questionnaire
an organized, systematic printed list of questions

quota sample
a sampling technique in which the first given number of people encountered who fit the research criteria are included in the sample

R

race
a large category of people distinguished from others by inherited physiological differences

racism
systematic prejudice and/or discrimination on the basis of physiological differences

random sample
a sample drawn purely by chance, in which every member of the population has an exactly equal chance of being selected

rate of natural increase (RNI)
the birth rate minus the death rate

rationalization
the redefining of a situation to make it seem less painful

reactionary social movement
a social movement that wants either to keep things as they are and prevent further changes or to restore some previously existing situation that is perceived as being better than the current situation

recidivism
the probability that a released offender will repeat his or her crime

red tape
the rigid application of regulations and routines

reference group
a group with which people compare themselves when evaluating themselves and their behaviour

reform social movement
a social movement that generally agrees with society's current goals but that seeks some modification or improvement in the way that society is trying to achieve its goals

relative deprivation
a sense that one is not getting a fair share of society's rewards

reliability
the consistency with which an instrument measures a response or an effect when the instrument is used by the researcher again or by another researcher under the same conditions

religion
a system of beliefs and practices surrounding a supernatural order of beings, places, and forces

response acquiescence
a tendency to agree with the statements of an authority regardless of their content

response deviation
a tendency to answer items in an uncommon direction

restricted language code
a speech pattern that consists of short, clipped sentences, with few adverbs and adjectives, used repetitiously, and lacks conjunctions and subordinate clauses

revolutionary social movement
a social movement that seeks to drastically redefine society's goals or the very nature and structure of society

riot
an explosive crowd bent on destruction and violence

rite of passage
a ritual or ceremony associated with a change of age status

role
a set of expected behaviours attached to a certain status

role conflict
the performance of one social role that detracts from the proper performance of other roles

role failure
the failure to meet the obligations of a clearly defined role that an individual is expected to perform

role set
the group that surrounds an individual in any given role

role strain
an individual's subjective and stressful feeling that role problems are burdens; a sense of discomfort or tension felt when we have difficulty meeting role expectations

rumour
a story that has no basis in fact but that is powerful because it makes an ambiguous situation meaningful

S

sample
a small group taken from the population in such a way as to represent that population

sanctions
negative and coercive techniques to ensure conformity

science
the pursuit of objective knowledge accumulated from observation

scientific medicine
the application of scientific methods to the study of disease and injury

scientific method
the process involved in acquiring objective knowledge

secondary deviation
deviant behaviour that occurs in part because of an individual's socially acquired self-image of deviance

secondary group
a collection of individuals who are brought together to achieve a common purpose

selection bias
the unconscious tendency of any individual to prefer some people to others

separation
the living apart of a still legally married couple

serial monogamy
a marital system in which an individual takes two or more marriage partners in succession

sex
the fact of being male or female as determined by chromosomes, hormones, anatomy, and physiology

sex ratio
the number of males per 100 females in the population

sex-specific birth rate
the number of live births per 1000 women in a population per annum

sex typing
the ascription of a status on the basis of gender

sexism
the act of prejudging a person in a negative way on the basis of gender

sickness
the recognition by society that one is unwell

significant other
a person who is extremely important to an individual's development

social change
any way in which society is now different from the way it was previously

social class
the social ranking of individuals on the basis of purely economic factors

social control
the process by which members of a group encourage desired forms of behaviour and discourage undesired forms; the forces that encourage individuals to abide by society's rules and that invoke sanctions against them if they break the rules

social Darwinism
the belief that competition results in progress because it eliminates weaker individuals

social desirability response
a tendency to answer questions in a direction that the respondent considers most socially acceptable

social distance
the point at which an individual thinks that another group should be prohibited from any further integration into society

social epidemiology
the study of the differential distribution of disease among various social groups

social facts
things that are outside the individual but that coerce or constrain him or her in some way

social issue
a controversial subject in a society on which there is no general agreement

social mobility
the ability of individuals to change their social standing

social movement
a secondary group whose aim is to promote or prevent social change

social problem
a social phenomenon that is perceived as detrimental to society by a large proportion of the population and, therefore, in need of correction

social stratification
the process of ranking people in status levels according to some criteria of inferiority and superiority

socialization
a complex, lifelong learning process in which an individual develops selfhood and acquires the knowledge, skills, and motivations that are needed to be a member of society

society
"the totality of social relationships and interactions among a collectivity of people occupying a territory who, over time, survive by meeting their needs and solving their problems" (Knuttila, 1993)

socioeconomic status
the social ranking of individuals on a combination of social factors such as occupation, lifestyle, and family lineage and economic factors such as income, property ownership, and investments

sociology
the scientific study of human relationships

spurious correlation
an apparent relationship between two variables that makes no sense

status allocation
the process of distributing individuals among the different positions in society

status inconsistency
the holding of two statuses that appear to be contradictory

status socialization
the process of teaching people to accept their position in the social stratification system

status
the social position of an individual in a group

stereotype
a generalized and exaggerated picture of an entire category of people

stigma
widespread and very strong disapproval of a behaviour or an individual

stratified random sample
a random sample that includes categories of people who are most important to a study; these categories are represented proportionately within the whole sample, yet within each category subjects are randomly sampled

subculture
a small group within society that shares most of the ways of the main society but that has some distinctive values and ideas of its own

subsequent state
the condition of a group at the prescribed end point (T2) of a study

suburbanization
the appropriation and use of productive farmland to build roads and residential and commercial areas

symbol
anything that is taken to stand for something else

symbolic interactionism
a theoretical perspective that seeks to describe how individuals interpret their environments and how these personal distinctions and meanings affect their interactions with others

T

taboo
a prohibited practice that is so horrific that it is impolite even to mention it

temprocentrism
the belief that one era in time is superior to all others and should be used as the standard by which other periods of time are judged

terror
an intense and enduring fear that emerges when an individual or a group is trapped in a dangerous situation for a period of time

theories
broad explanations and predictions concerning phenomena of interest

tokenism
the act of giving a person a position or an opportunity as a way of partially correcting previous wrongs, but not as a way of rewarding the person's merits

U

upper-lower class
a social class consisting of regularly employed but unskilled workers

upper-middle class
a social class consisting of professionals

upper-upper class
a social class consisting of individuals who were born into wealthy families

urban planning
the improvement of community living by the deliberate creation or changing of physical environments

urban village
a network of social relationships among some residents of a city

urbanism
the cluster of norms, values, and material possessions that originate from the requirements of city living

urbanization
the growth and development of cities, often at the expense of rural areas

V

validity
the degree to which a test actually measures what it says it measures

value
a socially shared idea about what is good, right, and desirable; the generally accepted standards of desirability of a society

value-free
the absence of personal biases in sociological work; to be unaffected by the biases and preferences of interested parties and by any potential consequences of the use of scientific findings

value judgment
an opinion based on personal biases about what is good, right, and desirable

variable
a characteristic that can change or differ

vertical mobility
movement up or down the social ladder

vertical mosaic
a social ranking that is affected by ethnicity or cultural heritage

vested interest
benefits that people receive from the society in exchange for fulfilling their obligations to that society

Z

zero population growth (ZPG)
a situation in which birth and immigration simply replace death and emigration

Index